Supercharge Professional Development for Early Childhood Educators

Supercharge Professional Development for Early Childhood Educators

101 Ideas for Designing and Facilitating Engaging Learning Experiences

Susan MacDonald, MEd,
and Nancy Toso, MEd

Foreword by Holly Elissa Bruno

www.redleafpress.org
800-423-8309

Published by Redleaf Press
10 Yorkton Court
St. Paul, MN 55117
www.redleafpress.org

First edition 2024
Cover design by Michelle Lagerroos
Cover photograph ©phive2015 / Adobe Stock
Interior design by Michelle Lagerroos
Typeset in Dapifer, Moonblossom, and Trade Gothic
Interior photos/illustrations ©siaminka / Adobe Stock
Printed in the United States of America
30 29 28 27 26 25 24 1 2 3 4 5 6 7 8

Material from *Inspiring Early Childhood Leadership: Eight Strategies to Ignite Passion and Transform Program Quality* by Susan MacDonald (ISBN 9780876596517), pages 14–16, is adapted and used with permission from Gryphon House, Inc., P.O. Box 10, Lewisville, NC 27023, (800) 638-0928, www.gryphonhouse.com.

Library of Congress Cataloging-in-Publication Data
Names: MacDonald, Susan, 1961 June 14- author. | Toso, Nancy, author.
Title: Supercharge professional development for early childhood educators : 101 ideas for designing and facilitating engaging learning experiences / by Susan MacDonald, MEd, and Nancy Toso, MEd.
Description: First edition. | St. Paul, MN : Redleaf Press, 2024. | Includes bibliographical references. | Summary: "Supercharge Professional Development empowers early childhood program leaders to transform their current professional development practices, offering innovative and concrete ideas for supporting educators. The timely and inspiring resources in this handbook will increase engagement, build collaboration, and enhance all aspects of any professional development program"— Provided by publisher.
Identifiers: LCCN 2023047090 (print) | LCCN 2023047091 (ebook) | ISBN 9781605548074 (paperback) | ISBN 9781605548081 (ebook)
Subjects: LCSH: Early childhood educators--In-service training. | Professional learning communities. | Early childhood educators--Professional relationships. | Early childhood education--Curricula.
Classification: LCC LB1775.6 .M34 2024 (print) | LCC LB1775.6 (ebook) | DDC 370.71/1--dc23/eng/20231116
LC record available at https://lccn.loc.gov/2023047090
LC ebook record available at https://lccn.loc.gov/2023047091

Printed on acid-free paper

We leave behind a bit of ourselves wherever we've been.—Edmond Haracourt

To Marlies Zammuto, our cherished friend and mentor, who inspired us to always look forward, to think outside of the box, to be authentic, to infuse joy and magic into every training and interaction, and to celebrate! Her wisdom, guiding thoughts, and empowering energy fueled our desire to create this book to honor her spirit and the lasting impact she had on so many early childhood educators, children, and families.

Contents

Foreword

What do we need to do this work of keeping our field geared up, tuned up, pumped up, well informed, and exquisite at everyday problem solving? How do we stay *supercharged* to model tireless curiosity?

Each time I step into an echoing convention center, slightly musty basement, well-lit university lecture hall, or restaurant ballroom with clinking glasses; whenever I greet tired teachers shifting on miniature chairs in an early childhood classroom or arranged in boxes across a video conferencing screen, I want to believe our time together will matter.

These hardworking, dedicated early childhood professionals deserve all good things. Let me give them my best.

Isn't that the heart's desire of trainers? We want to uplift deserving folk, inspire them, and leave them with useful insights and thought-provoking new practices as they return to the challenging work of educating young children.

We are early childhood trainers, lecturers, keynoters, and workshop facilitators—educators of educators. We "train" professionals who do miraculous work, often without the professional respect they deserve. We rekindle the wonder and awe we felt as children into passion for today's best practices and breaking research findings. There is something special about being an ECE trainer that the world barely grasps. We care about the people who care for young children. We bring our gifts and vulnerabilities, hopes and knowledge.

Readiness for each training matters. Readiness is studying up on and aligning with my clients' needs, knowing my material inside and out, preparing a stimulating slide deck to honor visual learners, posting relevant links to podcasts and articles, flying in a day early, and saying a prayer for all loving energies to fill the room so each person will gain something of value from our time together.

You have a strong sense of purpose. You have a likely jagged but clear (with hindsight) pathway that brought you to this day. You have a calling that brings you to choose to be an educator of educators. What calls you to do what you do? What's your gift as a trainer?

Here's my moment when I learned my calling. As you read my story, recall your own journey that brought you to this point in your professional life. I was twenty-two, a graduate student at the University of North Carolina at Chapel Hill, aiming for my PhD. Professor Eugene Watson asked me to help him with a conference on race relations he was presenting to educators. I agreed. Later Dr. Watson placed a group of us in front of teachers at a conference so we could share what heals and hinders racial conflict. The group's gut response may have been: "*Run!* What do we know? Who are we to speak?" But if Dr. Watson had faith in our truth-telling ability and vulnerable hearts, we could not let him down. Standing before those anxious teachers, I owned my anxiety and told my truth. When we spoke authentically, people listened. We formed trust with participants, trust in honesty without self-aggrandizement.

Something about the light in that room changed, shifting my confidence and convincing me that we are better together. From then on, whenever I took that "be curious, not judgmental" learning approach, everyday magic happened. At every training, I make sure safety is guaranteed, boundaries are honored, differences are shared, and bias is called out.

My trainings come to life when participants experience a sense of trust and can share their stories and insights in respectful safety without being judged, and we can thus build upon rather than tear down one another's budding insights. We begin by agreeing to ground rules for safety and respect.

Along the way, we will likely sing, bust some moves, meet and share with new folk, laugh at ourselves, sometimes cry, and find courage to speak difficult truths. Each training is a once-in-a-lifetime call to learn and grow in a supportive community honoring everyone's contribution. Did I mention I teach on legal issues? What better way than through compassion to figure out how justice can be done in everyday ways?

Training, like genius, is more than what we think it is. Training is pulling forth our own forged purpose, our pathway, our calling, to make a difference as only we can. This capacity to educate isn't easy stuff. It's not formulaic. It's not something we can imitate or borrow.

When I asked Nancy and Susan what their most compelling learning had been in creating this book, they reflected and sent me a list of what early childhood trainers seek and promote:

- shared learning
- exploring differing perspectives
- meaning, connection, caring
- laughter, playfulness, joy
- respect for our vulnerability and others
- a curious mind, an open heart, a seeking soul
- a love of children and of the child within each of us
- a desire to make a difference

Supercharge Professional Development for Early Childhood Educators offers us a vibrant cornucopia of vivid real-life strategies, tools, materials, and techniques on how to be like our students, upbeat and motivated to be our best. Whether your preference is for structure, playfulness, or a blend of both, you will find inspiration here. Susan and Nancy have gifted us with a thorough and detailed ECE professional development handbook both pragmatic and uplifting, realistic and inspiring, serious and humorous. Utilize this motivational handbook to make your presentations transformative for you as well as participants.

May you, as I do, find possibilities, solutions, support, and courage to continuously *supercharge* your professional commitment as an educator of educators of young children. Here's to each one of us every time we walk with hopeful dedication into a training room. Thank you for making a difference.

—HOLLY ELISSA BRUNO

Holly Elissa Bruno, best-selling, award-winning author and international keynoter, served as Maine's assistant attorney general and as dean and outstanding professor, University of Maine at Augusta. Alumna of Harvard's Institute for Educational Management, she taught leadership for Wheelock College, now Boston University.

Introduction

This book is rooted in our belief that thoughtfully planned, relevant, and dynamic professional development has the power to transform all aspects of the early childhood field by inspiring educators to embrace new thoughts and ideas for bringing their very best to their work. It fuels a commitment to grow and learn that in turn sparks creativity and builds confidence. Our journey to this book is the culmination of over twenty-five years of collaborative experiences, and we have seen firsthand how inspiring, effective, and engaging professional development can restore a sense of hopefulness during challenging times, revitalize teachers, motivate individuals to see new possibilities, and lead to transformative aha moments.

Our work together has grown out of our deep desire to provide trainers and leaders with fresh and easily accessible resources that will increase engagement, build collaboration, and enhance all aspects of the professional development they are providing. We share the belief that a strong commitment to ongoing professional development is an essential component of providing high-quality early learning environments where children, teachers, and families thrive.

Due to a variety of training requirements, most early childhood educators will experience hundreds of hours of professional development over the course of their career. The intent is that these hours will be crystallized in their memory as pivotal learning moments that significantly transform their thinking and enhance their daily practices.

The reality is that some will have little or no lasting impact. What's the difference? There are many factors to consider when answering that question, but *engagement* and *relevance* connect them all! How we design and deliver timely and inspirational professional development is directly linked to actively involving participants in their learning, connecting the learning to their goals and diverse experiences, and helping them put new knowledge and ideas into practice.

Consider how you provide professional development now. What do you do to spark a passion for learning? How do you plan it? How do you connect to new research that validates the lifelong effect of early childhood education? What activities do you include? How does it inspire teachers to reflect on their daily work, to embrace new knowledge, and to ignite positive changes in their practices? As you explore this book, you will discover a wide variety of ideas and resources you can use to design and deliver professional development that kindles participants' imaginations and helps them discover new ways to support children and families.

Our Intention

We have designed this book to be an inspirational and informative guidebook for facilitators to develop transformative professional learning experiences. *Supercharge Professional Development for Early Childhood Educators* offers a positive "you can do this" attitude to empower you to add new energy and concrete ideas for enriching your current professional development practices.

We hope that the strategies and activities in this book will ignite your passion for discovering new ways to approach professional development and expand your repertoire of techniques, practices, strategies, and activities. Our overarching goal in writing this book is to help you create and facilitate robust, holistic, and vibrant professional development sessions that provoke interest, generate excitement, energize educators, and ultimately shift practice forward. We are excited to share our techniques and insights to promote your ability and confidence to develop and present stimulating professional development that motivates educators to continually evaluate and enhance their knowledge and skills and moves participants forward in identifying and realizing their goals.

Be creative, inventive, and resourceful as you find ways to adapt the activities to your facilitation style and align them to your specific context. Explore new ways to be authentic and intentional about honoring the diverse needs and backgrounds of the participants. Deliberately design your professional learning experiences to respect and be inclusive of learning styles, abilities, culture, ethnicities, race, gender, and languages. Utilize these activities and the resources provided to engage participants in ways that give everyone a voice and an opportunity to contribute their ideas and unique perspectives.

We wrote this book for all individuals who provide professional development to the early childhood workforce. Throughout the book, we use the words *teacher* and *educator* interchangeably to refer to everyone involved in early childhood who are participants in professional development sessions or events, and *facilitator* to describe anyone who has the opportunity to teach, train, lead, and inspire others. The list is expansive and includes people with a variety of job titles, including these:

- directors of early childhood and school-age programs
- trainers
- workshop presenters
- pedagogical leaders
- curriculum specialists
- consultants
- coaches
- higher education instructors and professors
- child care resource and referral staff
- family child care coordinators and home visitors

In this book, you will find the tools you need to enliven your trainings with a wide range of activities designed to promote reflection, learning, collaboration, and interaction. We use the words *workshop* and *training* interchangeably to refer to any professional development experience that results in participants learning and being able to implement new information into their practice. The activities we provide can be adapted for specific professional development experiences, including the following:

- onsite workshops
- conference presentations
- keynote presentations
- professional development days
- staff retreats
- orientations
- college courses
- courses that provide continuing education credits
- weekly or monthly staff meetings
- team meetings
- board events
- Communities of Practice
- parent events

You will also find inspirational insights and ideas from a diverse group of colleagues and thought leaders who share their wisdom and unique strategies from their work. Look for our colleagues' activity suggestions and ideas throughout the book as an "Insight from the Field" or a shorter "Insightful Tip."

Tips for Using This Book

To guide facilitators in reimagining their professional development practices, we have created 101 specific strategies, tools, and activities presented in concise, easily referenced fact sheets. The book is divided into three sections:

1. The **first section** focuses on fundamental strategies for designing and delivering impactful professional development. Read these first for foundational guidance that applies to any learning experience you are developing and providing.
2. The **second section** furnishes a wealth of activities and fresh ideas to bring fun, joy, and positive interactions into your professional development sessions. These are grouped by the type of activity so you can read and use them according to your specific interest and need.

3. The **third section** contains a collection of templates and resources for structuring and enhancing professional learning experiences. You can tailor the templates to meet your specific needs or style. We encourage you to explore the resources to enrich your own development as a facilitator.

As lifelong learners, we have sought out new ideas and perspectives as we have built our own toolboxes and continually adapt to the changing landscape of professional development.

Many of the strategies and activities in the book stem from the wide variety of experiences we have participated in throughout our careers—workshops, courses, book discussions, staff meetings, and thousands of conversations with educators, leaders, and experts in complementary fields. As we continue to discover and explore current research, we have thoughtfully assembled ideas, techniques, and facilitation methods and tailored them to create relevancy for early childhood professionals.

The Five I's

The strategies and activities are all laid out using the following template:

- **Intention**—Clearly states the intended purpose of each strategy and activity.
- **Implementation**—Provides detailed steps for facilitating the activities and specific information for incorporating new strategies into your work.
- **Individualize**—Suggests adaptations and ideas for customizing the activities.
- **Investigate**—Offers current resources for further learning.
- **Illuminate**—Utilizes QR codes and links to short video clips of training activities and interviews with thought leaders.

We invite and encourage you to be creative in how you bring these ideas and strategies to life in your work. We like to think of the activities in this book like recipes in a cookbook. Select the ones that will add some zest to your presentations. Customize and adapt them to your individual style, the resources you have available, and the needs of your participants. Be adventurous, have fun, and try mixing things up in new ways. Most important, bring your joy, passion, and unique perspectives into each and every professional learning experience!

Section One

The FUNdamentals of Impactful Professional Development

Education is not the filling of a pail but the lighting of a fire. —Plutarch

This section will broaden your understanding of the strategies, techniques, and approaches that are fundamental for facilitating professional development that motivates educators and leaders to expand their knowledge and transform their practice.

As you design your training event, consistently stay focused on the overarching intent of professional development, as stated in the NAEYC Training, Technical Assistance, and Adult Education Glossary:

> *Early Childhood Professional Development is a continuum of learning and support activities designed to prepare individuals for work with and on behalf of young children and their families, as well as ongoing experiences to enhance this work. These opportunities lead to improvements in the knowledge, skills, practices, and dispositions of early education professionals.* (NAEYC and NACCRRA 2011, 5)

Explore each strategy to discover new ways to enhance how you design and deliver professional development. Notice how the strategies and activities can be woven together to help you create a memorable professional learning experience. Consider creating an actionable list of new ideas to incorporate into your current work. Small, consistent changes will get you started on the path to supercharging your professional development!

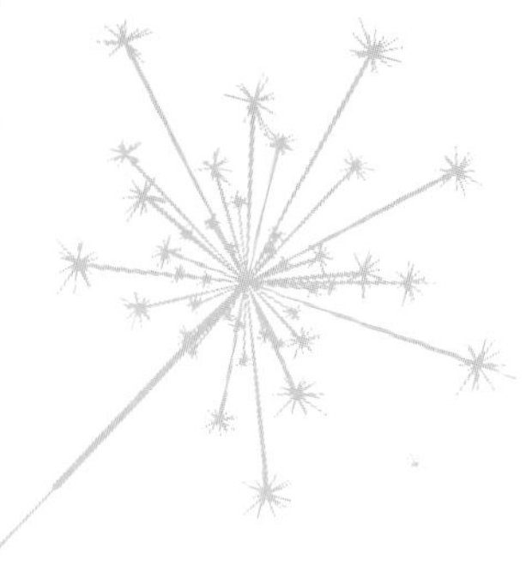

Strategy #1

Develop a Vibrant Learning Community

Intention

Whether you are a program leader or an outside facilitator, you want to cultivate an environment that values and supports professional growth. The purpose is to develop and provide dynamic professional learning experiences that energize and actively involve all participants. The aim is to connect timely and relevant professional development to the participants' and program goals to inspire teachers to learn and grow in ways that broaden their practices and perspectives.

Implementation for Program Leaders

- Build excitement and engagement in your staff from the very beginning! Ensure that strong, ongoing professional development is woven into your program's vision and values.
  - Include language in your recruiting materials that highlights how your program supports professional development and growth.
  - Ask questions in interviews that elicit a candidate's feelings about professional development and what they need for support. For example:
    - How have you continued your professional growth?
    - What are some topics or issues in early childhood that you would like to learn more about or skills you would like to improve?
    - What is a professional development event that has inspired you?
  - Add a professional development section to your employee handbook and contract. Consider including clear expectations related to ongoing professional growth, a description of your process for implementing individual professional improvement plans, a sample schedule for in-house professional development sessions, funding and resources for external learning opportunities, and any relevant regulations or accreditation standards.
- Commit to establishing and adhering to a consistent system of providing professional development and support.
  - Build connections to your program's vision, values, and goals at every opportunity—regular staff meetings, small team meetings, large professional development events, even parent events and board meetings.
  - Encourage staff to be involved in planning and implementing professional development activities that are relevant to them and highlight their culture, knowledge, experiences, and creativity.

- Provide pertinent examples showing how the information and activities in your professional development events link to the vision and goals.

- Create opportunities to be a learning partner with your staff.
  - Attend webinars, workshops, and conferences with your staff and schedule a time for debriefing with them after the event.
  - Attend any in-house training you provide for your staff and provide follow-up activities or observations.
  - Share perspectives gained from any professional development and develop action steps to put new knowledge and ideas into practice.

INSIGHTFUL TIP

from Luis A. Hernandez

"Make friends with participants before the session."

Take time to build a rapport with participants to show you are genuinely interested in them and to help foster interactive dialogue throughout the session.

- Recognize and appreciate each teacher's strengths, talents, and particular skills. (See Strategy #2—Be a Role Model for Ongoing Professional Development.)
  - Encourage teachers to use one another as resources. (See Activities #70—Choose an Item and #84—Scavenger Hunt.)
  - Curate resources to help teachers continue their own professional growth journey. Be sure the resources are accessible to all learners by including materials in a variety of languages and learning modalities that reflect a diverse, equitable, and inclusive community. Provide lists of websites with descriptions.
  - Create YouTube files of your favorite videos.
  - Keep your resource library up to date with current research.
  - Join a professional organization such as the National Association for the Education of Young Children (NAEYC) and gain access to journals and other resources.
  - Invite teachers to share their favorite resources.
- Establish Communities of Practice to bring individuals together in deeper reflection and understanding of a topic or practice, for instance, based on children's ages, a specific developmental domain, or designing developmentally appropriate environments and curriculum. (A Community of Practice is a group of practitioners—in this case early childhood educators or leaders—who come together over a period of time to share knowledge, perspectives, experiences, and resources around a topic of interest. Participants may belong to the same or multiple organizations. It provides a forum for the members to network, build relationships, learn collectively, and develop solutions and resources to respond to specific issues.)

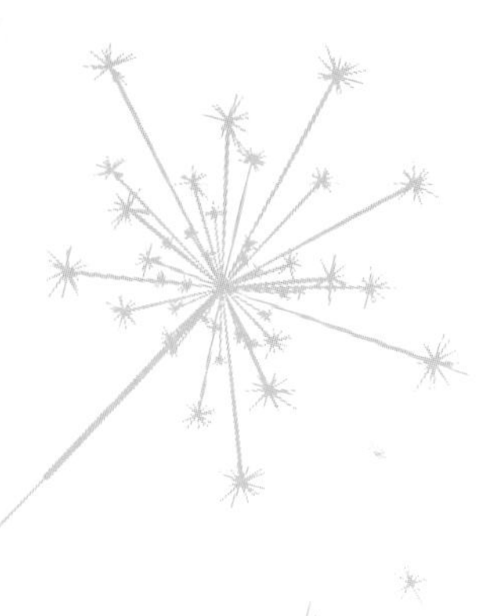

- Foster ongoing enthusiasm for staff to attend or create professional development experiences.
    - Include a line item for professional development in your budget.
    - Offer incentives for teachers to design and lead a professional development session. For example:
        - Grant extra personal time.
        - Pay for membership to a professional organization.
        - Give a gift card to a favorite store or restaurant.
        - Provide adequate time and coverage for teachers to attend or develop training activities.

Implementation for Outside Facilitators

- Consult with the program leader to identify the program's values and goals as well as the specific goals of the training.
- Conduct a pretraining survey of the participants to determine their interest in and current knowledge of the topic.
- Share a preliminary outline of the training with the program leader to ensure it covers the needed information and material.
- Send some material to the participants before the training for them to reflect on and to generate excitement and anticipation (for example, a list of quotes pertinent to the topic or a reflection sheet about current practices).

Investigate

- For more information on establishing a growth culture and professional development plans:

    Susan MacDonald. 2019. *Inspiring Professional Growth: Empowering Strategies to Lead, Motivate, and Engage Early Childhood Teachers.* Lewisville, NC: Gryphon House.

- For a comprehensive overview of professional development terms:

    NAEYC and NACCRRA (National Association of Child Care Resource and Referral Agencies). 2011. *Early Childhood Education Professional Development: Training and Technical Assistance Glossary.* www.naeyc.org/sites/default/files/globally-shared/downloads/PDFs/our-work/public-policy-advocacy/glossarytraining_ta.pdf.

Be a Role Model for Ongoing Professional Development

There is no end to education. It is not that you read a book, pass an examination, and finish with education. The whole of life, from the moment you are born to the moment you die is a process of learning.
—J. Krishnamurti

Intention

As a facilitator of professional development, your presence, knowledge, and energy influence the outcomes of the workshop. When you show up excited, with vibrant activities and relevant factual information, participants become engaged and invested in their own learning. Your own lifelong learning is essential to designing and delivering workshops that inspire the professional growth of the participants.

Implementation

- Align the professional development with topics you are passionate and knowledgeable about. Your enthusiasm will help bring the topic alive for the participants.
- Read! Expand your knowledge with current books. Share quotes and facts from your readings to add depth to your presentations.
- Stay current on issues affecting early childhood care and education. Subscribe to magazines, blogs, and newsletters that keep you up to date on the key issues and new research related to the early childhood field. (Use the references and resources provided in the appendices at the end of the book to find new sources of information.)
- Connect with early childhood individuals and groups on social media. Facebook, LinkedIn, and other platforms provide opportunities for you to gain insights, gather resources, and build relationships with a global early childhood community. Joining groups related to your specific interests helps you gather pertinent information to keep your trainings current and relevant.
- Take classes and webinars. Being a participant in professional development opportunities serves a dual purpose: while you gain knowledge you can also build your presentation skills by observing the presenter!

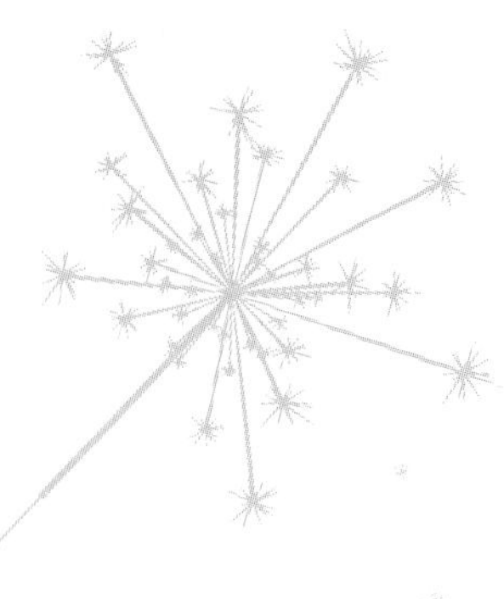

- Share what inspires you. Develop a collection of quotes and poems that have meaning to you. Weave the quotes and poems into your presentations as a way to inspire others and engage in reflective dialogues. Incorporate music and video clips that reflect your passions and interests to energize your presentation.
- Find a mentor. Reach out to someone who can guide you on your professional development journey. Having a mentor enables you to engage in focused conversations that will stimulate you in finding new ways to grow. Acknowledge and share stories of how your mentor has supported and influenced you.
- Be a mentor. Sharing your expertise is a valuable learning experience for you as well as the mentee that shows your deep commitment to supporting others.
- Be open and transparent about your own professional learning. Share your learning journey and the practices that help you continue to grow and develop.

Investigate

- Find current research, resources, and relevant video clips:

  Center on the Developing Child at Harvard University
  https://developingchild.harvard.edu

- Explore courses for your ongoing professional development:

  edX: free online courses from the world's best universities
  www.edx.org

- For a variety of articles on supporting the early childhood field, visit:

  The National Institute for Early Education Research Blog
  http://nieer.org/publications/blog

- For additional resources, see appendix: Resources for Professional Learning—Courses, Workshops, Conferences

INSIGHTFUL TIPS

from Beth Fredericks

"Be an ongoing learner as well as a teacher."

from Holly Elissa Bruno

"Every year, make a stretch to learn something new or deepen your understanding."

Strategy #3

Support Adult Learners

Intention

Building your understanding of adult learners as unique individuals with differing abilities, backgrounds, experiences, and learning styles is essential for creating relevant and engaging professional development. Design and deliver your professional learning experiences in ways that acknowledge and respect your target audience. Being intentional about creating opportunities for *all* participants to expand their knowledge will increase positive outcomes.

Implementation

- Discover what your audience is interested in learning. Conduct pretraining surveys, have individual conversations, or hold focus groups to learn about their specific interests, needs, and goals and to get their buy-in for the training. Be sure to gather input from individuals who represent the diversity of your intended participants.
- Clearly state the *why* of the session. Adult learners will be more motivated to engage in the session when they understand the relevance of the training to their work. Share specific objectives at the beginning of each session.
- Create a sense of safety and belonging. Start with a warm welcome. Introduce yourself, and allow time for the participants to introduce themselves, invite everyone to share their gender pronouns, and establish a group agreement to guide interactions throughout the session. (See Strategy #4—Create a Sense of Belonging, and Activities #22—Introduce Yourself, #23–26—Participant Introductions, and #30—Group Agreement.)
- Be intentional in designing your presentation to reflect and respect the participants' diverse backgrounds and experiences. This is an area of lifelong learning for many of us, and knowing where to begin can be challenging. You can start by making changes that ensure your language, images, content, resources, quotes, and video clips reflect the diversity of the early childhood workforce, children, and families. Commit to becoming more informed and developing ongoing changes to your presentation to create equitable and inclusive learning environments.
- Build engagement. Provide opportunities through various workshop activities for participants to connect the information you share to real-life problems and challenges they face. (See Activity #82—Scenarios/Case Studies.)
- Acknowledge and validate the expertise of the participants. Create opportunities for participants to share their expertise and prior experiences. Stress that you value their knowledge and want everyone to learn from and with one another! (See Activities #33—K-W-L and #35—Discovering What We Know.)

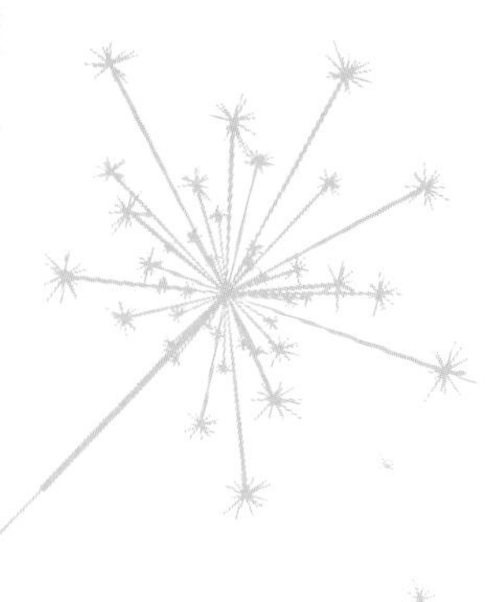

- Recognize that adult learners like to have some control over how they are learning. Provide options for participants to engage in ways that are comfortable and relevant to them. Allow participants to opt out or be an observer during activities they are not comfortable with.
- Encourage participants to share stories of their experiences as a way to expose people to perspectives that differ from their own. (See Activities #50—Defining Moments, #69—Hopes and Dreams, and #76—Chapters of Our Professional Lives.)
- Conduct evaluations to gather feedback on what worked well, what participants learned, what changes you can make to improve the session, and any issues needing follow-up. (See appendix: Sample Workshop Evaluation Forms.)
- Incorporate a variety of activities into each session to engage participants in ways that will increase their ability to learn and apply the information you are sharing. Howard Gardner's Multiple Intelligences theory is a useful lens for understanding the range of ways that individuals learn and for providing different methods for imparting information. Here are some examples of creative ways to incorporate activities to motivate different types of learners:

Learner Type:	Create opportunities to:
Verbal/Linguistic *"The Word Player"*	Share stories, work with a partner or small group
Logical/Mathematical *"The Questioner"*	Create charts, gather data, solve problems, work through critical-thinking scenarios
Spatial *"The Visualizer"*	Draw, build, design, and create; watch video clips and play games (Use visually appealing graphics)
Musical *"The Music Lover"*	Reflect on songs (Use music for opening presentations and transitions)
Bodily/Kinesthetic *"The Mover"*	Move throughout the session and take listening walks; do short energizers and mix-and-mingle activities
Interpersonal *"The Socializer"*	Pursue group work, share ideas, communicate with and listen to others, join professional learning communities
Intrapersonal *"The Individual"*	Reflect individually, do solo projects and activities
Naturalist *"The Nature Lover"*	Use natural materials to represent an idea or vision; spend time outdoors; do classification, observation, and organizational activities

Investigate

- Expand your knowledge of the principles of andragogy:

  www.thinkific.com/blog/principles-andragogy.

- Read an overview of Multiple Intelligences theory:

  Marenus, Michele. 2020. "Gardner's Theory of Multiple Intelligences." *Simply Psychology*. June 9. www.simplypsychology.org/multiple-intelligences.html.

- Learn more about supporting neurodiverse learners:

  Wood, Emily. 2021. "Design for Neurodiverse Learners." Association for Talent Development. April 30, 2021. www.td.org/magazines/td-magazine/design-for-neurodiverse-learners.

- Apply the Multiple Intelligences theory to your virtual professional development:

  Pappas, Christopher. 2014. "How Multiple Intelligences Theory Can Be Implemented in eLearning." eLearning Industry. March 29. https://elearningindustry.com/how-multiple-intelligences-theory-can-be-implemented-in-elearning.

Illuminate

- Watch Howard Gardner discuss Multiple Intelligences:

  Purefoy, Derrick. 2009. "Howard Gardner of The Multiple Intelligence Theory." November 7. YouTube video. www.youtube.com/watch?v=l2QtSbP4FRg.

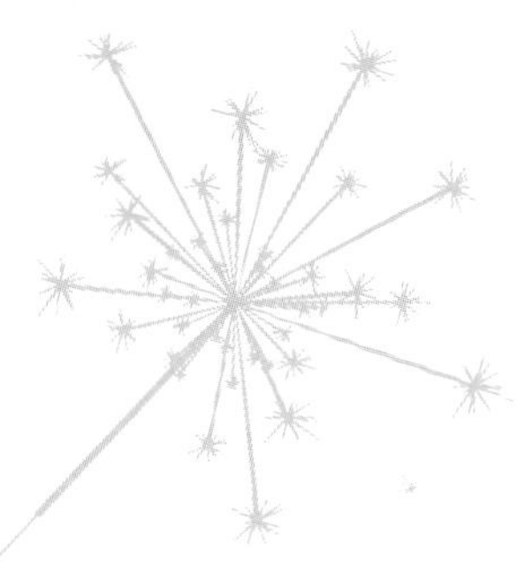

INSIGHT FROM THE FIELD

Ideas for Reaching Your Audience

Shared by Linda Schumacher

- As you plan your presentation, remember that the audience will contain all sorts of learners. By planning ahead and carefully balancing your presentation, you will reach everyone in your audience.
- Some will need to get up and move, so make sure you have one or more activities when they can get out of their chairs and move. It's especially important to do this in the second half of a long training day.
- Some learners will be visual and want to take notes, so provide handouts including spaces to write notes. The best handouts contain reflective questions, spaces to take notes, and resources to use later, all aligned with the agenda of your presentation. I even bring pens to give away, which encourages note-taking and are always a big hit.
- Some learners prefer to listen and not speak, so avoid requiring everyone to speak in a group. Even introducing oneself in front of a group of ten or more people can create anxiety for some people and will divert their attention from your presentation. Introductions are important, but they can be done through activities in small groups.
- Most learners have a lot to share, and they love to hear from their peers, so plan time to share and affirm the expertise of your audience in partners or small groups.
- Watch a video of Linda Schumacher sharing tips for supporting diverse learners (scan QR code or type URL into web browser).

https://vimeo.com/850578659

Create a Sense of Belonging

Connection is the energy that exists between people when they feel seen, heard, and valued; when they can give and receive without judgment; and when they derive sustenance and strength from the relationship. —Brené Brown

Intention

Deeply committing to cultivating cultural awareness and a sense of belonging will help provide a safe space for participants to interact, grow, and learn. When the participants feel welcomed, respected, valued, and appreciated, they will be more motivated to engage in the learning experiences and connect with others. Incorporating inclusive pedagogical practices will help you to create an emotionally safe environment in which all individuals are able to learn.

Implementation

- Use introductions and your individual and group interactions to acknowledge the diversity of the group you are working with. Recognize that individuals have unique perspectives based on their age, gender, sexual orientation, ethnicity, education, neurodiversity, socioeconomic status, and many other characteristics and demographic factors, as well as the intersections of all of the above. (See Activities #23–26—Participant Introductions.)
- Ask participants to introduce themselves with the name they would like to be called and to explain how to pronounce their name.
- Invite participants to share their gender pronouns as part of their introductions. Be intentional about using participants' pronouns to show respect and support an inclusive environment. To learn more about using gender pronouns, visit https://pronouns.org/how and watch "What Are Pronouns?" at www.youtube.com/watch?v=3xpvricekxU&.
- Rethink your language. Your choice of words can create or dissolve the sense of safety felt by participants. Stay current on words and phrases that reflect a commitment to diversity, and use language in ways that show participants you are striving to create an inclusive environment.

- Utilize key terms and relevant standards to build a shared understanding of the importance of creating welcoming and supportive learning communities. These statements are powerful examples for using standards to clarify expectations and springboard meaningful discussions.

  From the NAEYC Code of Ethical Conduct:

  "Ethical Responsibilities to Colleagues. In a caring, cooperative workplace, human dignity is respected, professional satisfaction is promoted, and positive relationships are developed and sustained. Based upon our core values, our primary responsibility to colleagues is to establish and maintain settings and relationships that support productive work and meet professional needs."

  From the National Board for Professional Teaching Standards' *Early Childhood Generalist Standards*, 3rd edition:

  "Standard III: Fostering Equity, Fairness, and Appreciation of Diversity. Accomplished early childhood teachers embrace diversity. They model and nurture treating others with equity, fairness, and dignity."

  See the Investigate section for additional resources for key terms and standards.
- Establish group agreements/guidelines to create a respectful and safe learning environment. (See Activity #30—Group Agreement.)
- Provide opportunities for participants to share stories that reflect their diverse backgrounds and experiences. (See Activity #28—Shoebox Autobiography and Insight from the Field: Learn about Your Colleagues on page 18.)
- Model and demonstrate active listening. Design small-group activities and interactions that help everyone feel seen and heard. (See Activities #67–80—Fostering Meaningful Interactions.)
- Make sure your visuals, resources, quotes, stories, and examples reflect and represent diverse people and situations without stereotyping. Be intentional about continually enhancing your materials, images, and researched facts from new and diverse sources. Consider creating a professional learning plan to guide you in building your understanding of diversity and inclusion. Use the resources listed in the Investigate section below as a starting point for enhancing your knowledge.
- Build an understanding of implicit bias:

  "Bias that results from the tendency to process information based on unconscious associations and feelings, even when these are contrary to one's conscious or declared beliefs." (www.dictionary.com/browse/implicit-bias)
- Discuss how implicit bias is part of all of us and share an example of how it affects our actions. A personal example will help create a safe place for others to share. Consider asking this question as a reflection: *How might our own biases influence our thoughts or actions?*

- Continually develop your working knowledge of cultural competency, implicit bias, and supporting diversity, equity, and inclusion. We have provided a range of resources to support your continued learning.
- Encourage feedback. Ask participants to speak up if they see, hear, or experience anything that feels uncomfortable for them.

KEY TERMS

"**Diversity** refers to anything that sets one individual apart from another, including the full spectrum of human demographic differences as well as the different ideas, backgrounds, and opinions people bring."

"**Inclusion** implies a cultural and environmental feeling of belonging and sense of uniqueness. It represents the extent to which employees feel valued, respected, encouraged to fully participate, and able to be their authentic selves."

"**Equity** encompasses fair treatment for all, while striving to identify and eliminate inequities and barriers."

Source: *Boden, Seth. 2020. "Start Here: A Primer on Diversity and Inclusion (Part 1 of 2)."* Leading the Way *(blog),* Harvard Business Publishing. *July 23, 2020.*

"**Implicit bias** refers to the attitudes or stereotypes that affect our understanding, actions, and decisions in an unconscious manner."

Source: *Staats, Cheryl. 2013.* State of the Science: Implicit Bias Review 2013. *Columbus, OH: Kirwan Institute, Ohio State University.*

Investigate

- Resources for enhancing your knowledge of key terms and standards related to diversity, equity, and inclusion:

  NAEYC Developmentally Appropriate Practice (DAP) Position Statement Glossary
  www.naeyc.org/resources/position-statements/dap/glossary

  NAEYC Advancing Equity Initiative
  www.naeyc.org/our-work/initiatives/equity

  Racial Equity Tools Glossary
  www.racialequitytools.org/glossary

  The National Board for Professional Teaching Standards' *Early Childhood Generalist Standards*, 3rd edition. See Standard III, page 34.
  www.nbpts.org/wp-content/uploads/2017/07/EC-GEN.pdf

  Karen Yin's Conscious Style Guide website—information and resources on using inclusive, empowering, and respectful language
  https://consciousstyleguide.com/about/

  NAEYC Code of Ethical Conduct and Statement of Commitment
  www.naeyc.org/sites/default/files/globally-shared/downloads/PDFs/resources/position-statements/Ethics%20Position%20Statement2011_09202013update.pdf

- Additional resources for creating a sense of belonging:

  Lewis, Greg. 2017. "Why Creating a Sense of Belonging Is a Gateway to Diversity and Inclusion." *LinkedIn Talent Blog*. November 2, 2017.

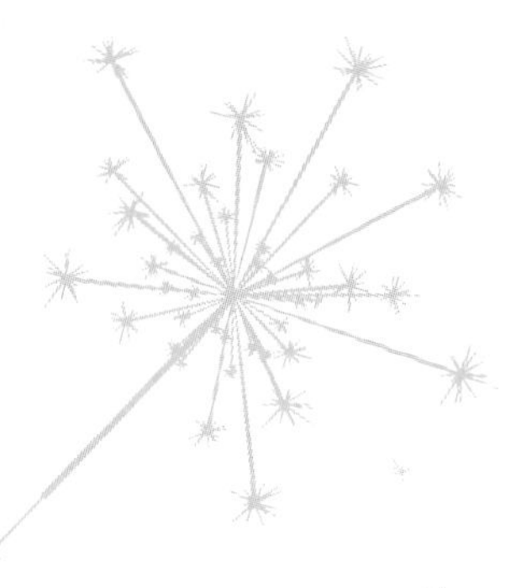

www.linkedin.com/business/talent/blog/talent-acquisition/why-creating-sense-of-belonging-is-gateway-to-diversity-and-inclusion.

Boudreau, Emily. 2020. "A Leader's Guide to Talking about Bias: How a Binary View of Racism Can Inhibit Productive Conversations about Race in School Settings" *Usable Knowledge* (blog). Harvard Graduate School of Education, August 3, 2020. www.gse.harvard.edu/news/uk/20/08/leaders-guide-talking-about-bias.

Marone, Mark. 2021. "4 Steps to Creating a Brave DEI Space in the Workplace." *Dale Carnegie* (blog). June 3, 2021. www.dalecarnegie.com/blog/create-a-brave-dei-spaces-in-workplace.

Mind Tools. n.d. "How to Thrive in a Multi-Generational Workplace: Avoiding Conflict and Creating Opportunity." *Mind Tools* (blog). Accessed August 16, 2023. www.mindtools.com/pages/article/multigenerational-workplace.htm.

INSIGHT FROM THE FIELD

Learn about Your Colleagues

Shared by Debbie LeeKeenan

Begin each session with an opportunity to learn more about your colleagues. You can do this in partners, trios, or the whole group, depending on the size of your group and the amount of time you have. This activity builds a culture of belonging, inclusion, risk-taking, and trust.

- Use different prompts, such as these:
  - Share something about your name—how you got it, what it means, and so on.
  - Share a memorable children's book or story from your childhood (it can be a positive memory or a negative memory) and tell why it is memorable.
  - Culture in your bag: share something from your handbag or wallet that tells something about you.
- Before you move on to another agenda item, be sure to acknowledge people taking risks by sharing something important to them. Other people can also express appreciation to the group.
- If you are leading a multi-session training or a staff meeting, use different prompts at each session.

Explore additional information and ideas:
Reflecting on Anti-bias Education in Action: The Early Years, a film by Debbie LeeKeenan, John Nimmo, and Filiz Efe McKinney.
www.antibiasleadersece.com/the-film-reflecting-on-anti-bias-education-in-action

Strategy #5

Use Strengths-Based Approaches to Build Trusting Relationships and Increase Engagement

Intention

Creating and supporting an engaged learning community is foundational to providing applicable and meaningful learning experiences. Integrate the five strategies of the Appreciative Inquiry approach into learning experiences to increase trust, participation, engagement, and positive outcomes.

Implementation

Bring the five strategies of Appreciative Inquiry—Inquire, Illuminate, Include, Inspire, and Integrity—into your professional development sessions:

Inquire—Strive to create a culture of inquiry by asking positive questions that guide people to share their best experiences, thoughts, or ideas linked to the focus of the workshop. Truly listen to their responses to let individuals know you value their contributions.

Illuminate—Become a strengths spotter! Build confidence by highlighting the best you see in each individual, the group, and the work they are doing. Simple statements can have a profound effect; consider using statements similar to these:

- *The story you just shared reflects your deep love of children.*
- *I can see by the expression on your face how much you value the support of your colleagues.*
- *I greatly appreciate your willingness to participate in this activity.*

Include—Create opportunities for the voices of the participants to be heard. Structure activities that encourage focused, inclusive conversations to occur between individuals from all positions, backgrounds, and experiences. (See Activities #67–80—Fostering Meaningful Interactions.)

Inspire—Give people hope by inquiring about their vision, dreams, and future aspirations! Provide a sense of direction by focusing on a brighter future. (See Activities #69—Hopes and Dreams, #80—Envisioning Future Success, and #81—Create a Vision Statement.)

Integrity—Establish an environment that lets the participants know they are expected to give their best and understand that everyone is held to the same standards. Be a role model by keeping your word and by creating and honoring group agreements, even in challenging situations.

Design and facilitate learning experiences throughout the session that allow participants to reflect on and share their strengths in partner or small-group activities. (See Activities #49—Make a Handprint and #70—Choose an Item.) Use these sample questions as a starting point. Be creative and customize the questions so they relate to the focus of your presentation:

- What brings you joy and a sense of satisfaction in your daily work?
- What is one story from your classroom that captures what you are proudest of as an early childhood educator?
- Over the last six months, when have you felt most alive and electrified by your work? What made this experience so exciting for you?
- What motivates you to do your very best?
- If you were to be given an award for your teaching, what would it be for? What specific skills would have helped you to win this award? Who do you think would have nominated you: Parents? Co-teachers? A supervisor? A community organization?
- What do your colleagues typically ask you for help with? What skills or talents do you feel you share with your colleagues on a regular basis?
- What is your perfect workday, from the moment you arrive until you leave at the end of the day? Share as many details as you can.
- What is something you accomplished in the past that you're proud of?

Investigate

- Resources to expand your knowledge of Appreciative Inquiry:

The Cooperrider Center for Appreciative Inquiry, Champlain College. https://appreciativeinquiry.champlain.edu.

Drolette, Ellen. 2020. "How Child Care Workers Can Find More Joy in Each Day: With Appreciative Inquiry, You Can Help Your Brain Pick Up the Brightest Moments." *Famly* (blog). December 16, 2020. https://famly.co/blog/appreciative-inquiry-child-care.

Stuart, David, Todd Nordstrom, Kevin Ames, and Gary Beckstrand. 2017. *Appreciate: Celebrating People, Inspiring Greatness.* Salt Lake City, UT: Trainer Institute Publishing.

Whitney, Diana, Amanda Trosten-Bloom, and Kae Rader. 2010. *Appreciative Leadership: Focus on What Works to Drive Winning Performance and Build a Thriving Organization*. New York: McGraw-Hill.

Design Compelling Presentations

Intention

A relevant and concise presentation by the facilitator is an essential technique for sharing new information and knowledge. To keep participants engaged, keep your presentations brief and provide opportunities for interaction and questions.

Implementation

- **Select a topic** that you are passionate about. Your enthusiasm will help the participants relate to the new information. Share why the topic is so important to you at the beginning of your presentation.
- **Hone the intent** of your presentation by asking yourself this question: "What are the key points I want the participants to take away?"
- **Be intentional** when deciding on the content. Select three or four main points to build your presentation around.
- **Develop an outline** for your presentation that includes factual information, relatable examples, and stories that illustrate the facts.
- **Focus on sharing information** in ways that are relatable to your audience. (See Activities #31–40—Presenting New Information and Knowledge.)
- **Consider using visuals** to enhance your presentations. Visuals can help keep the audience focused on your message. Become familiar with the technology you will use and practice setting up and sharing your presentation. Use the 10-20-30 Rule of PowerPoint, developed by Gary Kawaski, as a guide:
    - ten slides
    - twenty minutes
    - thirty-point font (this prevents you from putting too much information on each slide)
- **Present** with confidence and positive energy. Even if you are nervous, it always helps to smile, take a few deep breaths, and make eye contact with the participants! (See Strategy #12—Bring Positive Energy, Fun, and Memorable Moments to Your Workshops!)
- **Start strong!** Connect your topic to outcomes for children. Begin each session by establishing that a commitment to professional growth is fundamental to creating high-quality learning experiences. Consider starting your presentation using one of these reflective activities:

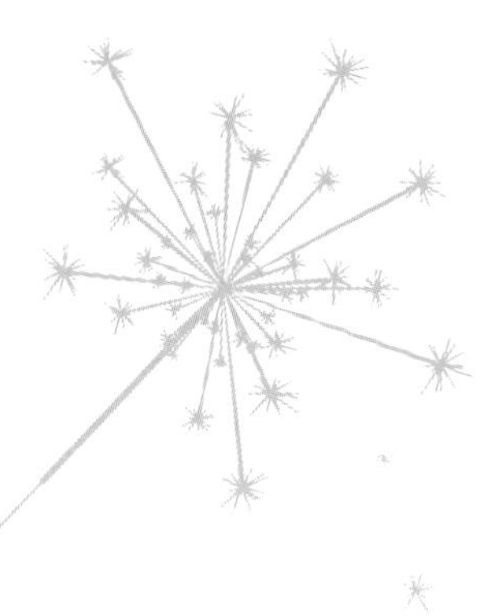

- Share a quote with a relevant message. This sample quote generates meaningful conversation:

We should remember that there is no creativity in the child if there is no creativity in the adult: the competent and creative child exists if there is a competent and creative adult. —Carlina Rinaldi, *In Dialogue with Reggio Emilia*

- Use current research and data points to stress the value and lasting effects of the work of early childhood educators. For example:

There are only 2,000 days between the newborn baby and when that child will show up in kindergarten. It is urgent that we use the best scientific information to make sure we support all our children so they can succeed in school. Our children can't wait. —Dr. Andrew Melzoff, University of Washington Institute for Learning and Brain Science

- Use quotes and data points that are timely and relevant to your presentation topic so they resonate with the participants.

- **Share a story** that captures the essence of your presentations. Participants are more likely to remember the key points when they are woven into a story.
- **Set a time limit** for your presentation. Ten- to fifteen-minute segments work well. Practice your presentation to be sure you can deliver it in the desired time frame. (See Strategy #8—Plan and Manage Time.)
- **Engage** the participants by asking questions during and following the presentation.
- **Follow presentations with activities** that allow participants to discuss or practice the information you shared.

Individualize

- Keep each presentation fresh and meaningful. Seek out new stories, facts, and visuals that bring the topic to life!
- Be sure that your presentation is culturally and linguistically responsive. Consider these questions from the National Center on Early Childhood Development, Teaching and Learning (https://eclkc.ohs.acf.hhs.gov/sites/default/files/pdf/clr-express-checkout.pdf):
    - "Is the content culturally appropriate for the intended audience? For example, does the content address topics that are relevant or familiar to the audience?"
    - "Does the content reflect the experiences and backgrounds of the audience?"
    - "Are people put first and then their language, culture, or disability put second (e.g., people with disabilities, children who speak Spanish)? Are abilities and strengths emphasized?"

- "Are the images of people and activities current and up to date? Do the images represent the intended audience in their demographics, physical appearance, behavior, and cultural elements?"
- "Will your audience be able to connect with the pictures and visual images used?"
- "Do the case studies, scenarios, and vignettes reflect diverse cultural perspectives and diverse families?"
- "Will your audience be able to relate to the information provided?"

INSIGHTFUL TIP

from Linda Schumacher

"If you are presenting virtually, it is important to be an expert at the online platform being used. Practice using all the tools available and use them to 'shake up' your presentation. Investing time in advance to learn the online tool will help you avoid embarrassing technology failures and will make your presentation more fun and varied."

Investigate

- Tips for enhancing your presentations:

  Stillman, Jessica. 2020. "Follow the 10-20-30 Rule for Killer Presentations." Inc. November 5, 2020. www.inc.com/jessica-stillman/presentations-guy-kawasaki-10-20-30-rule.html.

Illuminate

- Watch some TED Talks to inspire your presentation skills:

  TED Staff. 2021. "15 Most Inspiring TED Talks from Teachers and Educators." TopEducationDegrees.org. Updated November 2021. www.topeducationdegrees.org/15-inspiring-ted-talks-from-teachers-and-educators.

Strategy #7

Use Outcomes as a Foundation for Workshop Design

Intention

Begin with the end in mind! Take time to get clear on what you want participants to learn or do as a result of the professional development you are designing. Just as teachers plan activities for children based on the goals they have for children's development and the outcomes they are trying to achieve, you need to plan your workshop activities based on what you want participants to achieve. Specific outcomes are helpful for creating post-training assessments. (See appendix: Sample Workshop Evaluation Forms.)

Implementation

- Develop a description of the topic and content you want to cover.
- Create concrete learning objectives or outcomes for the session. Be careful of overload; three to four outcomes for a two- or three-hour session are enough.
- Outcomes should be written as active verbs and answer these questions:
  - What will the participants be able to do (what skill will they be able to demonstrate or master) as a result of attending the session?
  - What new information will participants be able to understand (describe, identify, explain)?
  - What will participants feel (consider new perspectives, have a shift in attitude)?
  - What impact will the workshop session have on children and families?
- Share the learning objectives with participants to build a shared understanding of the focus of the session.
- Incorporate an assessment of the stated learning objective as part of the evaluation form for the professional development session. (See the appendix for a workshop-specific evaluation form.)

Examples

- For a workshop on "Incorporating Literacy throughout Your Day"

  Participants will be able to

  - **Define** literacy and understand the developmental milestones
  - **Incorporate** literacy materials and learning experiences in all aspects of the day
  - **Choose** materials in all curriculum areas that support literacy

    - **Identify** the criteria for choosing books for infants, toddlers, and preschoolers
- For a workshop on "A Leader's Guide to Energize Professional Development: 25 Surefire Strategies"

  Participants will be able to

    - **Utilize** a variety of strategies, methods, and techniques to actively engage teachers
    - **Create** learning experiences that meet the needs of adult learners with respect for their diverse cultures, backgrounds, experiences, and learning styles
    - **Design and deliver** motivating and engaging staff meetings and professional development sessions that support the program and individual teacher's goals

Individualize

- Your objectives will likely vary depending on how many participants are in your workshop, their level of knowledge and experience, and how long your session is.
- Use Bloom's Taxonomy for a broad range of verbs to help you craft your objectives in a concrete, measurable way. (See below for resources.)

Investigate

- For an overview on writing learning objectives:

  How to Write Effective Learning Objectives in 5 Steps
  www.continu.com/blog/write-learning-objectives
- Learn more about Bloom's Taxonomy:

  Armstrong, Patricia. 2010. "Bloom's Taxonomy." Vanderbilt University Center for Teaching. https://cft.vanderbilt.edu/guides-sub-pages/blooms-taxonomy.

  Shabatura, Jessica. 2022. "Using Bloom's Taxonomy to Write Effective Learning Outcomes." *TIPS* (blog), University of Arkansas. July 26, 2022. https://tips.uark.edu/using-blooms-taxonomy.

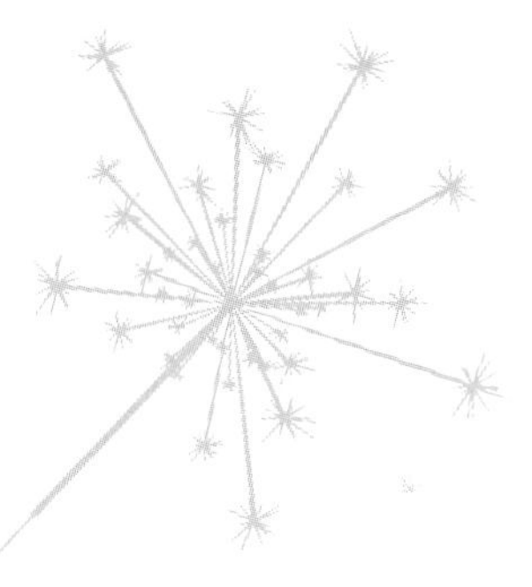

Strategy #8

Plan and Manage Time

You rarely have time for everything you want in this life, so you need to make choices. And hopefully your choices can come from a deep sense of who you are. —Fred Rogers

Intention

Thoughtfully plan how you will use the time available to help you deliver compelling professional development. Clearly communicate with participants about the schedule for the workshop to let them know you value their time and help you to stay on track to accomplish the goals for the session.

Implementation

- Determine the specific amount of time that you have. For workshops longer than two hours, allow for breaks.
- Review your goals for the session and be realistic about how much you can accomplish within that time frame.
- Develop a consistent structure for your workshops, similar to this example:

- Welcome and Overview
- Reflective/Centering Activity
- Presentation and/or Discussion of Key Issues
- Opportunity to Practice Applying Ideas
- Closing Reflection

- Create a schedule for the session to guide you. The more detailed your plan is, the easier it will be to stay on track. This type of chart is helpful:

  Workshop Title:

  Date: **Time:**

Time:	**Focus:** Presentation, Activity, Video Clip, Discussion	**Visuals or slide numbers**	**Materials Needed**

(See Workshop Planning Template in the appendix.)

- Share an overview of the agenda and schedule with the participants so they know what to expect. This helps participants focus and reduces the stress that some people feel when they don't have a clear plan. You can provide time check-ins during the presentation to help participants understand the flow of the session.
- Use a timer to remind you when to transition between segments of the schedule. This is especially important toward the end of the session so you have time for wrap-up activities and evaluations.

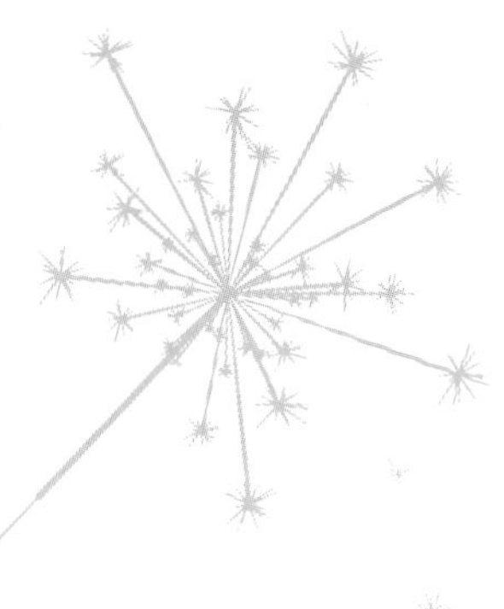

- Start and end on time. Let the participants know that you value their time. It can be helpful to let participants know you will be available for follow-up questions after the session ends. This allows people to leave on time while creating an extended opportunity for individual conversations.
- Provide specific time frames for individual reflections and group activities. For group work, ask each group to appoint a timekeeper, and then provide clear tasks and time frames. For example, if you are in groups of five, allot ten minutes for a task or a discussion point to allow each person to share for two minutes.
- Be intentional about keeping conversations focused on the topic you are discussing. Find a phrase you are comfortable with using to pause a participant's response that is off topic or taking too much time. Consider these options: "We are going to pause our conversation now to get back to . . ." "I appreciate your insights and would be happy to discuss this with you after the workshop." "Thank you for all of your thoughts and ideas. We are going to move on now."
- Be open to flexibility if the group is engaged in a topic or needs more information. Acknowledge the change to the group and adjust your schedule accordingly.
- Consider adding a question about time management to the workshop evaluation.
- Keep notes on each workshop—what worked well, what presented challenges, and what needed more or less time, and make revisions accordingly.

INSIGHTFUL TIP

from Linda Schumacher

"Do not pack too much content into one training. Give more time to exploring a concept and demonstrating it. It's better for learners to leave with one new idea very well learned than for them to be bombarded with too much new information."

Facilitate Group Discussion

Intention

Well-structured discussions energize and engage participants in the learning process. Working in pairs, triads, or small groups allows individuals to share their thoughts, experiences, and knowledge. Discussion groups also help create a collaborative learning experience in which everyone is gaining insights from the participants' diverse perspectives.

Many of the activities in this book include group work. These guidelines will help you form and manage the groups.

Implementation

- Provide clarity and focus for the discussion group. This can be a reflection, a set of questions, or a task.
- Structure the discussion groups. Divide participants into groups of the desired size. You can do this ahead of time or use some of these ideas:
  - When people arrive, give them a playing card. When it is time to form groups, have people who have the same suit work together.
  - If you are forming the group during the training, have people count off: 1 – 2 – 3 – 4 – 1 – 2 – 3 – 4 – 1. Then all the ones get together, all the twos, and so on.
  - Other options include dividing groups by specific roles or job titles, classroom teams, years of experience, or interest areas related to the topic.
- Provide a specific time frame; then establish guidelines for using the time. Example: "You will have eight minutes to share your thoughts, so because you are in groups of four, allow two minutes per person."

INSIGHTFUL TIP

from Debbie LeeKeenan

"A fishbowl model can allow for different learning styles. In this way, some people are observing, some participating, some documenting, and so on."

The fishbowl conversation model is an engaging strategy that has a small group of participants seated in a center circle to discuss a topic. The remaining participants are seated in a larger circle of chairs facing the inner circle so they can observe, listen, and take notes about the small group discussion. After the discussion has ended, participants can share their thoughts and reflections about what they learned and any questions they have. You can find an overview of this model on the Facing History and Ourselves website: www.facinghistory.org/resource-library/fishbowl.

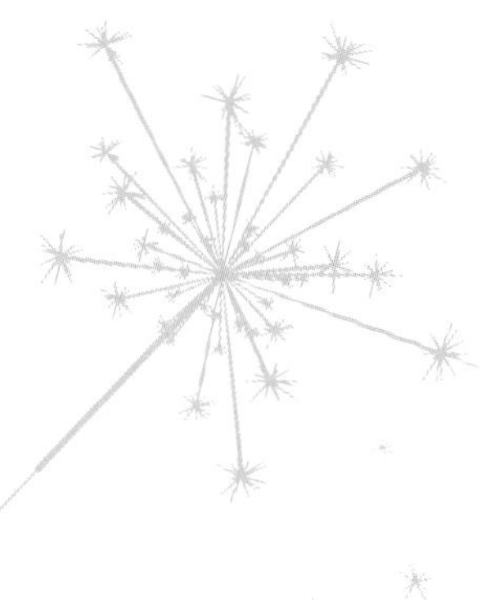

- Vary the group size based on the activity, the learning goal, and the time available.
- Pairs work well for introductions, listening activities, building connections between individuals, and short reflective exercises.
- Triads are useful for practicing communication skills and exploring issues or challenges in a supportive way. Triads are structured around three roles:
  - Speaker—the person who shares a situation or issue that is the focus of the exercise
  - Listener—the person who is listening to the speaker share their story
  - Observer—the person who observes the speaker and listener, takes notes, and provides feedback

Triads benefit from explicit time frames. This is one option that works well: five minutes for the speaker to share a specific situation, three minutes for the listener to ask reflective questions, and two minutes for the observer to share feedback. If time allows, it is helpful to have participants switch roles so each person has an opportunity to share, listen, and observe.

An example of a triad exercise:

ACKNOWLEDGE AND VALIDATE STRENGTHS

1. Ask the speaker to share a story about a challenge they recently faced and how they dealt with it. Encourage them to share how they used their strengths and past experiences to move past the challenge.
2. Have the listener focus on listening to the story and use keywords from the speaker's story to validate the speaker's strengths.
3. Ask the observer to provide feedback on the listener's paraphrasing and strengths-based validations.
4. Give each person a chance to experience each role.
5. Debrief by discussing how validation and rephrasing are powerful communication skills.

- Small Groups: Four to six participants can work together on a specific task. It can be helpful to have groups working on tasks that are similar but not the same. This helps keep the reporting back from being repetitive and generates a wider range of responses. Example: For a workshop on positivity, give each group a slightly different focus to brainstorm a top-ten list—top ten ways to bring more positivity to your work with children, to create positive relationships with parents, or to build positive relationships with your colleagues.
    - Appoint a group leader to keep track of time and record key points. Provide an easy way for the groups to select a group leader, for example, the person who is wearing the brightest color or whose birthday is closest to today.
    - Facilitate group sharing. Give the groups a specific focus for sharing their work. For example, ask each group to share two highlights from their discussions or talk about a change they would like to make. Then ask them to present their responses as a song, skit, or rap, or illustrate their response on large chart paper.
    - Wrap up and refocus. Be intentional about connecting the information the groups shared to the focus of the presentation. Be sure to thank the groups for their work and insights.

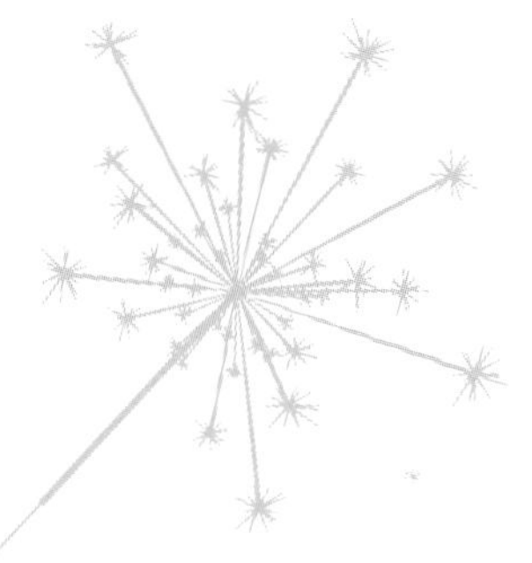

Strategy #10

Troubleshoot Challenges with Participants

When teachers are filled with a sense of their own strengths, vitalities, and aspirations, and when they are invited to imagine the possibilities that would make their life and work more wonderful, they get fully engaged in self-directed learning. Their energy goes up and their resistance goes down. —Bob and Megan Tschannen-Moran, *Evocative Coaching*

Intention

For some participants, resistance to professional development may begin before the training even starts. Educators may feel pressured to attend a session they don't think will be significant, or they may feel overwhelmed with other responsibilities. This resistance will likely become evident during the training through a variety of disruptive behaviors. As the facilitator, you will need to pay attention to the dynamics in the room and to individuals to address challenges and provide a meaningful session. It is helpful to remind yourself that everyone will engage with the presentation in their own way, based on their unique backgrounds, opinions, and experiences. Make sure to assume good intentions and avoid embarrassing or ostracizing any participant. Navigating resistance requires self-reflection, skill, and practice.

Implementation

UNENGAGED OR DISRUPTIVE PARTICIPANTS

Unengaged or disruptive behavior can range from participants focusing on their phones to having side conversations to giving themselves a pedicure! Some behaviors you may be able to ignore; others will require intervention.

- Move around the room during the session to help keep people focused.
- Pause and ask questions to assess the mood and needs of participants:
    - I can see this activity is not engaging you. Please share with me what you are experiencing.
    - I am hearing some concerns about today's topic. Can you help me understand what they are?

- Use a break time to talk to the disruptive or unengaged participant individually. Ask questions that help them share what they are experiencing (*"How can I best support you in today's session?* or *"What is the biggest challenge you are facing?"*). The personal connection you make helps them feel more invested.

DOMINATING OR HIJACKING THE DISCUSSION

Making sure that everyone has a chance to speak up can be challenging if there is a participant who dominates or derails the discussion by interrupting, always shouting out an idea, or going off topic.

- Redirect the participant to the goals of the session.
- Have participants share in pairs or small groups; then have each pair/small group report.
- Ask for hands when soliciting input and call on different people.
- Set a time limit for talking.
- Use a quota system (each person gets to express X number of ideas).
- When someone shares a thought or idea that cannot be addressed at that moment, let them know you are making a note of their comment. You can weave it into a segment of the presentation, discuss it during the question-and-answer session, or offer to talk about it after the session.
- Use a round-robin response strategy.
- Call a time-out, summarize what the participant has said, thank them for their contribution, and move on.

BEING OVERLY NEGATIVE, ARGUMENTATIVE, INAPPROPRIATE, OR CRITICAL

Negativity and criticism can cause discomfort among participants and alter the mood of the gathering. Participants may turn off and become disengaged or resentful if you don't keep people on track. Try one of these useful tactics:

- Acknowledge the person's comment and thank them for contributing.
- Ask the group for their ideas or thoughts.
- Brainstorm pros and cons of an idea.
- Look beyond the statement. Is the person trying to solve a particular issue or problem?
- Refer back to the group agreement you developed at the beginning of the workshop. (See Activity #30—Group Agreement.)

INSIGHTFUL TIP

from Debra Sosin

"Listen with your eyes and ears. Be observant of the participants and how they are receiving the information. Always allow space to hear from the participants."

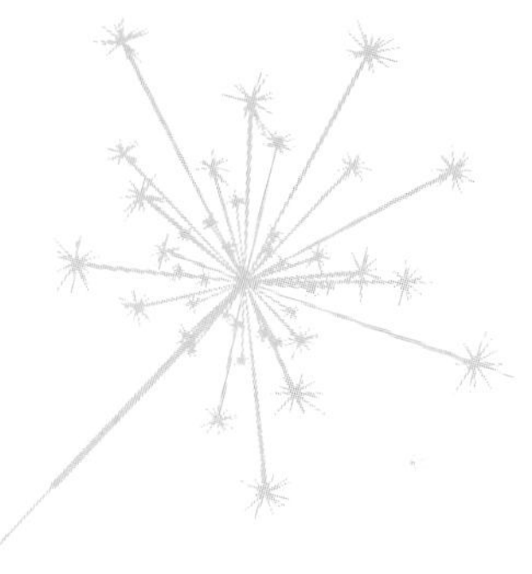

NOT PARTICIPATING

People may not participate in discussions or activities for a variety of reasons. Perhaps they don't feel well or they don't have the confidence to speak out. And remember, just because someone does not fully participate doesn't mean that they are not attending to or benefiting from the session.

- Let people know at the beginning that they can pass on any activity. Encourage them to observe the activity or write a reflection related to the activity to keep them engaged.
- Be sure to include a variety of learning experiences in your workshop to increase the likelihood of everyone feeling comfortable to participate in some way.

Notice when you are being triggered by someone's resistance. Practice self-regulation and mindfulness exercises to manage stress and develop some coping strategies to use in the moment, for instance, deep breathing. Build resilience through maintaining connections or creating joy or gratitude lists. Remember—behavior is communication. Consider the message in participants' behavior and try to address that in a supportive way. (See Insight from the Field—Navigating Challenges with Participants, below.)

Illuminate

- Listen to recordings of relaxation exercises (available in English and Spanish):
  Center for Early Childhood Mental Health Consultation
  www.ecmhc.org/relaxation_exercises.html

INSIGHT FROM THE FIELD

Navigating Challenges with Participants

Shared by Dr. Jayne Singer

Adapt this advice from Dr. Singer to help you navigate challenges with participants, such as disruptions. Consider this as a parallel process, in that how you deal with your adult participants mirrors how Dr. Singer recommends dealing with children, so in turn the adults treat children in this manner.

- When you find yourself challenged by a child's behavior, pause to let yourself become aware of where and how in your body you are feeling stress.
- Give yourself a moment to take care of yourself by pushing your breath out and then breathing in deeply and slowly.
- When a child is out of control, remember that your goal is to practice your own self-control first. That helps you not to get engaged in a control battle with the child, models self-regulation, and gives the child a chance to practice their own self-regulation in response to your co-regulation. (Compare this with engaging in a verbal disagreement or an emotionally charged discussion of ideas with a participant.)
- This also helps you both stay in relationship with each other as you focus on the person rather than the behavior.

Cultivate and Utilize External Collaborations

Collaboration allows us to know more than we are capable of knowing by ourselves. —Paul Solarz

Intention

Community building is a critical element of quality early childhood care and education and is just as important outside of a program as it is within it. Exposure to and collaboration with the wider community enriches a program and multiplies the resources that are available. Getting to know and engaging with the broader community engenders goodwill, builds connections, and provides opportunities to advocate (for individual programs as well as the early childhood field). Teachers who are involved with the larger community are more likely to be invested in their own programs and can become ambassadors representing them.

Implementation for Program Leaders

- Encourage your teachers to visit other programs.
    - Work with other directors to do a teacher swap or arrange for educators to go to observe another program.
    - Provide your teacher with some prompts regarding what to notice or look for, such as:
        - New and interesting curriculum ideas for relevant age groups
        - Ideas for family engagement
        - Ideas for documentation
        - Methods for guiding behavior
        - Evidence of team spirit
    - Share teachers' experiences at staff meetings. Determine whether there are ideas you would like to incorporate into your program and make an action plan.
- Invite outside specialists and/or parents to share their expertise at staff meetings or do a workshop.

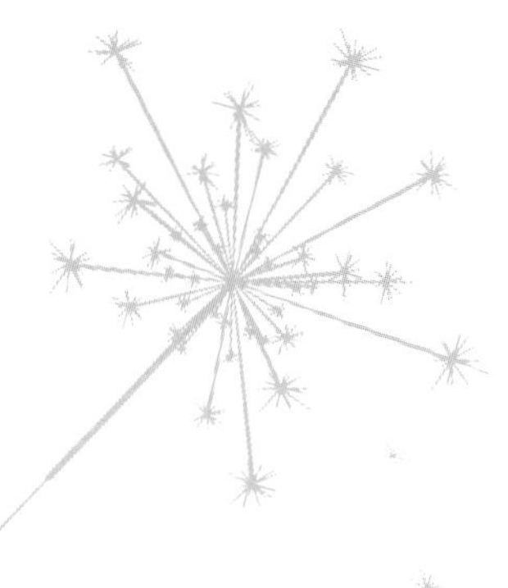

    - Research community organizations that provide services for families and children (for example, WIC, medical/dental, early intervention, recreation, museums, libraries).
    - Invite representatives from those organizations to present at a staff meeting or training; include guidance about the topic and prepared questions from staff.
    - Follow up with a thank-you and description of how your program benefited from their presentation.
- Partner with other programs for professional development. Find common topics or issues that will strengthen your programs and combine resources to bring new knowledge and ideas to your staff. Engaging in rich dialogue and receiving feedback from others adds new perspectives to their professional learning and the work they are doing.
    - Identify an outside trainer who will be able to provide a relevant and engaging session; be sure to talk with them first so they can be aware of the goals and values of the programs involved.
    - Facilitate a book group with educators from multiple schools.
    - Have a documentation sharing event with educators from local schools, presenting documentation on a specific topic.
- Get involved in a community service project that has meaning and relevance to your school community. Working together toward a goal of improved services for children and families cements relationships and can lead to new insights that guide curriculum and policies.
- Encourage your teachers to become members of community early childhood organizations (local affiliates of NAEYC, state-funded alliances). Invite them to share new information, perspectives, and knowledge at staff meetings or ask them to deliver a workshop.

Implementation for Outside Facilitators

- Be familiar with the local, regional, or statewide community and services available to early childhood constituents.
- Include outside experts or community agency representatives in live or virtual panels as part of your trainings.
- Utilize outside resources and perspectives (websites, videos, and so on) in your sessions.
- Add examples of community resources into your discussions when appropriate and relevant.
- Encourage participants to be positive advocates for the field in the outside community.

Strategy #12

Bring Positive Energy, Fun, and Memorable Moments to Your Workshops!

Nothing without joy. —Widely attributed to Loris Malaguzzi

Intention

The presence and energy you bring to your workshops will significantly affect the learning experience for participants. Facilitators must tap into what makes them unique as an individual and as an adult educator to create authentic and memorable workshops. Inspirational, relevant, fun, and interactive sessions will help participants fully engage with the information you are presenting and increase the likelihood that they will apply it to their practice. Be adventurous, step away from the comfort of using the same methodologies, and embrace new ideas.

Implementation

- **Set a positive intention.** Visualize your intention for the workshop coming to life. Keep your thoughts upbeat and focused on the outcomes you want to achieve.
- **Energize!** Prepare for the start of your presentation in ways that focus and energize you. Taking a quick walk, meditating briefly, reading a favorite poem, or hearing an uplifting piece of music can help you feel ready to begin your presentation.
- **Dress for success.** What makes you feel most confident? What colors invigorate you? What jewelry or

INSIGHTFUL TIPS

from Beth Fredericks

"Make your interest in and enthusiasm for what you are teaching visible to adults. They don't care if you don't care."

from Holly Elissa Bruno

"Use humor, movement, singing, and inspiring questions to engage participants."

from Linda Schumacher

"Humor! I find being a good trainer and facilitator includes entertaining people. Use humor, smile a lot, and be affirming and positive to your audience. Practice saying 'yes and . . .'"

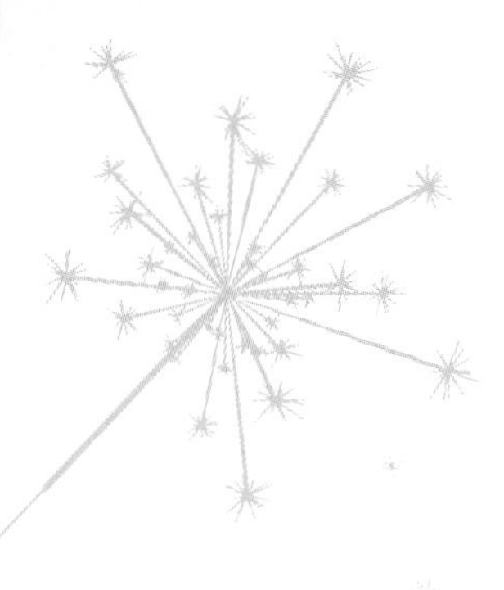

accessories can give the participants a sense of who you are? Bring vibrancy and pizzazz when you show up!

- **Smile.** Remember the words from the song in the musical *Annie*: "You're never fully dressed without a smile!"
- **Warmly greet participants.** Be available to welcome participants as they are entering the session.
- **Share a story.** Storytelling is a powerful way to draw participants into the material you are sharing. Develop an authentic and meaningful story that highlights your unique purpose and passion. Let the participants know where your enthusiasm for working in the early childhood field comes from. Vignettes from your work and life that illustrate a key point will help participants connect to and retain the information. Weave in some facts about your background that shaped your views on the information you will share. Encourage participants to share a story that relates to the topic, either with the whole group or in pairs. (See Activities #43—"Where I'm From" Poem and #50—Defining Moments.)
- **Play music.** Use music to keep the energy flowing. Develop a playlist to use when participants enter the session, during breaks, as backgrounds for activities, and as participants are leaving. Choosing music you love and that is relevant is another way to share something about yourself with participants. Here is an example of a playlist that Susan uses in her vision workshops:
  - "Pachelbel's Canon"—London Symphony Orchestra
  - "This is Your Fight Song (Rachel Platten Scottish Cover)"—The Piano Guys
  - "A Thousand Years"—The Piano Guys
  - "One Direction—What Makes You Beautiful (5 Piano Guys, 1 piano)"—The Piano Guys
  - "What a Wonderful World (instrumental)"—Richard Clayderman
- **Share images.** Incorporate photos from your life and your work that reflect your values and interests in ways that are pertinent to the presentation.
- **Laugh.** Adding appropriate humor and funny anecdotes can generate laughter and ease tension. Be sure that you are not making any negative connotations or using offensive language.
- **Listen to yourself.** Pay attention to your tone of voice. You want to portray both confidence and energy. It can be helpful to record yourself during a session and listen to the recording to see if there are ways you could enhance your delivery. Solicit a friendly critique by inviting a trusted colleague or friend to attend a workshop and give you feedback.

- **Provide creative table materials.** Set out exciting and engaging materials on the tables. Consider displaying images; natural items, including flowers, rocks, and shells; or a sign that relates to your message and values. Sharing hands-on materials like play putty, stress balls, small fidget toys, fun pens, or stickers helps participants focus. Tablecloths enhance the beauty of the tables. (See Strategy #14—Preparing the Space.)
- **Express gratitude.** Take a few moments throughout your session to thank participants for attending, sharing their thoughts, or volunteering to be part of a demonstration or exercise.
- **Finish on a high note!** Ask participants to share how they will use what they learned from the workshop. (See Activities #89–97—Wrap-Up Activities.)

Investigate

- For a variety of videos, articles, quizzes, and podcasts related to happiness and strengths-based approaches:

  Greater Good Magazine from The Greater Good Science Center at the University of California, Berkeley
  https://greatergood.berkeley.edu

Strategy #13

Celebrate! Document and Share Ongoing Stories of Growth and Change

Intention

Finding creative ways to acknowledge the professional growth of the educators you are working with will help build the momentum needed to fuel an ongoing commitment to continued learning. Celebrating and documenting the learning that is happening weaves the value of professional development into the culture of the participants' programs.

Implementation for Program Leaders

- **Make it visible.** Highlight the focus of the professional learning and the positive changes that are occurring. Invite participants to create documentation that can be displayed throughout the program (entranceways, classrooms, hallways, staff rooms). Keep the documentation fresh, relevant, and exciting.
    - Example: *A program that worked collaboratively to create a new vision for their program posted the vision statement on a large poster at the entranceway of their building. Each month on the day of their staff meeting, a different classroom team posted photos of how they were bringing the vision to life! This document inspired rich dialogue between the staff, current and future families, board members, and visitors.*
    - Create a "Magic Moments" board where you and the teachers post pictures or descriptions of interesting and impactful interactions and activities, especially those related to professional development topics.
- **Share stories.** Provide opportunities for educators to share highlights from their daily work that link to the areas of professional development that you have been focusing on. Asking the following questions will help to spark relevant dialogue:
    - *What is an exciting change that you are seeing in your classroom related to __________ (a topic or area of professional growth you are focusing on)?*
    - *Share one example of a beneficial effect of our professional learning. How has our focus on __________ influenced you? The children? The families? Your colleagues?*

Have people share in the full group or in pairs; then work with the group to summarize the key points on a flip chart or digital whiteboard. (See Activity # 55—Create a Success Board.)

- **Present your work.** Hone the stories of your professional growth into a presentation for a local or national conference. Support educators in understanding the process of writing and submitting a conference proposal and formatting the presentation.
- **Write about it.**
  - Include stories that highlight everyone's professional growth in newsletters, blogs, and annual reports and on your website.
  - Write an article for a local paper or an early childhood publication that focuses on the impact of your professional development work.
  - Don't forget personal thank-you notes! Take time to write heartfelt notes that share specific reflections and observations to show participants that you are noticing the positive changes.
- **Celebrate!** Let the participants know that you value their dedication by finding unique and joyful ways to celebrate the achievements that are being made. Gestures of appreciation do not need to break the budget; finding small ways to consistently show that you value the work they are doing will boost morale and keep the focus on learning and growing together!
  - Share a special meal or snack to mark the end of the multi-session series.
  - Provide a small gift related to your vision and goals. (Consider cards with quotes, a group photo, an item from nature, or something similar.)
  - Extend opportunities to connect with others in the field.
  - Arrange a team outing to a museum or event.

Implementation for Outside Facilitators

- **Train leaders.** Provide professional development focused on leadership to empower leaders to implement effective professional development strategies in their own programs.
- **Make it visible.** Provide suggestions for and encourage teachers to document their own learning and make it visible in their program.
- **Share stories and experiences.** Include opportunities within your training for participants to relate the content to their own practice and accomplishments.
  - Ask questions that encourage participants to consider how they will use new information and ideas to enhance their practice.
  - Encourage participants to envision how what they are learning will improve their skills and enhance the quality of their program. Implement training activities that inspire participants to highlight positive aspects of their work. (See Activity #80—Envisioning Future Success.)
- **Celebrate!** End your session with appreciation and joy. Share an inspirational quote or small token.

Investigate

- Teacher appreciation ideas:

  8 Simple Ways to Make Teachers Feel Appreciated
  www.teachthought.com/pedagogy/teachers-feel-appreciated

  Fun gift ideas for teachers
  www.joyintheworks.com/25-free-printable-teacher-appreciation-gift-tags/

- Information on writing articles for publication:

  Writing for *Young Children* (NAEYC)
  www.naeyc.org/resources/pubs/yc/writing#writingforyc

  Writing for *Child Care Exchange*
  www.childcareexchange.com/opportunities-for-you/write-for-exchange

Section Two

Designing and Delivering Engaging and Impactful Professional Development Experiences

There's nothing better than people talking to each other, sharing best practices, and opening up communications. —Dan Gilbert

This section leads you through the key components of well-planned and engaging learning experiences. Here you will find a wide variety of specific, concrete examples of activities to set expectations, spark interest and curiosity, create excitement, energize participants, and promote reflection. Beginning with setting up the environment, you are guided through introductory activities that immediately involve the participants, as well as reflective practices, team-building activities, and interactive exercises to make sure that everyone's voice is heard and to foster a collaborative learning community. Finally, you will discover closing activities that inspire teachers to engage in ongoing reflection, implement next steps, consider new perspectives, assimilate new research, and integrate new ideas into their practice.

Workshop Basics

Follow these foundational guidelines to make any professional development experience a success:

- Gather and organize all your materials beforehand.
- Do a technology check to be sure everything is working properly. Be sure to test your videos, sound, links, internet connections, and for live events, your projector.

- Introduce an activity with a description of the intent—how does it fit into the overall workshop and topic?
- Provide an overview of the activity to the participants.
- Post instructions for activities (on a presentation slide, handout, or chart) so participants can refer to them.
- Inform participants of time allotted for an activity or discussion and provide warnings before time expires.
- Debrief the activity or discussion with the whole group to summarize and provide any additional information.
- See Tips for Facilitators in the appendix for additional guidance.

For virtual workshops, learn and utilize the various engagement options on whatever platform you are using: chat, question boxes, whiteboards, polls, games, or information sharing apps.

Setting the Stage

If we want teachers to offer well-designed and pleasing environments for children, we must design an environment like that for teachers. —Aarie Ward, Baxter Community Center

Creating a welcoming, inspiring, and comfortable environment lets participants know that you value their time and ideas and helps them feel invested in learning. Make sure to plan for how you are going to set up the space to foster the activities you have planned—individual reflections, pairs and small groups, and whole group interactions. Will you need space for people to move around? What about wall or table space to display resources?

You will also want to know something about your audience to help you connect with them (even before the workshop if possible). If you are a program leader providing a professional development session for your staff, you will likely know more about their needs (as individuals and as a group). If you are an outside facilitator, you want to determine what background information will most help you design a meaningful experience and connect with participants (for instance, their experience levels, individual learning styles, or interests), and how you can collect that information. You might have a conversation with the person arranging the session or create a survey that can be distributed with results sent to you before the session.

Planning and preparing ahead—for your activities, for designing the space, and for connecting with participants—will help ensure a successful workshop that will engage and inspire participants.

INSIGHTFUL TIP

from Karen Nemeth

"The most important thing I do to keep participants engaged is to learn about where they work and tailor my content to fit their curriculum, rules, and students! No one-size-fits-all workshops!"

Strategy #14

Preparing the Space

Intention

Space and environment play a major role in shaping behavior and fostering attentiveness, as well as sending a message about how we value the participants. Ideally, you want your training space to be comfortable, accessible, and visually pleasing (while not distracting). Space that is uncomfortable, drab, or aesthetically unappealing can cause participants to feel less energized and involved. The workshop space helps set the tone for the event.

Implementation

- Know your space.
    - Where is it located?
    - How do people get in? Is it accessible to everyone?
    - Is it near other spaces in the building that house potentially distracting activities?
    - What is the layout of the building—where are the restrooms, where can participants get water or snacks, where are the emergency exits?
    - What kind of technology is provided? What equipment do you need to bring? How will you set up your things?
    - What kind of seating arrangements are there?
        - While adult chairs and tables for small groups are often a preference, we might find ourselves having to deliver training in a school cafeteria, a theater-style room, or a children's classroom with adult participants sitting in preschool chairs or on the floor.
    - Could you do any activities outside if you want?
    - Make sure you are aware of any space constraints so that you can plan accordingly to best meet the needs of the participants.
- Confirm that you will be using the space in advance. Will there be any support people available to help with setup and technology? If you are not using your own space, make sure to get a contact person and phone number in case of any emergency.
- Personalize the space to make it comfortable for you and the participants. What can you add to make it feel less institutional? How can you best utilize the space to make it efficient, welcoming, and engaging for the participants? Use some items that are special and meaningful to you as decor—perhaps a quilt or interesting tablecloths, some nature items, inspirational books, or plants. Consider some items that would resonate with educators from a variety of backgrounds and with diverse learning styles.

- Arrive early enough to make sure the space is arranged for maximum effectiveness and that all your equipment is working, and to allow you time to greet participants as they arrive.

Investigate

- Explore how to set up your space:

    Room Arrangements for Training Sessions
    www.dummies.com/article/business-careers-money/business/human-resources/room-arrangements-for-training-sessions-142474

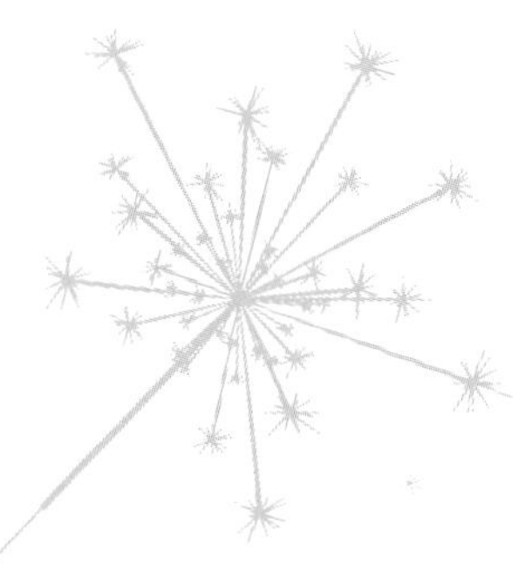

INSIGHT FROM THE FIELD

Create a Sense of Welcome and Belonging

Shared by Beth Fredericks

- I love greeting participants at the door. A fist bump on the way in is how I like to connect in a respectful, trustworthy, and caring way, affirming that each person has valuable things to contribute.
- The next "message" to participants is how the environment looks and feels. I put "stuff" on the table—materials we may use in the session, something from nature, a few sweets, and maybe something to fidget with to help participants pay attention. This visual lets them know that I was there early, I set up the room, I am paying attention to them, and, again, that I care about this time together.
- Finally, I intentionally structure the learning to build relationships among pairs of learners, small groups, and the whole group. This ensures that they learn to listen to and talk with one another, identifying ways they can learn from one another.
- For virtual presentations:
    - I See You: Take a moment to have people look at every other person in the group, and occasionally hold the gaze of the camera. Play some background music to get grounded and centered.

I bring my whole self to the job of facilitator. I embrace whoever is in the room and work toward creating an ongoing community of learners—even if it's only for sixty minutes.

Watch a video interview of Beth sharing her tips and strategies for creating a sense of welcome (scan QR code or type URL into web browser)!

https://vimeo.com/861361288

Strategy #15

Troubleshoot Space and Equipment Challenges

Intention

Ideally all the logistical details that help make your session successful will proceed smoothly. But, as we know, something always comes up that has the potential to derail your carefully laid plans! The strategies below can help you troubleshoot some of the obstacles that create barriers to effective professional development.

Implementation

CHALLENGE: LESS-THAN-IDEAL SPACE

Sometimes you just have to make the best of the space you have. Consider how you can most effectively arrange the space and add your personal touches to make the space more welcoming and inviting.

- Make sure chairs are arranged so that everyone can see the front where you will be presenting and using audiovisuals or charts.
- Leave as much space as you can so that people are not overcrowded and can move about the room for any activities you have planned.
- If there is wall space available, post inspirational pictures or quotes.
- Include a variety of activities that allow for some movement, and insert energizers as needed. (See Activities #61—Energizers and #62—Shake Down, Warm Up!)
- Acknowledge space issues when you start the workshop and encourage participants to make themselves as comfortable as possible based on their own needs.

CHALLENGE: EQUIPMENT FAILURE

You're about to get started when your computer or projector stops working. There is an unexpected power outage. Or perhaps it's just that all your markers have dried up.

- Always have a Plan B (and C and D)!
- Check your equipment the day before, and if possible, test it in the space you will be using for the training.
- Have your slides on a thumb drive as well as a printed copy. You can also email them to the host or technical support person beforehand.
- Have alternate ways to present the training in the case of glitches.
- Keep your cool and remain professional.

- Acknowledge the problem and solicit help or ideas for alternatives from the participants. There just might be a tech expert among them!
- Use the situation as a learning opportunity to help participants explore problem solving and flexibility.

INSIGHTFUL TIP

from Beth Fredericks

"#%^ happens. Don't stress, just fix the A/V, fix the lighting, open the window, find your notes. Whatever it is, it's a real moment. People are human (you included)!"

Building Engagement through Opening Activities

First moments matter. —Jane Dutton

Start strong! The opening minutes of the workshop are important for setting the tone of the session. Find unique ways to help participants to connect with you and one another. When working with groups who don't know one another, these opening activities provide an opportunity to build connections. For in-house groups, these activities provide new ways to learn about one another and strengthen relationships.

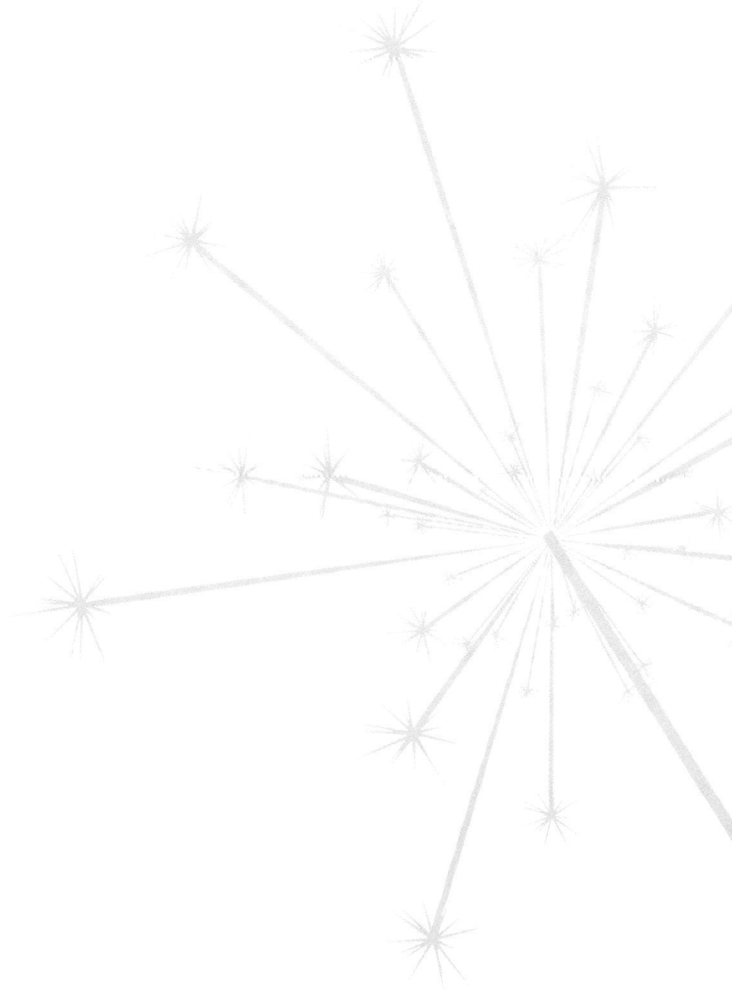

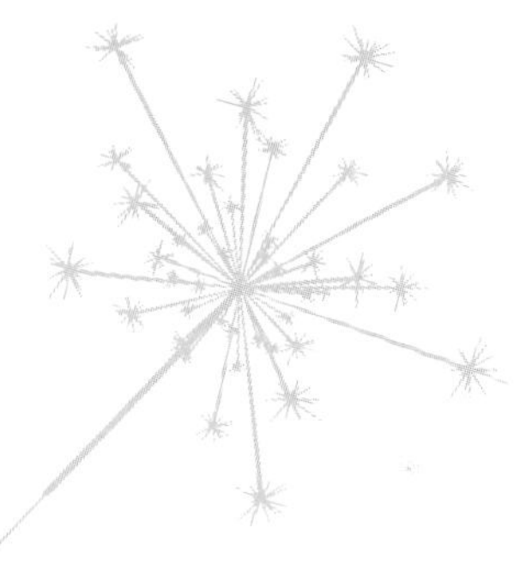

Activities #16–21

Warm-Up Activities

Intention

Generate excitement and curiosity in your workshop before it even begins! Warm-up activities engage participants as they are arriving, before the official start of the session. They pique interest and start connecting people to the topic. For facilitators, these activities also provide key insights into participants' knowledge, experience, perspectives, hopes, and beliefs.

Implementation

- Design warm-up activities with content that relates to the topic of the workshop.
- Prepare the warm-up activity and materials, and have it set up before participants start arriving.
- Provide instructions (slide, handout, or posted on the wall) so that participants can be involved right away.
- As participants arrive, greet them and invite them to engage in the warm-up activity.
- As people settle in, gather the group and begin the session. Thank people for participating in the activity. Note the work that was done and let people know that you will be addressing key points during the session.
- After (or as part of) introductions, return to the warm-up activity and debrief, noting trends or similarities. Keep charts posted to refer to during the session.

Activity #16: Dot Voting

- Write a series of nonjudgmental statements related to the topic on a poster or chart. Provide participants with dot stickers and invite them to "vote" by putting a dot on the statements they agree with. For example:
    - In a session on process art: *"I feel comfortable with children getting messy." "Children need an opportunity to express themselves." "We use many materials from nature for children to create art."*
- As a variation, you could draw a continuum line after the statement and ask participants to put their dot along the line to indicate how much they agree with it.
- In the debrief, note the trends and assure participants that there will be opportunities to further explore these ideas during the training.

Activity #17: Sentence Completion

- Have the first part of a statement related to the topic posted as participants arrive. For instance:
  - For a workshop on environments: "*The most important part of a quality early learning environment is . . .*"
- Invite participants to complete the sentence by writing their answer on an index card and putting it in a basket (or another container), or on a sticky note on the posted chart. This process can be anonymous.
- At the beginning of the workshop, or as part of the introductions, note the answers on the chart or pass the basket around and have each participant pick a card to read (and chart the answer).
- During the debrief, reflect on how the unique perspectives and diverse backgrounds of the group are reflected in the responses.
- This activity can also be done as an opening activity in small groups or at tables. Have a series of sentence stems written out on separate cards. Provide each group with a couple of cards to discuss.

Activity #18: Opening Mini-Reflections

- Provide a reflection sheet/question for participants to consider and fill out as they arrive. For example:
  - In a workshop focused on the environment, have people reflect and write on a prompt such as, "*The thing I like best about my work environment is ______ because ______.*"
- In the debrief, ask for some volunteers to share their responses and chart them.
- To follow up on this in the introductions, you can have people pair up to introduce themselves and share their reflections.

Activity #19: Alphabet Chart

- Post a chart with the letters of the alphabet listed vertically. If the group is large, post two or more charts around the room, or have one chart at each table for small groups to work on.
- Provide a prompt for participants to consider words that relate to the topic. List the prompt at the top of the chart.
  - For example, "*Find a word that exemplifies a quality environment for each letter,*" or "*What is a word that relates to teamwork?*"
  - Participants add words that start with each letter to the chart(s).

- Variation: Provide a handout of an alphabet chart for individuals to complete on their own. Solicit responses and chart them as part of your welcome and introductions.

Activity #20: Joys and Challenges Chart

- Post two charts—one for joys and one for challenges—related to the topic. For example:
    - The Joys and Challenges of Engaging Families in your Program
    - The Joys and Challenges of Reading and Talking with Young Children
    - The Joys and Challenges of Staff Meetings
- Participants add their thoughts as they arrive.
    - If tables are set up for participants to sit at, this activity can also be done at the tables as people are coming in and getting settled. You can also use the charts as a prompt for when participants introduce themselves.

Activity #21: Word Association

- Post chart paper with a word (connected to the topic) at the top and invite participants to write words they associate with that title word.
    - For example: *"Separation," "STEM,"* or *"Teamwork."*
    - This could also be done as a word cloud or web. Write the word in the center of the chart with stems for people to build on.

For virtual workshops, consider using polls, the chat box, or online apps such as word clouds to generate participation.

Introduce Yourself

Intention

As the facilitator, you will be introducing yourself first. This is your opportunity to establish credibility, create a connection with the audience, share your passion, and develop trust. What do you want people to know about you? Prepare your introduction ahead of time and vary it according to the audience and topic.

Implementation

- Build a connection with the group by sharing something you have done that relates to their work. Participants value experiences that are connected to their roles.
  - If you are familiar with the participants already, this might be more of a welcome than an introduction. You can add any new and relevant information.
- Identify your *why*—what connects you to the topic? Use an anecdote that highlights your experience with the topic. Where does your passion come from?
- Share a personal hobby or interest, or any fun fact, that people may relate to.
- Consider sharing a photo that captures the essence of your work, an interesting fact about yourself, or a passion you have.
- Express your appreciation for the participants' attendance and their dedication to the field.

Individualize

- Give just your name and ask participants what they would like to know about you. If you face a wall of silence, let it be for a few seconds. You may invite engagement by saying something like "Who will ask the first question?" If there are still no questions, you can convey that you understand that it is sometimes hard to be the first person to speak, and proceed with an introduction of yourself.

Investigate

- Tips for introducing yourself:

  The Training & Development World, "Trainer Introduction: How to Introduce Yourself at a Seminar with Purpose: The Do's" by Robert Bacal
  http://thetrainingworld.com/faq/startintrotrainer2.htm

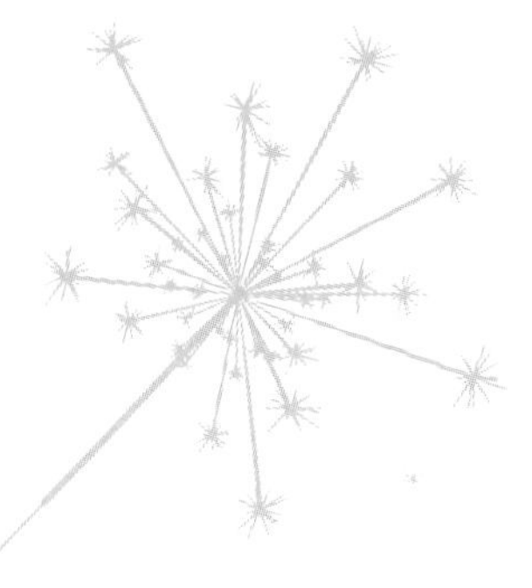

Activities #23–26

Participant Introductions

Intention

Participants like to know who else is in the session to recognize the diversity of the group and acknowledge the common goals they share. Introductions are the beginning of creating connections and nurturing a learning environment that welcomes all participants and their ideas. Ensuring that everyone has been introduced helps establish a safe and positive climate in which participants can feel energized and motivated. These activities are also useful for in-house groups to learn about one another in new ways and for you to learn more about the participants.

The following activities provide an opportunity for participants to be actively engaged while learning (or learning more) about one another. If the group is large, there likely won't be enough time for everyone to introduce themselves. You can have smaller groups or pairs introduce themselves to one another. You can also ask people to raise their hands or stand up according to different criteria to find out more about who is attending. For instance, ask who works with certain age groups or how long participants have been in the early childhood field.

Implementation

Activity #23: The Basics

- Ask participants to share basic information about themselves:
    - Their names and preferred pronouns
    - Where they work and what age(s) they work with
    - What role they play in their program
    - One thing they hope to get from the workshop. (This will help give you an idea of the group's expectations. You will be able to acknowledge what people hope to learn and let them know how that will be addressed.)
- Ask participants to share their name and one thing they know about the topic and one thing they want to learn.
- Note the variety of roles and experiences that are represented.

Activity #24: Weather Report

- Have participants share their names and where they are from (or where they work).

- As part of their introductions, ask participants to compare their knowledge or feeling about the training topic to a weather condition. This will give you a more general idea of people's experience and the climate of the group.
- Note the range of feelings or knowledge represented by the group.

Activity #25: Favorite Things

- Ask participants to say their names and their favorite items that relate to the training topic. For instance:
    - For a training on children's literacy, ask participants to name their favorite children's book (one that they read to children now or one that they remember having read to them).
    - For a training on self-care, you can ask them to name a favorite thing that brings them joy.
- Note the variety of answers and highlight that we all have unique preferences.

Activity #26: Pairs Interviews

- Pair up the participants and give them a few minutes to interview each other, framed around the training topic. For instance, they could ask about their favorite thing about the topic, a positive experience they've had related to it, and a related challenge they've faced.
- Give each interviewer one or two minutes.
- Each person introduces their partner, choosing two things to share about them.
- Partners can ask each other if it is all right to share those things first to ease any anxiety.

Individualize

Which introduction activity you choose will depend on the size of your group as well as how much time you have and how often the group will be meeting together. For a short, onetime workshop, introductions can be a quick sharing of names and a couple of facts; for a longer training or for a group that will be meeting more regularly, introductions can be a more involved activity that produces a deeper conversation.

Illuminate

- Watch a demonstration of participant introductions:

    North Star Facilitators. "5 Ways to Introduce Group Participants." YouTube video. www.youtube.com/watch?v=49qtagvxldA&t=9s.

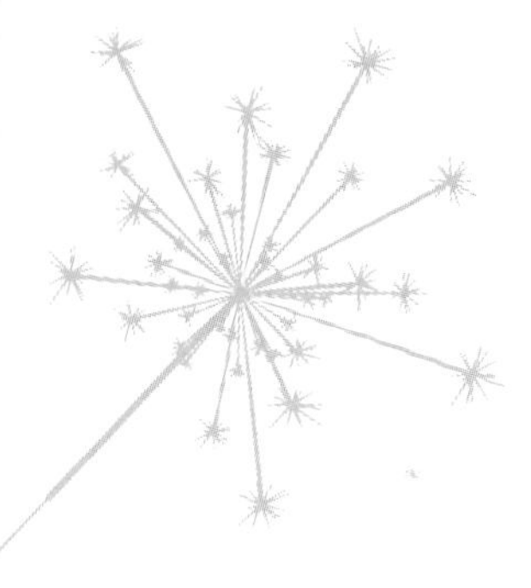

Activities #27–29

Opening Activities

Intention

Opening activities help provide context for the training and prime the participants to begin thinking about the content you will be sharing. These activities are typically implemented in small groups, after formulating the group or community agreement (see Activity #30—Group Agreement). The purpose of these activities is to build a community of learners who are ready to engage in the workshop and develop relationships. Many of these activities, as well as others in this book (such as Activities #41—Quotes That Resonate and #69—Hopes and Dreams), can also be used as introduction activities (if there is time for lengthier introductions). The key is to find compelling ways to structure the activity so it relates to your topic and allows participants to connect their knowledge and skills to the new information you will be providing.

Implementation

- Choose an opening activity that aligns with the topic of the workshop to elicit meaningful discussions.
- Have the materials for the activity prepared and ready before the workshop begins.
- Break the large group into pairs or small groups of three to five people, or have participants work together at their tables. (See Strategy #9—Facilitate Group Discussion.)
- When you bring the group back together to debrief, solicit some highlights from the small-group discussions. What did people learn about each other? What were some connections they found to the topic of the training?

Activity #27: Grab Bag

- Prepare a bag or basket with a variety of items that could represent something related to the topic.
- Give participants a couple of minutes to explore the items.
- Invite participants to introduce themselves to one another with one of the items and describe how they see it relating to the training topic.

Activity #28: Shoebox Autobiography

- Ask participants to bring with them a shoebox (or other container) of items that tell the story of their professional journey or how the workshop topic is relevant to their lives. These can include pictures, books, special mementos, and so on.
- Invite the participants to introduce themselves to one another by sharing their items, talking about their importance and how that might relate to the topic of the training.

Activity #29: Commonalities

- Invite participants to introduce themselves and to find three to five things they all have in common.
    - These commonalities cannot include being an educator or other obvious attributes such as physical or visible characteristics.
    - In the debrief, discuss the strategies that participants used to find out about what they all had in common. Highlight that despite our differences, we should always strive to find common areas of agreement.

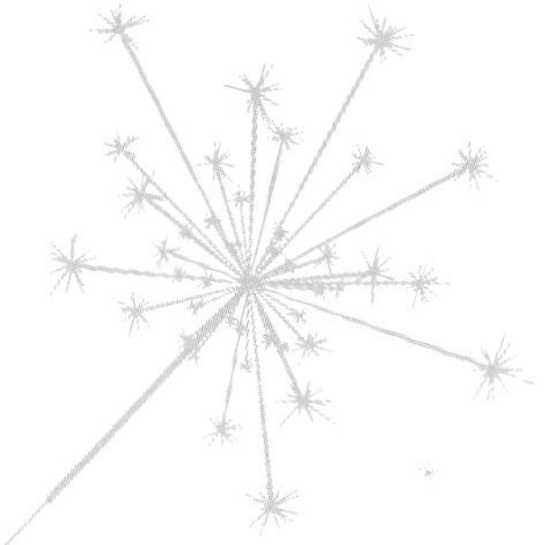

Activity #30

Group Agreement

A consensus on what every person in our group needs from each other and commits to each other in order to feel safe, supported, open, productive and trusting . . . so that we can do our best work, achieve our common vision, and serve our [students/families/constituents] well. —Definition of community agreements, National Equity Project

Intention

Begin any meeting or workshop with this activity to construct a set of group norms (ground rules) to guide interactions during the session. This will help establish a psychologically safe environment in which every individual can feel comfortable fully participating and contributing. Even onetime or short sessions need to be grounded in clear expectations. Just as having clear expectations helps children feel secure in their environment, adults will feel more secure and at ease about sharing when they know the parameters of appropriate behavior. Group agreements should be simple, direct, and concrete; have a limited number of statements; and be visible throughout the session.

Implementation

- After welcoming the group and engaging in introductions, pose the following question: What are the elements of a learning environment in which you can feel safe, comfortable, and able to fully participate and learn?
- Ask participants to individually reflect and think about their responses.
- Invite participants to share their responses using one of these methods:
    - In a round-robin, ask each participant to name one thing on their list and chart the responses. Continue until all ideas are shared.
    - Share in a popcorn response method and chart responses.
    - Have participants write their words or phrases on sticky notes and post them on a board or chart paper.

    - Create a group mural or word cloud of words and phrases.
    - Share with a partner and agree on their top priority. Have someone from each pair share their response and chart them.
- Include anything you need as a facilitator to run an effective session, stating, for example, that participants should remain present (physically and mentally), engage in respectful discussion, be open to diverse opinions, take responsibility for their own learning, and assume good intentions.
- Review the responses and construct them into a list of agreements. Explain that the list will be a guide to group interactions during the session. Remind participants that they are making a commitment to themselves and one another.
- Let participants know that, as the facilitator, you are making a commitment to apply these agreements evenly and consistently, especially with regard to watching for bias.
- Refer back to the list as necessary during the session to keep the group process on track.

Individualize

- For a short workshop with more limited time, consider one of these variations:
    - Solicit a few ideas from the group and synthesize them into an agreement by consensus.
    - Have a few guidelines prepared and ask the group to contribute their ideas. These could include statements like *"Respect others' time and ideas," "Be nonjudgmental," "What we say in the group remains confidential," "Look at issues through an anti-bias and equity lens,"* and *"Embrace differences to foster meaningful conversations."* For additional ideas, explore the resources listed in the Investigate section.
- If the group is going to be engaging in multiple sessions together, this process should be conducted in a more in-depth manner.
    - After constructing the list from all the responses, read through it together and ask if any need clarification.
    - Consider whether any responses can be consolidated to keep the list manageable.
    - Engage participants in a discussion to establish whether everyone accepts all the agreements and will be able to follow them. If there is disagreement, discuss and determine whether to modify it, discard it, or keep it on the list while noting the objection. You may also decide to try it out and reevaluate it later.

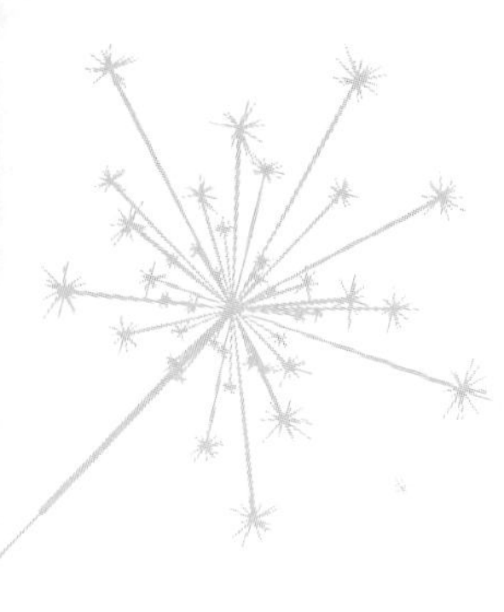

Investigate

- Explore resources for group agreements:

  Courage & Renewal Touchstones
  https://couragerenewal.org/wp-content/uploads/2022/06/CCR_Touchstones_V4.pdf

  "Developing Community Agreements" by the National Equity Project
  www.nationalequityproject.org/tools/developing-community-agreements

- For additional guidance and helpful language:

  NAEYC Code of Ethical Conduct, Section III: Ethical Responsibilities to Colleagues

  www.naeyc.org/sites/default/files/globally-shared/downloads/PDFs/resources/position-statements/Ethics%20Position%20Statement2011_09202013update.pdf

Presenting New Information and Knowledge

Sharing knowledge only occurs when people are genuinely interested in helping one another develop new capacities for action; it is about creating learning processes. —Peter Senge

Igniting a passion for learning and applying new information is at the heart of all professional growth experiences. This section provides a variety of activities that will expand your repertoire of creative ways to share relevant information.

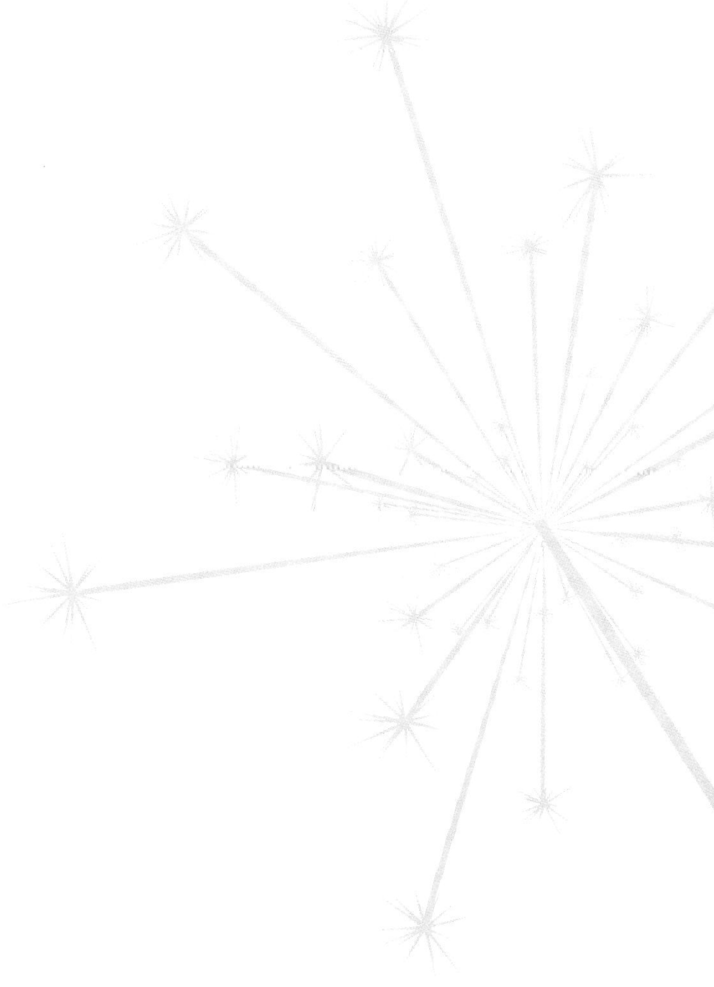

Activity #31

Brainstorming Techniques

Intention

Brainstorming is a simple, quick, and energizing way to promote creative thinking and generate a wide range of ideas. The technique allows everyone a chance to share their unique and diverse perspectives. The goal is to get a large number of ideas for participants to sort, prioritize, and discuss.

Implementation

- Determine a focus. Provide clarity on the issue or question you want the participants to respond to. Relate the focus to your workshop topic. Some examples include the following:
    - All the ways you know to calm an upset child
    - Mindfulness practices to reduce your stress after a difficult day
    - Characteristics of the most influential teacher you ever had
    - Your ideas for making this the best school year ever
    - Keywords that capture the effect of high-quality early childhood programs
- Divide into groups. Groups of four to five work well, as smaller groups may have trouble keeping the ideas flowing. Use a flip chart to capture the responses.
- Provide ground rules:
    - Record all ideas and responses without comment, discussion, or judgment.
    - Quantity is more important than the quality of ideas.
- Create an energizing atmosphere. Consider playing some fast-paced music (the theme from *Jeopardy* works well). Encourage participants to have fun with the process.
- Set a time limit. Five to eight minutes is usually plenty. Be sure to give a one-minute reminder.
- Group discussion. Allow the group five additional minutes to review their lists. It is helpful to ask the group to do a specific task, such as
    - determine their top three ideas;
    - pick the most and least likely response to be implemented; or
    - rank their ideas from ten to one.

When time is up, have each group appoint a spokesperson to share their group's responses to the brainstorming exercise.

- Wrap up. Acknowledge the ideas the brainstorming generated and encourage participants to bring the ideas to life in their work.

Individualize

- Creating a top-ten list can be a fun way to set up the brainstorming session. Ask groups to brainstorm their top ten thoughts and ideas on a specific topic and then have them rank their ideas. Encourage participants to incorporate a bit of humor into their lists.
- For groups that are less comfortable sharing their thoughts verbally, try this:
    - Provide a pile of index cards to each group.
    - Have participants write one thought or idea related to the focus on each card. Allow three to four minutes.
    - When the time is up, everyone passes their cards to the person next to them so they can build on and add to the ideas on the cards. Repeat this process two or three times, depending on the size of the group.
    - Allow the group five minutes to create a master list of their ideas on a flip chart.
    - Continue with the group discussion, sharing, and wrap-up ideas listed above.

    Or

    - Provide packs of sticky notes to the group. Encourage participants to write one idea per sticky note and post it on the group's flip chart.

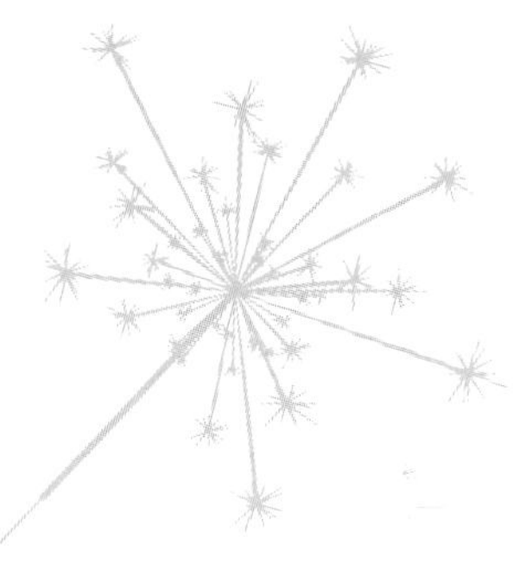

Activity #32

Demonstrations

Intention

Effective demonstrations arouse curiosity, promote observation skills, and stimulate group discussions as participants see and experience new ideas and strategies. Including participants in the demonstrations or inviting them to do their own demonstration builds a collaborative learning environment where each person's skills and perspectives are valued.

Implementation

- Plan demonstrations that illuminate a particular skill or idea that is an important component of your topic. Here are some workshop examples:
  - **Parent Communication**—Conduct a role play highlighting positive communication skills with a disgruntled parent. Invite a participant to role-play the parent.
  - **Children's Literacy**—Read aloud children's books, highlighting specific read-aloud techniques and skills. Invite participants to demonstrate as they read a favorite book.
  - **Creative Classroom Activities**—Plan a variety of demonstrations that help participants think beyond their tried-and-true activities. Share new materials and innovative ways to use traditional materials. Invite participants to demonstrate activities to the group. (See Activity #60—Supporting Children's Play with Intentionality to use in combination with this activity.)
  - **STEM (Science, Technology, Engineering, Math)**—Conduct an easy-to-replicate experiment for participants to use in their classrooms.
  - **Health and Safety**—Demonstrate a specific skill or technique, such as diapering, hand washing, or disinfecting.
- Practice your demonstration beforehand to be sure you have everything you need and to build your confidence.
- Set up the space so participants can clearly see the demonstration.
- Provide an overview of the demonstration to the group. Explain why you are doing it and how it relates to the workshop content.
- Present the demonstration to the participants in a positive and engaging way. Consider using humor, props, or funny images to add elements of fun!
- Involve the participants by asking questions and incorporating their thoughts and ideas.
- Wrap up by having the participants share something they learned or are excited to try.

Individualize

- For in-house workshops, consider having a sign-up for teachers to share ten-minute demonstrations at staff meetings. Encourage them to demonstrate creative classroom activities, games, songs, fingerplays, behavior management strategies, a children's book, a planning technique, a technology skill . . . The possibilities are endless when you tap into the varied expertise of the teachers! These demonstrations are an opportunity to showcase and value the diverse talents that everyone brings to the program.

Illuminate

- Watch Cathy Weisman Topal demonstrate her Thinking with a Line Tools: https://vimeo.com/user45942720

Activity #33

K-W-L (What I Know—What I Want to Know—What I Learned)

Intention

Teachers often use the K-W-L format with preschoolers when introducing a new topic or concept, and it can easily be adapted to use with the educators themselves. It invites participants to be engaged and invested in their learning by using their own background knowledge, experience, and interests to construct their new knowledge.

Implementation

- Determine what topic you want to explore (for instance, Process Art, Creating a Welcoming Environment, Engaging Families).
- Prepare three charts: What I Know; What I Want to Know; What I Learned.
- Generate a list of what people already know about the topic (What I Know).
  - Have people individually write on sticky notes and add them to the chart.
  - Brainstorm the list.
  - Do a round-robin response.
  - Consider how you want to address misconceptions—amend them right away or wait to see if they get corrected in the next phase as the participants learn new things.
- Develop a list of questions (What I Want to Know). You may want to come prepared with some prompts (such as "who, what, when, where, how") to stimulate participants' thinking. These questions will help keep discussion on track and focused on the purpose.
- Break participants into small groups for discussion and research. Assign each group one or more of the questions. Provide resources (tablets, books/articles, lists of websites) for people to use to answer the questions.
- Bring the group back together to debrief.
  - Were the questions answered? (What I Learned)
  - What resources were most useful? What other resources would have helped?
  - Discuss the process of people collaborating to research and share perspectives and ideas. How does collaboration broaden the scope of the research and benefit the learning?

Individualize

- Add columns, for example:
  - How do I know it (the context)?
  - Why is this important?
  - What do I still want to know or wonder about?
  - How will I use this in my practice?

Illuminate

- Watch a teacher explain the benefits of using K-W-L with students in a bilingual classroom:
  www.youtube.com/watch?v=keXLRM-VkUI

Activity #34

The Question Formulation Technique

Great questioning, great enlightenment; little questioning, little enlightenment; no questioning, no enlightenment.
—Attributed to Dōgen

Intention

Helping adult learners ask insightful and relevant questions is an essential component of supporting them. Learning to ask questions has many benefits, including increased engagement and confidence, improved learning outcomes, and the generation of new ideas. The Question Formulation Technique, created by the Right Questions Institute, is a fun, fast-moving way to guide participants in developing their questions. It is important to note that not every question has to be answered, since the act of generating and sharing the questions is the focus of this process.

Implementation

STEP ONE: DESIGN A FOCUS STATEMENT

This positive and clear statement directly linked to your session's content and desired outcomes will form the basis of this interactive process. Here are a couple of examples from Susan's workshops:

Workshop: Finding the Spark! Bringing Passion, Intentionality, and Engagement into Your Work

Focus Statement:
Teaching with passion, intentionality, and engagement has a positive and lasting impact on the lives of young children.

Workshop: Strengths-Based Communication to Support Positive Team Relationship

Focus Statement:
Strengths-based communication is essential for creating positive team interactions and learning environments where children, teachers, and parents can thrive!

Workshop: Innovative Professional Development Projects

Focus Statement:
High-quality professional development experiences are essential for transforming the quality of early childhood programs.

STEP TWO: PROVIDE AN OVERVIEW OF THE QUESTION FORMULATION PROCESS

1. Explain that this process will help you:
   - Produce questions
   - Improve questions
   - Prioritize questions
2. Break participants into groups of four to five. Ask each group to select a recorder who will write down all the questions. Provide flip chart paper and markers if you would like to post the questions in the workshop space.
3. Review the process:

   Provide five to ten minutes for groups to generate their questions using these guidelines from the Question Formulation Technique:
   - Ask as many questions as you can.
   - Do not stop to discuss, judge, or answer the questions.
   - Write down every question exactly as it is stated.
   - Change any statement to a question.

   It is helpful to provide a couple of general questions to get the groups started. Keep the energy high by sharing the amount of time left and letting everyone know if they get stuck to quickly review the list and ask, "What else?"

   After the time is up, pause the group discussions and ask the groups to spend the next five minutes prioritizing their questions:
   - Choose your three most important questions.
   - Why did you choose these three as the most important?
   - Rank your top three questions and discuss why you decided on the ranking order.

STEP THREE: SHARE AND REFLECT

- Ask for a volunteer from each group to share their number one question. Then, after each group has shared once, ask the groups to share their top two or three other questions that have not been shared.
- You can create a combined list of questions based on what was shared. The goal is not to answer every question, but it is helpful to reflect on common themes in the questions and address them. You can work with the group to decide how the questions will be used in your work together. Some possibilities:
  - Highlight for participants that many of their questions will be addressed in the workshop.
  - Select a few questions that seem pressing or relevant to all groups to answer briefly.

  - Provide each group with the opportunity to discuss one of their top three questions and share their thoughts with the larger group.
  - Encourage participants to bring some questions that intrigue them back to their programs for further discussion.
  - You can use the questions to shape future content if it is a multi-session workshop.
- Close the activity by asking participants what the experience was like for them. Highlight the importance of developing and asking questions that support ongoing professional growth.
- Remind participants that this process can be used with children and as part of their work with colleagues to explore an issue and generate questions.

Adapted from: Rothstein, Dan, and Luz Santana. 2017. Make Just One Change: Teach Students to Ask Their Own Questions. *Cambridge, MA: Harvard Education Press.*

The Question Formulation Technique (QFT) was created by the Right Question Institute. Learn more at https://rightquestion.org/what-is-the-qft.

Investigate

- Learn more about the Question Formulation Technique:

  Rothstein, Dan, and Luz Santana. 2017. *Make Just One Change: Teach Students to Ask Their Own Questions*. Cambridge, MA: Harvard Education Press.

  "What is the QFT?" Right Question Institute. https://rightquestion.org/what-is-the-qft.

Illuminate

- Ideas for using the Question Formulation Technique in groups:

  Right Question Institute. 2018. "Using the Question Formulation Technique (QFT) in Groups." YouTube video, November 1, 2018. www.youtube.com/watch?v=aaUMHshUTbk&t=1s.

Discovering What We Know

Intention

You may want to quickly assess what your participants already know about a topic to help you frame a discussion and do a deeper dive into the content or adjust content according to their current knowledge. It likewise gives you the opportunity to dispel any myths or misinformation in a diplomatic manner. These quick activities can provide useful information, especially when time is limited. They also allow for adult learners to share their prior knowledge and experience and promote more active engagement from the participants.

Implementation

- **T-Chart:** Use this method to compare two ideas or concepts. This is an effective way to get information about what people think or know about a topic or idea before delving into the content.
    - Divide a chart paper or whiteboard into two columns, with a heading for each column.
    - Solicit input in a popcorn response format from the group and add to the chart or ask participants to write responses on sticky notes and put them on the chart.
        - Examples: Joys and challenges of outdoor play; children's and parents' feelings about separation; elements of process vs. product art
    - Make sure to debrief by noting any themes, discussing different perspectives, and adding any other suggestions.
- **Beach Ball Toss:** This is an active and fun way to get pertinent information about participants' experiences or assess the group's knowledge about a topic.
    - Write a question on each portion of a beach ball. Make the questions related to the topic. For example:
        - For Child Development: At what age would we expect a child to willingly share materials? What is one way you could set up the environment to encourage infants to interact with one another?
        - For Language and Literacy: What is your favorite children's book? How many languages were spoken in your childhood home? What are examples of items in a print-rich environment?
    - Have everyone stand in a circle. Throw the beach ball to one person. They answer the question on whatever section one of their hands lands in (or specify which hand) or pass.

- Chart the response.
- That person then throws the beach ball to someone else.
- Continue the procedure until everyone has had a chance to answer a question.
- Debrief by affirming correct responses and providing accurate information for incorrect ones or noting themes or similarities in responses. Continue with a deeper dive into the content.

Activity #36

Mind Mapping

Intention

Mind maps are a creative and engaging way for individuals to think more deeply about a keyword or phrase. They are a form of reflective brainstorming that encourages participants to think outside the box and make concrete connections between ideas. This activity is helpful for a group to develop new ideas on a key issue they are exploring or struggling with. Creating mind maps will provide participants with a visual representation of a wide range of thoughts and information on a focus area.

Implementation

- Provide participants with three sheets of blank paper, pens, and pencils.
- Share a visual of a mind map to be sure everyone understands the process.

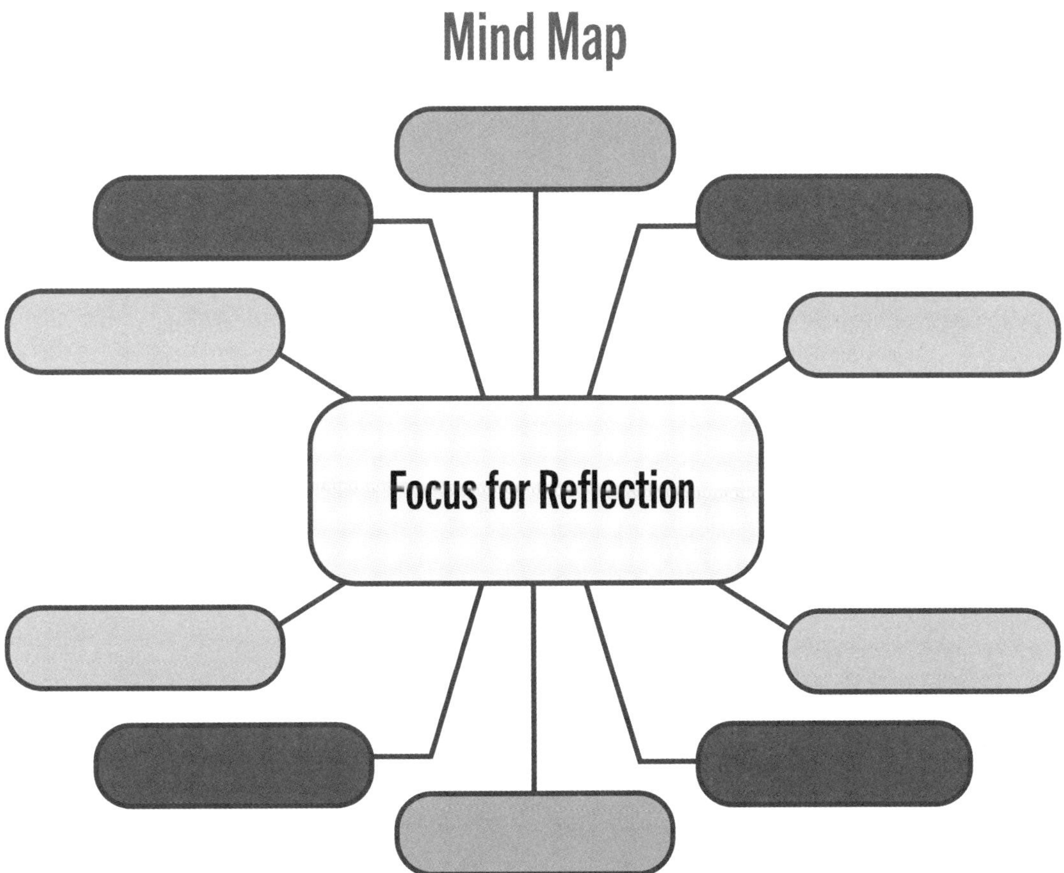

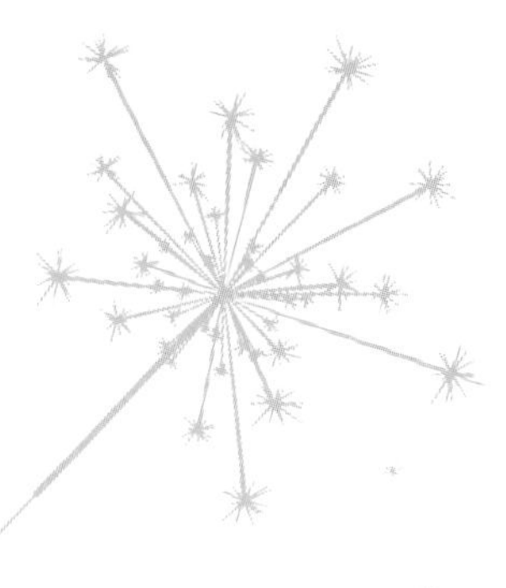

- Establish the focus of the mind map. The group can all do a mind map based on a keyword or phrase related to the presentation (*intentionality, developmentally appropriate practice, child-centered*), or they can choose a word related to their individual work in the course (their word of the year, a phrase from their vision statement). Examples:
  - To get a group energized to bring new ideas into their work during a particular season, use the season with the word *fun—Winter Fun, Summer Fun.*
  - To explore solutions to challenges, rephrase the problem into a positive statement. For example, if the program is struggling with loud, chaotic environments, use *peaceful environments* as your focus phrase.
- Ask participants to write the word in the center of the circle, and then give them two minutes to fill their page with thoughts and ideas. Encourage participants to keep going. Remind them to ask themselves, "What else?"
- At the end of two minutes, ask the participants to take the very last word or phrase they wrote and put it in the center of the second piece of paper. Restart the two-minute timer to continue the mind mapping on this page. Repeat this process with the third piece of paper.
- After the third round is complete, give participants two more minutes to review their mind maps and summarize the key message they derived from this exercise. These questions are insightful reflection points:
  - *"What key thoughts or new ideas emerged as you moved through this exercise?"*
  - *"What do you feel is the main message you received through this exercise?"*
  - *"Summarize two action steps you are inspired to take."*
- Then break into small groups to create a list of all the ideas. Post the lists around the room and ask a volunteer from each group to share three ideas. Once all the ideas are shared, discuss which ideas the group would like to implement.
- Ask for volunteers to share what the process was like for them and their key messages.

Note: This activity can be shortened or expanded based on the time available. Doing as few as two or as many as five rounds can be effective.

Investigate

- Explore more about mind mapping:

  Sicinski, Adam. "The Complete Guide on How to Mind Map for Beginners." IQ Matrix blog. Retrieved September 9, 2022. https://blog.iqmatrix.com/how-to-mind-map.

Video Clip Reflections

Intention

Video clips energize a presentation with new concepts, ideas, and knowledge and provide a jumping-off point for the participants to engage in focused discussions.

Implementation

- Develop a listing of video clips you like to use in your presentations. It can be helpful to put the topic of the video you are looking for into Google and then click on the video option to see what video clips are available. YouTube and TED Talks are also good places to start searching. Be sure to determine whether any permissions from copyright holders are necessary given your situation and usage. (See Resources for Videos in the appendix.)
- Be selective. Find a clip that emphasizes a key point of your workshop. The clips can be light, humorous, or factual, as long as they are relevant and stimulate conversation.
- Keep the video clips short—three to five minutes is long enough.
- Turn on closed captioning to support a variety of learning styles and preferences.
- Introduce the video clip by aligning it with the message you want the participants to take away.
- Before showing the clip, provide reflective questions for the participants to be thinking about as they watch the video.
- Allow time for participants to share their reflections. This can be done with the whole group, in small groups, or with a partner, depending on the size of the group and time frame.
- Debrief key thoughts from the discussion before resuming the presentation.

Individualize

- For child-centered curriculum, intentional teaching, developing learning projects, or creating how-to books:

  Rivard, Melissa. 2014. "The Color Investigation." *Project Zero*. Video. Cambridge, MA: Harvard Graduate School of Education. www.pz.harvard.edu/resources/the-color-investigation.

  Discussion Questions:

  - *What did you find most exciting about this video?*
  - *How would you describe the role of the teacher?*

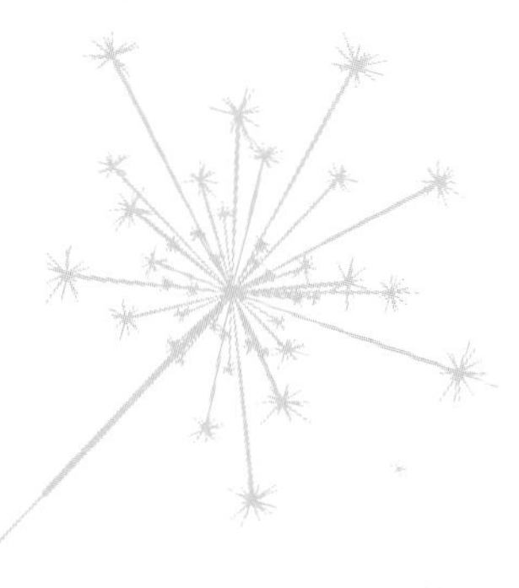

  - *How did the teacher's observations inform the learning environment she created for children?*
  - *What is one change you would like to make in your own work as a result of watching this video?*
- For a goal-setting workshop:

  Goldsmith, Marshall. 2016. "The 6 Daily Questions." YouTube video. August 9, 2016. www.youtube.com/watch?v=YWpUqXFe4Fw&t=6s.

  Participants will watch a three-minute video clip and then reflect on these questions:

  - *Did I do my best today to . . .*
    - set clear goals?
    - make progress toward goal achievement?
    - be happy?
    - find meaning?
    - build positive relationships?
    - fully engage?
  - *How could the six daily questions provide useful insights for you? Which question is most relevant to your own professional growth?*
- For a strengths-based communication workshop:

  Harvard Graduate School of Education. 2016. "Dean James Ryan's 5 Essential Questions in Life." YouTube video. May 29, 2016. www.youtube.com/watch?v=bWoNguMGIbE&t=19s.

  1. Wait, What?
  2. I Wonder?
  3. Couldn't We at Least?
  4. How Can I Help?
  5. What Truly Matters?

  Discussion Questions:

  - *How could the five essential questions enhance your work?*
  - *Which questions will you commit to using in your work with your colleagues? Parents? Administrators? Share examples.*

Investigate

- Find ideas and resources for locating video clips:
  Appendix: Resources for Videos

Activity #38

Using Children's Books for Professional Growth

Intention

Children's books can be a powerful tool for adult learning. A well-chosen children's book can highlight key points, lead into a reflection, or prompt insightful discussion. Select books that have a message related to your topic, provide unique perspectives, and represent the diversity of the educators and their learning communities.

Implementation

- Select a children's book (or a few books) that will add new perspectives to your presentation. (See sample ideas and resources below.)
- Decide how you will share the book with participants. Consider:
  - Reading the book aloud to the group
  - Asking a volunteer to read the book to the group
  - Providing multiple copies of the book for the participants to read in small groups
  - Showing a video of the book being read in a powerful way. A couple of favorites:
    - For a workshop on diversity and inclusion:
      Mem Fox reading her book *Whoever You Are*
      www.youtube.com/watch?v=VSCbCuGxkVc
    - For a workshop on creativity:
      The Dot by Peter H. Reynolds
      www.youtube.com/watch?v=vKCsqbiCxE8&t
- Provide a few different books on a similar topic for the groups to read, discuss, and report back.
  - For a behavior management workshop, consider:
    - *Calm-Down Time* by Elizabeth Verdick
    - *Rex Wrecks It!* by Ben Clanton
    - *Hands Are Not for Hitting* (Best Behavior Series) by Martine Agassi
    - *Sometimes I'm Bombaloo* by Rachel Vail
- Provide some focus questions to explore the messages in the book (see examples below).

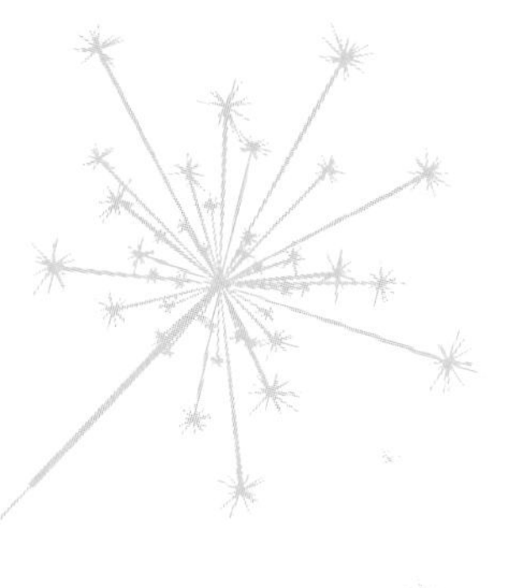

- Lead a discussion with the whole group or ask participants to discuss the questions in small groups.
- Wrap up by highlighting the key points of the discussion that relate to the workshop and encourage participants to share other children's books that have a connection to the workshop topic.

Individualize

- For a workshop on social-emotional topics/friendship:

  Friends by Helme Heine

  Focus questions:

  - *How do the three friends use their unique strengths and attributes to accomplish their goals?*
  - *Consider the concept of fair. How do the friends embody fairness?*
  - *What are some of the ways you demonstrate friendship?*
- For a workshop on team building or communication:

  Wilfrid Gordon McDonald Partridge by Mem Fox

  Focus questions:

  - *Consider the word* memory. *How do people's different descriptions of memory contribute to Wilfrid's understanding of it?*
  - *What are the advantages of building relationships with people who have a variety of perspectives?*
  - *How did Wilfrid's project benefit both Wilfrid and Miss Nancy?*

Investigate

- Connect with your local library for children's book suggestions!
- Guides to choosing anti-bias children's books:

  www.antibiasleadersece.com/wp-content/uploads/2018/05/Guide-for-Selecting-Anti-Bias-Childrens-Books-_-Teaching-for-Change-Bookstore.pdf

  www.antibiasleadersece.com/wp-content/uploads/2020/06/ABELiterary-LensesDLKdocx.pdf
- Books that promote social-emotional development and skills:

  https://challengingbehavior.org/implementation/program-wide/books
- ¡Colorín Colorado! is an educational service of WETA (public broadcasting station). The website has a wealth of resources, including recommended books for young children that include culturally relevant and diverse content and feature a diverse range of children and families.

  www.colorincolorado.org

Sharpen Your Observation Skills (Penny Exercise)

Intention

Educators are responsible for observing children for a variety of reasons—for example, to assess progress in their skills and development, to determine their interests, and to help inform curriculum planning. To accurately interpret their observations, it is important that educators notice the details and record them in a timely manner. This activity provides a visual approach to help teachers understand the importance of focused observations and how relying on memory to record an observation is not always effective.

Implementation

- Explain the purpose of the activity as it relates to your workshop.
- First, ask participants to give you words that describe a penny (without looking at a penny).
- Write each word on a chart.
- Next, hand out a penny to each participant (have a variety—shiny or dull, different years and images, and so on).
- Invite participants to focus their attention on the details of the penny and add any words to the list.
- Debrief:
    - Ask participants what they noticed. Responses will likely include comments related to memory and the importance of focusing on something to get all the details.
    - Summarize:
        - We may think we know about something because we have seen it already, but focusing on the details provides a richer and more accurate picture of what we are observing.
        - It is important to have a workable system to record our observations when we make them instead of relying on our memory to record later.

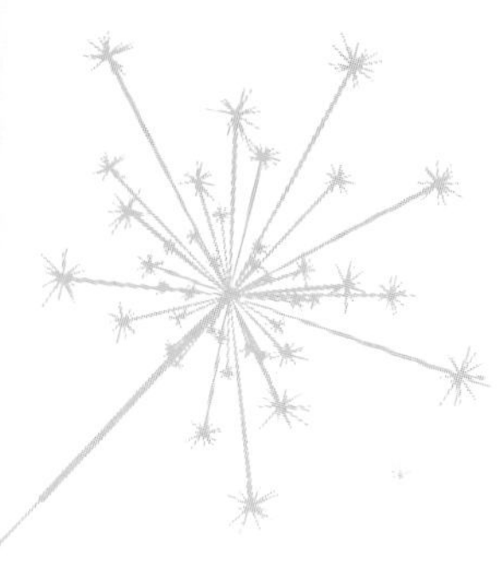

Individualize

Use this activity to highlight the importance of focused observations in a variety of workshops, for example:

- **Supervision**—Your focused observations add detail to a practice you want to work on with an educator.
- **Child Development or Parent Communication/Conferences**—Focused observations are critical to assessing children's growth in all developmental areas and gaining insights into their skills.
- **Environments**—Focusing your observation on a specific area or material can help with curriculum planning and gathering information and insight into designing space for effective use.

Investigate

- "A Closer Look at Observation Methods, Tools and Techniques" by Gina Peterson and Emily Elam:

  https://socialsci.libretexts.org/Bookshelves/Early_Childhood_Education/Book%3A_Observation_and_Assessment_in_Early_Childhood_Education_(Peterson_and_Elam)/03%3A_Using_Observation_Methods_Tools_and_Techniques_to_Gather_Evidence/3.04%3A_A_Closer_Look_at_Observation_Methods_Tools_and_Techniques

Illuminate

- The Infants & Toddlers website by Mary Johnson contains a wealth of video clips that you can use to do practice observations:

  http://toddlers.ccdmd.qc.ca

Design Effective Handouts

Intention

Handouts reinforce and highlight the key facts related to the presentations and provide opportunity for reflection. Participants appreciate handouts that help keep them focused and provide resources for their ongoing professional growth.

Implementation

- Be sure the handout has a clear purpose linked to the content of the workshop.
- Make the handouts appealing. Pay attention to the fonts, text sizing, and layout. You can find useful handout design tips in this blog post on the Presentation Load website: "Creating a Handout to Support and Enhance Your Presentation!" https://blog.presentationload.com/handouts-presentation.
- Consider the diverse backgrounds of the participants. Strive to have resources that are accessible to a wide variety of users; for example, consider reading level, clarity of writing, adaptations for readers with disabilities, translations, and so on. (See this handout from the National Center on Early Childhood Development, Teaching and Learning on culturally and linguistically responsive resources: https://eclkc.ohs.acf.hhs.gov/sites/default/files/pdf/clr-express-checkout.pdf.)
- Ideally, your handout will spark interest, build engagement, meet the learning needs of the participants, and enhance their knowledge. (See Strategy #3—Support Adult Learners.)
- Avoid unnecessary abbreviations and jargon that can confuse the reader.
- Consider the following suggestions for designing and using handouts to enhance the content of your workshop:
    - Use quotes, poems, or inspiring facts that can springboard individual, partner, or small-group discussions.
    - Provide specific instructions for small-group activities.
    - Create reflection sheets that help participants process their thoughts on a specific topic.
    - Summarize key facts and data points from the presentation.
    - Develop action sheets that encourage participants to plan how to use the workshop information in their daily work.
    - Provide a resource list that has current and accessible books, videos, TED Talks, podcasts, and blogs for participants to further their learning.

Individualize

- A variety of sample handouts are provided in this book.
    - SOAR (page 123)
    - Create a Professional Shield (page 93)
    - "Where I'm From" Poem (pages 90–91)
    - Video Clip Reflections (pages 77–78)
    - The Win List (page 109)
    - Support Systems (page 101)
    - DAP for Adults (page 178)
    - Human Skills and Experiences Scavenger Hunt (page 173)
- For outside facilitators, handouts provide a way to share your contact information with the participants. Adding your website, social media links, and email allows participants to reach out to you in the future.

Facilitating Reflective Practice

Reflective practice is the ability to reflect on one's actions so as to engage in a process of continuous learning.
—Donald Schon

Reflective practice has many benefits; it enables participants to gain insights, increase their self-awareness, understand different perspectives, and engage in creative thinking. The activities in this section provide opportunities for individuals to self-reflect and also participate in group reflections. Find meaningful ways to incorporate reflections into your professional development sessions to increase positive outcomes.

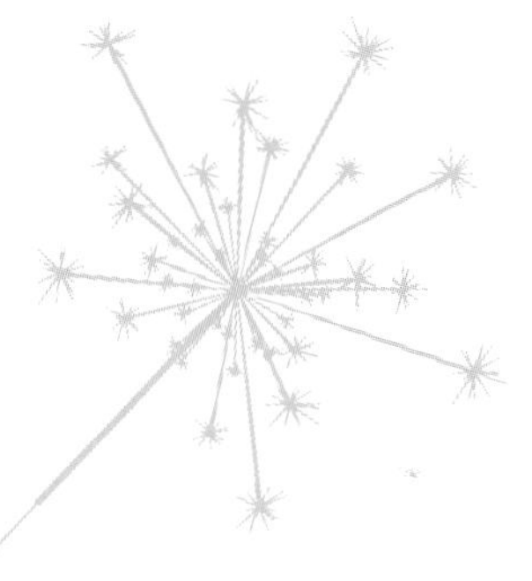

Activity #41

Quotes That Resonate

Intention

Quotes spark discussion, stimulate dialogue, provide inspiration, and generate ideas and insights. Participants reflect on a quote, consider how it resonates with them, relate it to their own thoughts, values, and beliefs, and determine how it can influence their practice. They can then converse with other teachers to reflect on their perspectives and motivations.

Implementation

- Gather a variety of quotes. Choose quotes that are inspirational, aligned with the training topic, represent a diverse group of thinkers and communities, and draw from a variety of fields (not just from early childhood). Make sure you have a reliable source for the quotes, preferably the original or primary source for the material.
- Post the quotes around the room (on nice paper and large enough to be easily read) or print them on a handout.
- Invite participants to read and linger with the quotes.
- Ask participants to choose a quote that resonates with them and reflect on it individually.
- Provide a reflection sheet for them to write their thoughts.
  - What about the quote resonates with you?
  - How does the quote relate to the training topic?
  - What implication does it have for your practice?
- Form pairs or small groups for participants to share their reflections. Or, if quotes are displayed around the room, have people gather at the quote that resonates with them and discuss with others in that group.
- Encourage participants to discover insights through their conversation. What new perspective does the dialogue evoke? How does the discussion help them look at things differently?
- Bring the whole group together to debrief. Note any themes and relate them to the topic.

Individualize

- Invite participants, individually or in small groups, to create their own quotes, or research and discover others that relate to the topic and consider how that quote might inspire other teachers.
- Use quotes as an introduction or warm-up activity. Have the quotes prepared and posted as participants arrive at the session, and invite them to reflect on them before the session begins. Then have participants introduce themselves and comment on the quote that resonates with them.
- Use quotes as a transition back from lunch or as an energizer when you see the group needs to refocus or reengage. Invite participants to choose a quote; then pair up participants and have them move around the space together as they converse. This gets people moving and energized, especially for that after-lunch period!

Activity #42

Questions and Reflections for Energized Interactions

Always the beautiful answer who asks a more beautiful question.
—e. e. cummings

Intention

Asking questions that spark curiosity and interest encourages participants to have vibrant conversations. It is amazing how a well-planned question can build engagement and foster new insights.

Implementation

- Energizing questions can be woven throughout your workshop. Consider using them as an opening activity, energizer, or closing reflection.
- Keep the questions fresh and open-ended, and introduce them with a positive tone in a way that makes clear the purpose and intent of the questions. Use simple introductory statements like, "Your unique ideas and perspectives are a valuable contribution to our learning together" or "Let's take a few minutes to hear what everyone is thinking about our topic today."
- The questions can be general or specific to your topic or group. Use these examples as a starting point for crafting your own questions:
    - What is one surprising thing that happened to you this week? Since our last session?
    - What is the very best thing that has happened to you since starting this course? Since redesigning your classroom environments? Since rethinking your behavior management strategies? Today? This month? This year?
    - What is one aha (new perspective or idea) you are taking away from this workshop? From your discussion group? From the reading?
    - What is one word that describes your passion for the early childhood field? For the topic of the workshop? The best day you have had in your current role? If

time allows, ask participants to share a one-minute reflection on the word they selected.

  - Think of a story that captures your professional journey to your current position. Share only the last line of the story. Consider sharing one or more of these prompts to help participants generate ideas: *It turns out . . . I was so surprised . . . I never expected . . .*
  - What helps to recharge your battery when __________ (planning curriculum, preparing for parent-teacher conferences)? Encourage participants to share self-care strategies and concrete ideas for making the task selected less stressful.
  - Ask "if only" questions. Relate the question to an aspect of the workshop: If only I had known about __________ (strengths-based communication, curriculum planning, behavior management strategies, and so on). Encourage participants to think about what would have been different if they had learned this information earlier in their career.

- After asking the question, give participants a couple of minutes to think about their responses. Depending on the size of the group, you can have participants share as a large group, with a partner, or in a small group. To keep the conversations focused, limit the sharing time to no more than two or three minutes per person.
- Debrief this activity by asking participants to share any new insights, takeaways, or aha moments. Be sure to comment on what you observed about the participants' interactions, the energy in the room, and their responses. Use your comments to build a connection back to the focus of the workshop.

Individualize

- Add another layer of creativity by asking participants to sketch their responses to the question and then share their sketches.

Investigate

- To gain new ideas for building engagement and utilizing Appreciative Inquiry strategies, see:

  Stavros, Jackie, and Cheri Torres. 2018. *Conversations Worth Having: Using Appreciative Inquiry to Fuel Productive and Meaningful Engagement*. Oakland, CA: Berrett-Koehler.

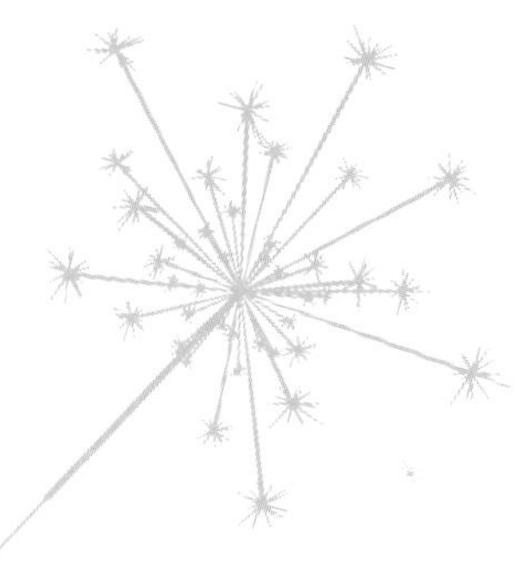

Activity #43

"Where I'm From" Poem

Intention

Learning about the members of your learning community helps deepen relationships and create a richer understanding of the diverse experiences of each individual. This activity provides a creative way for participants to share aspects of their unique life journeys with one another.

Implementation

- Provide a context for the activity. Discuss the importance of learning about one another as a way to strengthen the learning community.
- Distribute the "Where I'm From" template.
- Optional: You can share a video of a "Where I'm From" poem being read:
    - "Where I'm From," a poem by George Ella Lyon www.youtube.com/watch?v=ZdnHl_yW1dQ
    - "Where I'm From" by Julia Daniel www.youtube.com/watch?v=QGb40iUqlhA&t=1s
- Ask each participant to create a poem using the template as a guide.
- Encourage people to be creative. Remind them that the template is just a guide to get them started, and they are free to write something unique.
- Create an opportunity for participants to share their poems. You can do this in small groups or in the full group. If the participants are reluctant to share their full poem, ask them to select three to four lines to share.
- Wrap up this exercise with a discussion about what the process was like for the participants and what they learned about one another.

Sample Template

This template is based on the George Ella Lyon poem and is from the Freeology website: https://freeology.com/worksheet-creator/poetry/i-am-from-poem/

> Your Name
> I am from (a specific item from your childhood home)
> from (two products or objects from your past).
> I am from (a phrase describing your childhood home)
> and (more description of your childhood home).
> I am from (a plant, tree, or natural object from your past)
> whose (personify that natural object).

I am from (two objects from your past)
from (two family names or ancestors)
and from (two family traits or tendencies)
from (another family trait, habit, or tendency).
I am from (a religious memory or family tradition)
from (two foods from your family history)
from (a specific event in the life of an ancestor)
and from (another detail from the life of an ancestor)
(a memory or object you had as a child)
I am from the moments . . .

Individualize

Consider providing an alternative way for individuals to share their "Where I'm From" stories:

- Have a variety of materials (paper, magazines, markers, glue sticks, stickers) for individuals to create a collage board.
- Provide an assortment of natural items (rocks, sticks, moss, dried flowers, sea glass, and so on) and a tray or mat for participants to design a representation of their "Where I'm From" story.

Investigate

- Learn more about creating "Where I Am From" poems:

  "Where I'm From" by George Ella Lyon
  http://georgeellalyon.com/where.html

  "How to Write a 'Where I'm From' Poem" by Danna Smith
  https://poetrypop.com/2021/03/20/how-to-write-a-where-im-from-poem-with-template

Illuminate

- Watch a video of Susan MacDonald sharing the impact of this process and her "Where I'm From" poem (scan QR code or type URL into web browser).

https://vimeo.com/861357878

Activity #44

Create a Professional Shield

Intention

The Professional Shield activity creatively helps participants get to know one another by sharing some information about their backgrounds, values, and professional experiences.

Implementation

Step One: Distribute the Professional Shield template; have a variety of pens, pencils, and markers available. You can also provide large flip chart paper posted on the wall and have participants draw the shield outline.

Step Two: Ask participants to fill in each category of information to be represented on the shield. Announce one category at a time and remind participants to leave space on their shield for all four. Allow them approximately two minutes to draw each response.

These are the categories for each quadrant:

- Two of your strengths
- The part of your current job you like best
- Two values that influence your work
- A recent success or accomplishment

Step Three: Ask the participants to complete their shields by writing their family names on the shield and adding a personal motto they try to exemplify. If they wish, they can embellish their shields with other graphics or designs.

Step Four: Encourage participants to explain what they have included on their shield and why. This can be done as a full group or in small groups. Set a time limit for each person to share. Participants may only have time to explain some of the sections.

Step Five: Briefly discuss how our backgrounds, values, and personal philosophies affect the ways we interact, teach, and lead. (See Strategy #4—Create a Sense of Belonging, and Activities #67—Sharing Our Viewpoints and #68—Exploring Culture and Identity.) Tie what is shared by the participants into the content of the workshop.

Step Six: Debrief Questions:

- *Which quadrant was the easiest to complete and why?*
- *Which quadrant, if any, reveals something about you that others might not know?*
- *What questions did this activity raise for you?*

SHIELD TEMPLATE

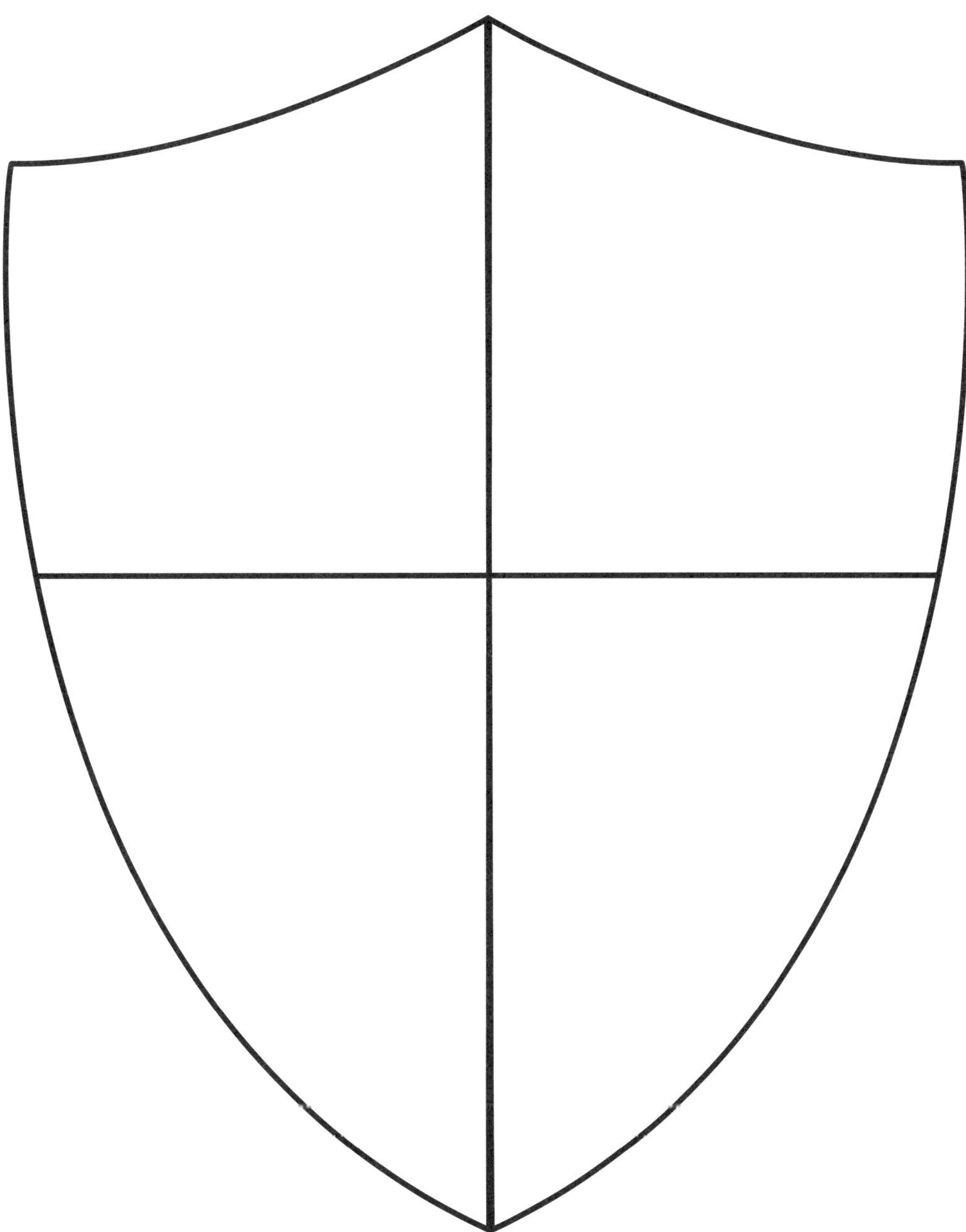

Activity #45

Learning Experience Visualization

Intention

What factors make a learning experience meaningful and sustainable? As participants consider, visualize, and reflect on a time from their own lives that they learned something, they can consider what elements contributed to their learning. They can then apply those qualities to the experiences and activities that they plan for children.

Implementation

- Begin with a discussion of the importance of intentionally planning activities and creating opportunities for learning, and what characteristics influence how children experience those activities.
- Invite participants to individually think about a time (any time in their lives) when they learned something, and to visualize that experience as they consider the following questions:
  - *What were you doing?*
  - *Who were you with? What was their relationship to you?*
  - *Where were you (your surroundings)?*
  - *How did you feel?*
  - *What did you learn?*
  - *Why was it transformational or important?*
- Have participants engage in a pair-share to discuss their reflections.
- Bring the group back together. Ask for volunteers to share responses and chart them.
- Debrief: Review the responses and discuss the factors that contribute to learning.
  - **Who are the people?** Learning takes place in the context of positive, supportive relationships. Teachers who are knowledgeable about child development plan learning experiences that foster relationships and positive interactions with adults and peers.
  - **Is the environment welcoming and enriching?** How are materials organized and displayed? Is there a consistent schedule that balances the variety of activities and routines that children engage in? Is the space arranged to facilitate safety and ease of movement? Do children have time to play outside and explore nature? Are children, their families, and their communities well represented in the books and materials present?

    - **What will children be doing?** Do children have ample opportunity to choose their own materials and activities? Are the activities purposeful as well as developmentally and age appropriate? Do the activities connect to children's outside experiences and interests? Do the activities offer the children possibilities for exploration and discovery?
    - **How does it make children feel?** Do adults provide children with a sense of security? Are children able to be successful and feel confident? Do adults help children identify and manage their feelings?
- Form small groups and have participants share concrete examples of how these factors are demonstrated in their programs.

Individualize

- If there is only a little time, instead of a pair-share, go right to the step of asking for volunteers to share their responses, and chart them.
- Continue the activity by having teachers create an action plan, individually or in teams. Have them determine how they can incorporate more of the factors that make learning meaningful into their current practice. Encourage them to create concrete, realistic steps that will positively influence how children grow and learn.

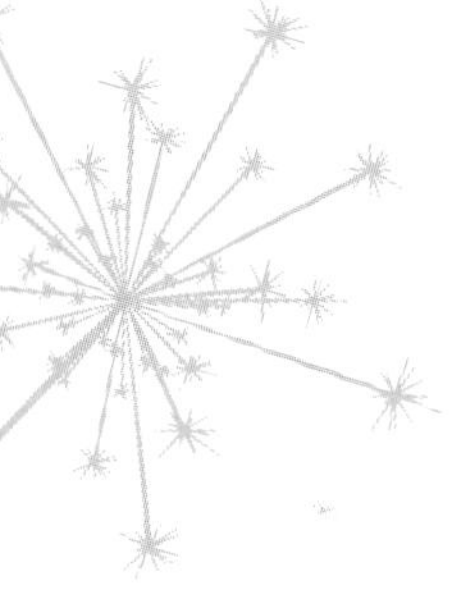

Activity #46

Your Image of the Child

Intention

Your image of the child influences how you plan curriculum, how you view your role as an educator, and how you interact with children. This activity gives participants an opportunity to reflect deeply upon and discuss their thoughts on their image of the child and how that image guides and influences their work with children.

Implementation

- Before the workshop:
  - The article "Your Image of the Child—Where Teaching Begins" by Loris Malaguzzi provides a lead-in to this activity. Send the article link to participants beforehand and ask them to read it in preparation for the training. http://reggioalliance.org/downloads/malaguzzi:ccie:1994.pdf
  - Ask participants to bring with them to the training one digital or printed photograph that captures their image of the child.
- Reflect on the article:
  - Begin by asking participants to share a thought, idea, or quote from the article they found insightful.
  - Ask participants to reflect on this quote:

  It's necessary that we believe that the child is very intelligent, that the child is strong and beautiful and has very ambitious desires and requests. This is the image of the child that we need to hold.—Loris Malaguzzi

- Individual Reflection: Ask participants to take five minutes to individually reflect on the photograph they selected. Provide a reflection sheet to the participants with these questions:
  - *Reflect on the photo you selected that captures your image of the child. Why did you choose this photo? How do you describe your image of the child?*
  - *Thinking about your own image of the child, describe how this image of the child is made visible in your daily work.*
  - *What ideas do you have for bringing your image of the child to life in new and different ways?*
  - *How will creating new ways to keep your image of the child at the heart of your work influence your relationship with all children and families? How will it affect your daily work?*

- Group Work: Divide participants into groups of four. Have each teacher share their photo and a short statement about how this photo reflects their image of the child. Have each group appoint a recorder to take notes on the common themes that emerged within the group and list ideas for keeping the image of the child at the center of their work.
- Group Sharing: Allow each group to share some key thoughts from their work.
- Wrap-Up: *What is most important for us to remember in our daily work with children? What did we learn by reflecting on the image of the child?*

Individualize

- For in-house workshops, it can be helpful for classroom teams to do their group work together so they learn more about their unique perspectives. Have each team come up with a list of ways they will work together to bring their image of the child into their daily work.

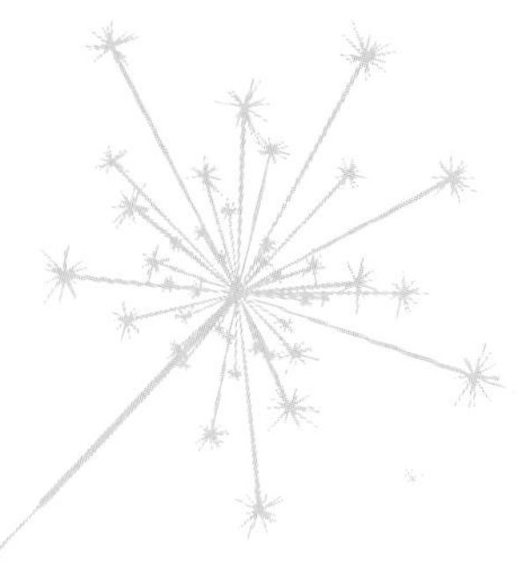

Activity #47

Affirmation Statements

We always attract into our lives whatever we think about the most, believe in most strongly, expect on the deepest levels, and/or imagine most vividly. —Shakti Gawain

Intention

Creating affirmation statements will highlight participants' positive thoughts and boost their confidence. Affirmation statements move us beyond the negative, self-limiting thoughts that are barriers to growth and lasting change. Encourage participants to write affirmation statements that reflect their hopes, dreams, and goals for their professional life.

Implementation

Step One: Review these guidelines, developed by Jack Canfield, for writing affirmation statements:

- "Start with the words 'I am.' Write the affirmation statement in the present tense as though it is already happening."
- "Include an action word ending with –ing. The active verb adds power by evoking an image of doing it or experiencing it right now." For example, "I am confidently expressing my needs to my colleagues."
- "Make it specific." Clearly stated affirmations will help you achieve the results you desire.
- "Keep it brief." It should be "short enough to be easily remembered."
- "Use at least one dynamic emotion or feeling word. Include the emotional state you would be feeling if you had already achieved the goal, such as: enjoying, happily, celebrating, peacefully, lovingly, and triumphant."
- "Make affirmations for yourself, not others. Construct your affirmations by describing your behavior; it has nothing to do with anyone else."

Adapted from: Canfield, Jack. 2020. *The Success Principles Workbook: An Action Plan for Getting from Where You Are to Where You Want to Be.* New York: William Morrow.

Step Two: Writing the affirmation statements

- Provide materials, a reflection sheet or blank paper / index cards, markers, and pens.
- Give participants a specific time frame for completing their affirmation statements.
- Consider playing soft background music to help participants focus.
- Share a sample or form:
  - I am so happy and grateful that I am ________________.
  - I am consistently expanding my comfort zone and joyfully bringing new ideas into my work.
  - I am enthusiastically creating meaningful learning experiences for children.

Step Three: Sharing and wrap-up

- Provide an opportunity for individuals to share their affirmations with the group. Hearing the affirmations of the group can be a powerful experience. Remind everyone they do not have to share if they are not comfortable.
- Highlight that affirmation statements are a way to focus your brain on what you want to achieve, and they are most effective when they are reviewed one to three times a day. Repeating affirmation statements daily and keeping them visible will help your positive thoughts become an integral part of the life you are creating.

Individualize

- Affirmation statements can be created to align with the specific focus of the workshop. For example, create affirmation statements linked to your daily work with children, your professional colleagues, or your vision statement.

Investigate

- Additional ideas for using affirmations:

Canfield, Jack. 2019. "Daily Affirmations for Positive Thinking." Medium blog. January 17, 2019. https://medium.com/@officialjackcanfield/daily-affirmations-for-positive-thinking-e4538336b90b

Canfield, Jack. 2020. *The Success Principles Workbook: An Action Plan for Getting from Where You Are to Where You Want to Be*. New York: William Morrow.

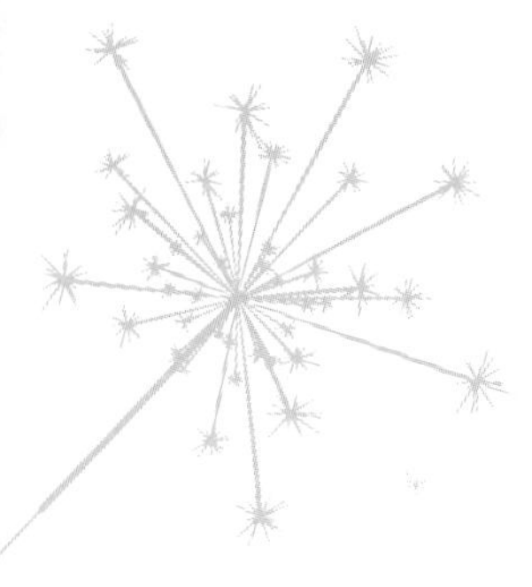

Activity #48

Support Systems

Intention

The job of an early childhood educator is often stressful, and teachers may feel overwhelmed and drained. It is important for teachers to develop strategies to take care of themselves so they can remain positive and energized. We typically rely on a variety of other people and resources to help us through changes or challenges. This reflective activity invites participants to consider the different support systems they have available to help them recharge and stay grounded.

Implementation

- Use this activity in a training focused on self-care, avoiding burnout, professionalism, or mindfulness. The reflection can follow a discussion or presentation on the self-care topic.
- Provide an overview of the activity, and have these reflective questions posted.
  - *What support systems do I currently have in place?*
  - *Who can I rely on to help give me perspective?*
  - *What resources do I have or need to help me reflect?*
  - *Who at work has the potential to be a support person or mentor for me?*
  - *Who will just listen to me without judgment or giving advice?*
  - *Do I have a special place I can go to reflect and decompress?*
  - *What activities do I engage in that bring me joy?*
- Provide paper and a variety of art materials to encourage reflection and creativity.
- Invite participants to respond to these prompts through writing, drawing, or creating a visual representation.
- Establish a specific time frame for completing the reflection.
- Create a soothing, relaxed environment by playing soft music.
- Invite people to share.
  - Engage participants in a pair-share. Have them share their reflections with a partner; then bring everyone back to solicit thoughts from the group.
  - Have participants post their creations around the room and go on a walkabout or gallery walk. Encourage them to leave comments or questions. (See Activity #85—Gallery Walk.)

- Bring the group back together to debrief. Note any themes and highlight the fact that we need a variety of strategies for support. Also note the importance of support systems for others (parents, coworkers, children) and consider how we can help them recognize the supports they have.

Individualize

- See Activity #51—Drawing for additional ideas.
- Create a template such as this one to encourage participants to consider their broader communities of support.

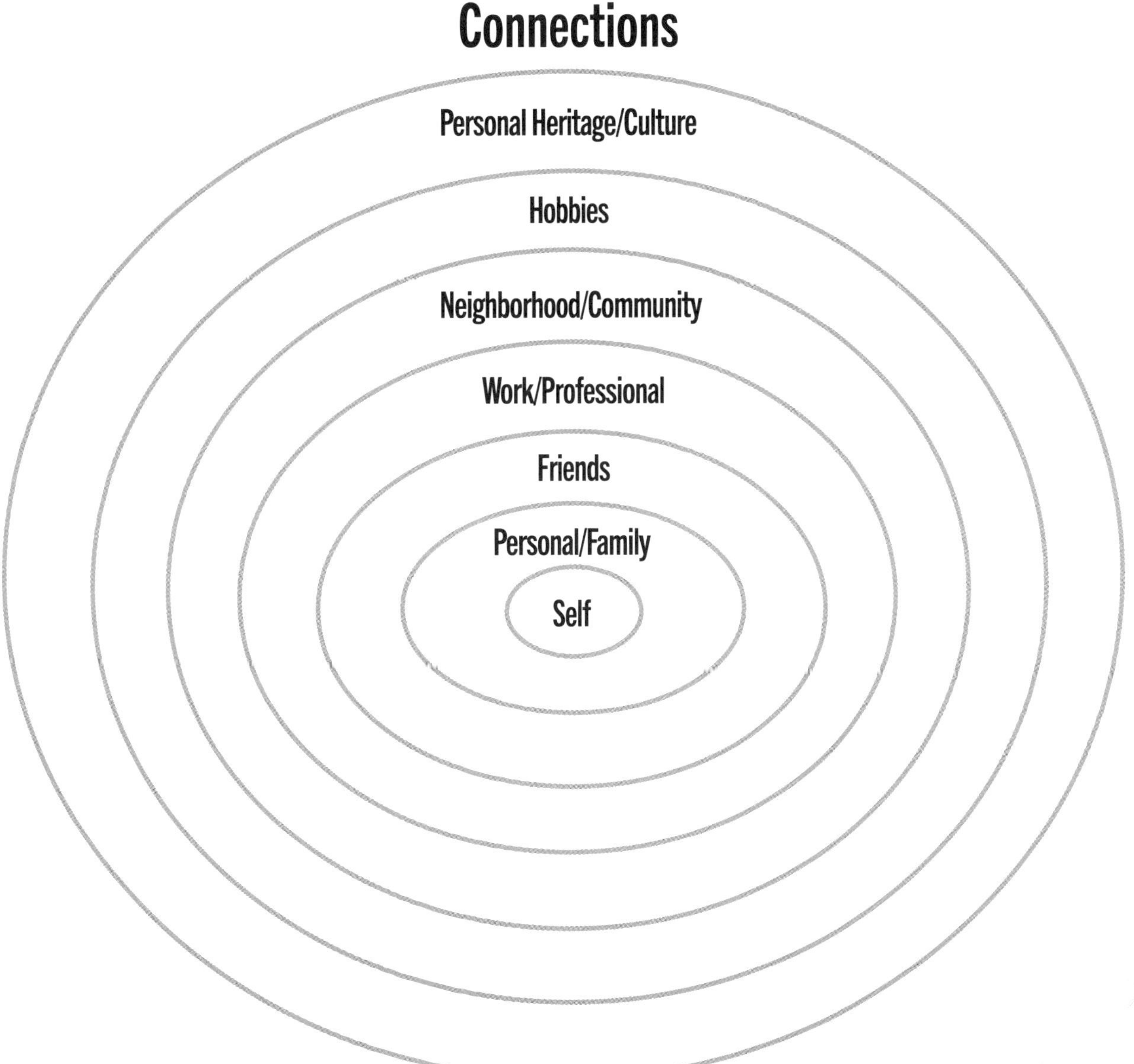

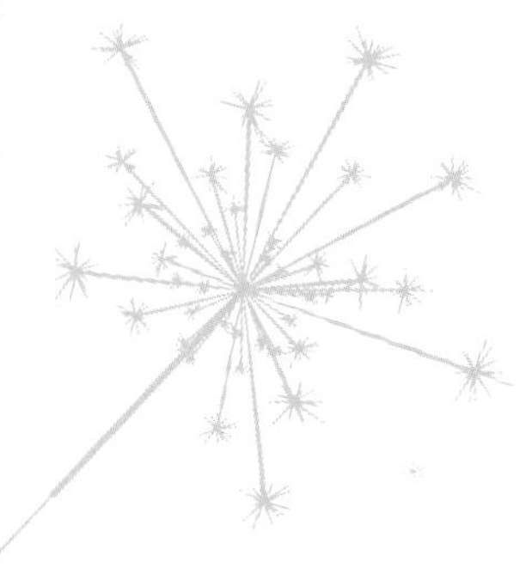

Activity #49

Make a Handprint

Intention

In a strengths-based environment, we learn to recognize the strengths, skills, and talents we bring to our jobs that contribute to the quality of our work with children and families. We also continually strive toward gaining information and improving our practice. In this reflection activity, educators identify their strengths and determine a specific skill to build.

Implementation

- Prepare a handout of a handprint (large enough for people to write inside the fingers). Have one copy for each participant.
- Use the Handprint activity at the beginning of the session, after the welcome and introductions. Invite participants to reflect on specific strengths or skills they have related to the topic being discussed and write one of those in each of the fingers (and thumb) of the handout. For instance,
    - *Strengths they bring to their practice of supporting children's social-emotional development*
    - *Strengths they have in building relationships with families*
    - *Strengths they have in creating developmentally appropriate curriculum*
    - *Strengths they have in communicating with coworkers*
- Have participants work in pairs to share one of their strengths and discuss the influence that strength has on their practice.
- Bring the group back together and instruct participants to put aside their handprints; you will come back to them later.
- At the end of the session, as a concluding exercise to the training, invite participants to revisit their handprint and reflect on the strengths or skills they identified. Ask participants to think back on the training content and consider anything they found particularly interesting or surprising. What information validated their strengths? What would they like to investigate further, or what skills would they like to acquire to strengthen their practice?
- On the back of their handprint, have participants write something about the topic of the training they would like to know more about or gain more skill in. These will guide their future professional development choices.
- Invite participants to share their strengths and goals. Note any themes that emerge, and identify possible topics for future professional development.
- Encourage participants to keep their handprints where they can remain visible, as well as in their personnel files so they can notice their progress and celebrate their successes.

Individualize

- Have materials available for participants to make and decorate their own handprint.
- For a workshop focused on team building, in the first step have teachers make a handprint identifying a coworker's strengths or describing how other people in the program have used their strengths to support that teacher.

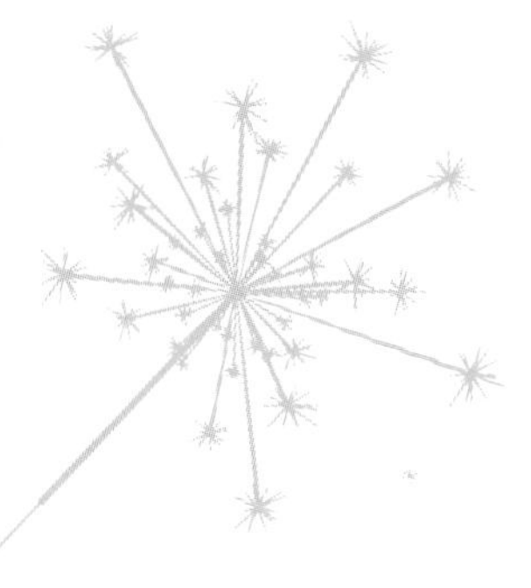

Activity #50

Defining Moments

Intention

People enter the field of early childhood for many reasons. This activity provides an opportunity for participants to reflect on their purpose and motivation as well as their journey to date, and to realize one or two defining moments or turning points during their career. A defining moment is a time when you have had an experience that has influenced or changed your attitudes, thoughts, feelings, actions, or behaviors in important ways. This would be a good activity to use in a training focused on professionalism, advocacy, or taking care of yourself.

Implementation

- Engage participants in a discussion of how they chose early childhood care and education as their career. What attracted them to the field? What were their attitudes and expectations of what the work would be? What was the actual reality of the work in an early learning program? How were their expectations met, and where was there any dissonance? This could be a full- or small-group discussion, depending on the number of participants. You could also use a protocol like the Carousel activity. (See Activity #77—Carousel.)
- After this discussion, share the concept of a defining moment, experiences that provide that aha moment when we recognize that our perceptions have shifted. Provide some time for individuals to reflect on their journey in the field, using these guiding questions:
    - *What was a kind of turning point—a moment, event, or experience—when a light came on? For example, think of a time when you realized something different about yourself or about a change in your relationships and interactions with the children, your colleagues, supervisors, or parents. What happened to shift your thinking, feeling, and/or behavior?*
    - *Consider how your defining moment affected your viewpoint, practice, or identity as an early childhood educator.*
- When individual reflections are done, divide the group into pairs. Have each person share a story of one defining moment, describing what it was and how it transformed their attitudes or behavior. Make sure to set a time frame for this discussion so that each partner has time to share.

- Bring the group back together and debrief.
  - Ask participants how it felt to recognize and share their defining moments.
  - Emphasize the importance of understanding your purpose and motivation to help keep you energized and grounded.
  - Note any themes and consider how these stories help illustrate the importance of our work.
  - Discuss how these stories might be used in advocating for the field.
  - Point out that we are lifelong learners and that each experience we have contributes to our knowledge and understanding.

Individualize

- Use a defining moments framework to help teachers recognize the impact of professional development. What training have they had or what material have they read or researched that provided new insights that changed their perceptions or practice?
- Create a reflection form that participants can complete after a professional development event or after they have done any reading or research about a particular topic. See the appendix for a sample Professional Development Reflection Sheet.
- Use some of the suggestions in Strategy #13—Celebrate! Document and Share Ongoing Stories of Growth and Change.

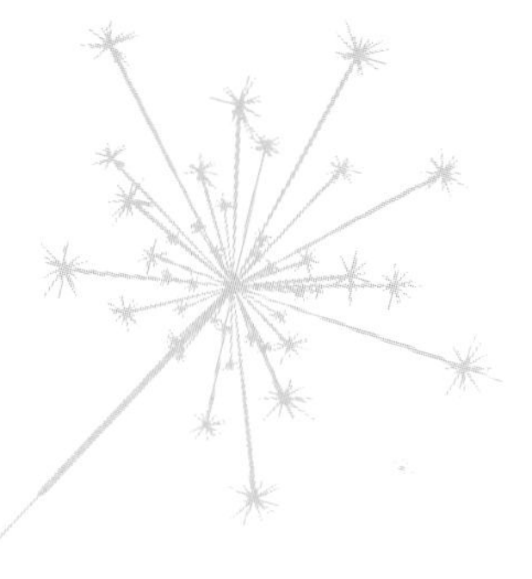

Activity #51

Drawing

Intention

Drawing exercises engage the creative side of the brain and give participants a chance to get a new and often more creative perspective on a topic. A picture or graphic can convey a message in ways that are different from words alone.

Implementation

Materials: an assortment of paper (standard size and flip chart size), markers, pens, and colored pencils

- Provide a focus for the activity that is linked to the workshop. The following are examples for different types of workshops:
    - Leadership skills workshops—ask participants to illustrate their leadership journey.
    - Workshop on challenging behaviors—have participants illustrate how they feel when they are dealing with high-stress moments in their classroom or when their classroom is calm and peaceful (or both, and discuss the differences).
    - Child growth and development workshop—ask participants to illustrate a favorite memory from childhood.
- Have the materials readily available and encourage participants to spread out in the room to work on their drawings.
- If using large flip chart paper, consider hanging sheets up on the walls so participants work on their drawings standing up.
- Play background music and encourage participants to work silently on their drawings.
- Bring the group back together after a set time or when most of the group has finished.
- Invite participants to share their drawings and discuss what they represent.
- Wrap up the activity by connecting the thoughts shared by the participants to the focus of the workshop.

Individualize

- Combine this with Activity #85—Gallery Walk.
- For creative and engaging in-house team-building workshops, you can set large pieces of paper (rolls of butcher paper work well) on the table and divide participants into groups by classroom teams. Have the members of the group collaborate on a shared drawing that illustrates how they work together.
- For vision workshops, you can ask individuals to draw two images, one that depicts how they are working now and the other that shows the way they would like to work in the future.
- For groups or individuals that are hesitant to draw, provide an interesting variety of materials for people to create a collage image; magazines, calendars, photos, stickers, newspapers, scissors, and glue sticks are good starting points.

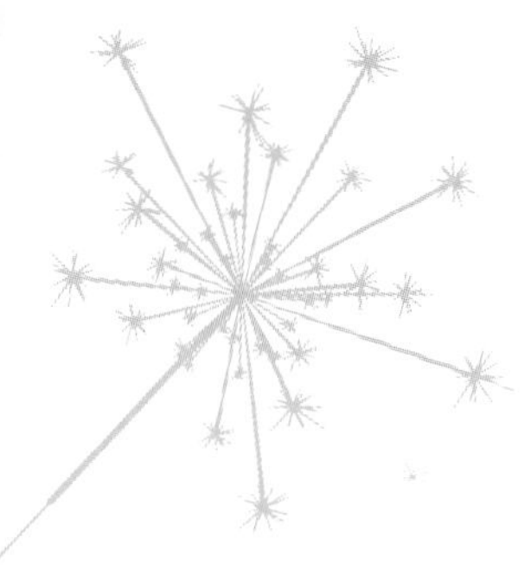

Activity #52

Create Win Lists

Intention

This quick activity focuses participants on their own accomplishments, no matter how big or small! Listing wins related to any topic helps to build confidence and fuels momentum for continued learning.

Implementation

- **Provide a positive focus.** Ask participants to create a win list directly related to the topic of your presentation. For example, a win list of . . .
    - the ways you soothe an upset child.
    - the positive impact your work has on children and families.
    - the creative activities you develop to engage children in your classroom.
    - the ways you honor the diversity and uniqueness of all the individuals in your program community.
    - the steps that you have taken to complete a project or assignment. (See sample below.)
- **Set a time limit.** Five minutes is usually plenty.
- **Establish guidelines.** Ask participants to think of positive experiences related to the focus. Encourage them to think of small everyday experiences. It can help to reflect on things other people have complimented them on—kind words from parents, a coworker, or a supervisor are good starting points. You can suggest a target range—such as five or more, or ten or more—but to reduce pressure, remind participants there is no set number of responses. You can ask the participants to write their responses on blank paper or provide a handout.
- **Small-group sharing.** Provide five additional minutes for participants to share the highlights of their list with a partner or in a small group of three. Sharing helps spread positive energy across the group. Observe the expressions on people's faces and the energy in the room. Share your observations during the wrap-up.
- **Wrap-up.** Ask everyone to share their thoughts about this activity. What surprised them? What did they learn about themselves? Use their thoughts as transition points as you resume the workshop.

THE WIN LIST

Think about all the work you have put into your professional development project. Create a list of all that you have done that will help to bring this project to life! Include every action, thought, new idea, and resource you have discovered since our last session.

1. ______________________________

2. ______________________________

3. ______________________________

4. ______________________________

5. ______________________________

6. ______________________________

7. ______________________________

8. ______________________________

9. ______________________________

10. ______________________________

INSIGHT FROM THE FIELD

Who Saw You and Who Believed in You?

Shared by Holly Elissa Bruno

Relationships are the foundation of young children's learning and can help mitigate toxic stress and trauma. It is crucial for educators to provide the positive environment and interactions that enable children to play, explore, and thrive. This activity provides an opportunity for participants to reflect on and share a story of an individual who made a difference in their own life.

- Have participants find a partner.
- Invite each person to reflect on these questions and then share with their partner:
    - What is the name of the person (teacher, neighbor, relative, and so on) in your young life who saw you, listened to you, believed in you, and let you know how special you are?
    - How did this person's actions influence your life?
- Share specific thoughts and details.
- Lead a wrap-up discussion focused on the lasting impact one person can have and the importance of being a person who reaches out to children to let them know you see their unique gifts and strengths.
- For virtual presentations: Use the breakout group function to set up pairs.

To learn more about the crucial value of mentorship for traumatized children, see the following resources:

Happiness Is Running through the Streets to Find You: Translating Trauma's Harsh Legacy into Healing by Holly Elissa Bruno

"Broken into Wholeness: Transforming Trauma into Practical Wisdom" by Holly Elissa Bruno in *Exchange Magazine*. www.hollyelissabruno.com/wp-content/uploads/2021/04/Broken-into-Wholeness.pdf

Illuminate

- Watch a video of Holly discussing the importance of this activity (scan QR code or type URL into web browser).

https://vimeo.com/861347379

Incorporating Team-Building Activities

If everyone is moving forward together, then success takes care of itself. —Frequently attributed to Henry Ford

Part of your role as the facilitator is to help build a sense of community and trust for the participants. Team-building exercises help teachers feel involved in the session and connected to one another. When participants work together to solve a problem, learn more about one another, discover new approaches to learning, and celebrate success, they are more likely to use their insights to strengthen their practice.

Activity #53

Human Timeline

Intention

Participants are instructed to create a human timeline according to a set of criteria that you explain. This interactive activity helps you assess the group's experience and provides an opportunity to get people up and moving.

Implementation

- Choose the criteria you want to use to determine the order in which people will line up. Some possibilities include the following:
    - age
    - years of experience (be specific—as an early childhood educator, as an infant or toddler or preschool educator, as a human being?)
    - something topic oriented (for instance, for a communication workshop, it could be, *"Line up according to how long you have been communicating."* You can clarify this with a statement that we've been communicating since we were born—or before!—or leave it vague. That leads into a debrief discussion about how we interpret words: How did people decide what *communicate* means?)
- Instruct participants to line up according to your criteria *without talking*.
    - Make sure to identify the starting point of the line.
- Give people just a few minutes to create their line.
    - Notice how they are determining where to place themselves.
- When the line is formed, start at the beginning and have everyone share (their age, years of experience in early childhood, or other).
    - Allow people to change positions based on this new knowledge if you want.
- Debrief
    - Invite people to share how they figured out where to place themselves in the line. How did they communicate? Comment on anything you noticed.
    - Discuss the many modes of communication, especially nonverbal communication. Note that we all have our own unique styles of communication. Also note the importance of paying attention to nonverbal communication when working with preverbal or nonverbal children, or children whose primary language is not English.
    - Note the range of experience in the group.

Individualize

- First, have people line up according to their age. Have everyone say their age and shift positions accordingly.
- Next, have participants line up according to how many years of experience they have in early childhood education.
    - You could also use a "four corners" activity for this part; have participants go to a corner that represents their experience (freshman, sophomore, junior, senior).
- Debrief:
    - Make note of the number of years of wisdom and experience contained in the group.
    - Discuss the benefit of having both experienced and newer people involved in a program and the fact that age and experience don't always correlate.
    - If the group has a majority of people with high levels of experience, you may comment on the need to bring more people into the field and discuss advocacy issues.
    - Pair up less-experienced people with more-experienced people to share advice and questions.
- Bring the group back together and invite participants to share any highlights (advice they received or answers to any questions).

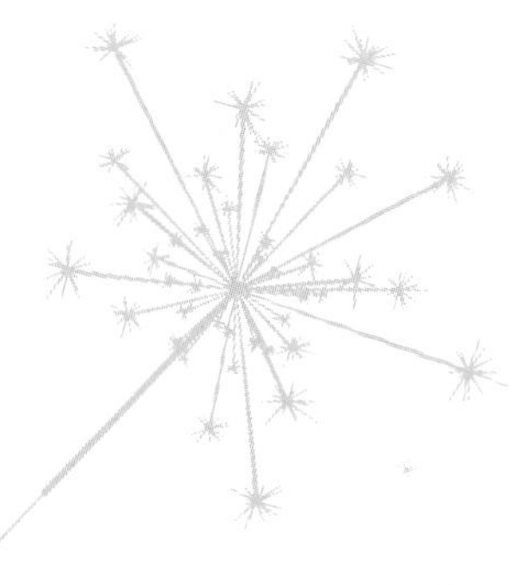

Activity #54

Yarn Web

Intention

Create a visual representation of how ideas and concepts are interrelated and connected. This activity inspires participants to broaden their understanding and perspective of an idea and develops team building through getting to know more about one another.

Implementation

- Identify what question needs to be answered. This will depend on the topic you are exploring. For example:
  - For a workshop on "Creating an Enriching Environment for Young Children," ask participants to identify one element of an enriching environment.
- Have participants stand up and form a circle. Provide an overview of the activity and instructions.
- The first participant holds the yarn ball and answers the question. The facilitator charts the response.
- Holding the end of the yarn, the participant throws the ball of yarn to another participant (anyone in the circle), who answers the question or passes.
- Follow this process until everyone has had a turn.
- When everyone has had a turn, have people share what they notice; a typical response will be that they have formed a web with the yarn and are all connected.
- Debrief:
  - Go over the list of responses and note how they are interrelated.
  - Note that people had different ways of approaching the task of throwing the yarn ball (for instance, throwing it overhand or underhand, winding it up first, and so on). This represents a parallel process, as we work with children who have different approaches to learning.
  - Also point out that if someone made a mistake or needed assistance (forgot to hold their end of the yarn before throwing it, overthrowing it, and so on) people offered support and encouragement.
  - Summarize by tying responses back to the original topic and reflecting on commonalities and connections.

Individualize

- If your group is going to be together for multiple sessions, this is a great activity to use for introductions (even if they already know one another). Participants can share their name and something about themselves. Use a question that would connect to the topic of the training. Some possible questions to ask include the following:
    - *What is your favorite activity to do with children?*
    - *What is your favorite way to communicate with coworkers?*
    - *What is a strength or talent you bring to your job?*
    - *What attracted you to work with young children?*

When Nancy did this activity with a group of leaders in a session on "Maintaining Quality and Morale," the central question was "What attracted you to the field of early childhood?" As the yarn ball was passed around and participants shared their stories, the passion they felt was so evident and palpable. They smiled, laughed, and glowed—one even cried. As they debriefed the activity, people noted the enthusiasm and joy shared by everyone, and the feeling of community that was created, laying a foundation to anchor their discussions.

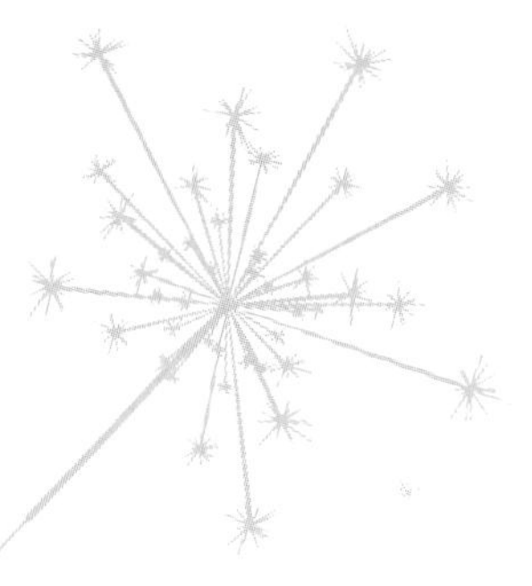

Activity #55

Create a Success Board

You need to be aware of what others are doing, applaud their efforts, acknowledge their successes, and encourage them in their pursuits. When we all help one another, everybody wins. —Jim Stovall

Intention

Illuminate the positive experiences of your learning community by highlighting what is working. A success board is a fun, energizing way to capture the high-point experiences of individuals and the group visually. This activity helps acknowledge and validate current success and build momentum for continued success.

Implementation

- **Set the tone.** Welcome participants into the activity with an energizing piece of music. Check out the article "31 Best Songs about Winning, Celebration, Victory, and Success" in the resources below to find a song that will inspire your group.
- **Be creative.** Have fun materials available to encourage participation—multicolored pieces of paper in different sizes and shapes, a variety of markers, colored pens, and stickers.
- **Reflect.** Ask participants to reflect on their individual moments of success over the past school year (or pick a suitable time frame). Encourage them to think about all aspects of their work with children, colleagues, and parents, as well as their professional growth. Remind them that successful moments are not just major achievements, but that small, everyday moments also have an extraordinary impact. Sharing an example from your own work can help others begin to think about their successes.
- **Share.** Fill the room with positive energy by asking individuals to share their successes. Depending on the group size and time constraints, you can do this as a whole group or break into smaller groups (classroom or age-group teams work well). If you use small groups, ask each group to share a couple of highlights with the whole group. Debrief after the sharing with a few questions:

  - *What are some common themes?*
  - *What do our successes say about the impact of our work?*
  - *What helps us create these positive experiences?*
  - *How can we continue to be successful in our work together?*
- **Document.** Ask for a couple of volunteers to create a success board that you can display in your program. Having a visual reminder of the positive effects of your daily work is inspirational and energizing!
- **Celebrate.** After the exercise is complete, have a small celebration for the group. Consider a special treat; some ideas include a sparkling cider toast, a cheese tray, a cake with a thank-you message written in frosting, or a handwritten thank-you card (with or without a small gift item).

Individualize

- **Parent Success Board.** Invite parents to share special moments they have experienced at a parents' night event, or provide individual opportunities for sharing. Encourage them to think about everyday moments of joy, wonder, and connection. Consider asking parents to share their thoughts by sending them a letter about this activity and asking them to fill in slips of paper or send their thoughts to you electronically. Adding the parents' thoughts and ideas to your success board will help everyone see how their work matters!

Investigate

- The following are ideas for celebrating success:

  "31 Best Songs about Winning, Celebration, Victory, and Success" by Liam Flynn
  www.musicgrotto.com/songs-about-winning-celebration-victory-success

  "Beyond 'Great Job': Meaningful Ways to Celebrate Success in the Workplace" by Carrie Williams Howe
  https://carriewilliamshowe.com/celebrating-success-at-work

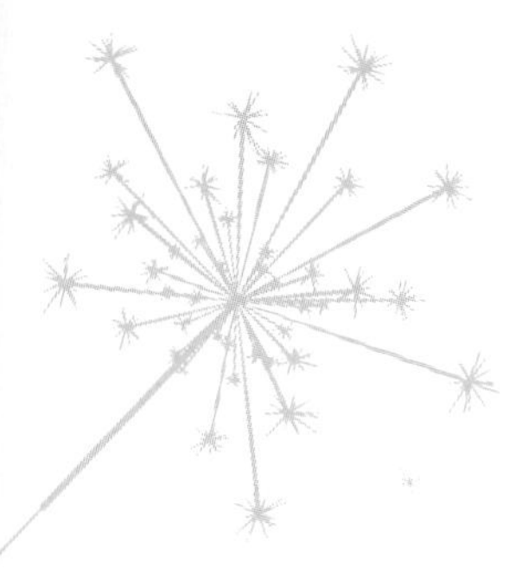

Activity #56

Collaborative Building Tasks

Intention

Working together to complete a fun task can help invigorate teamwork. Challenging building activities lead people to collaborate in creative and innovative ways and see things from a variety of perspectives.

Implementation

OPTION ONE: THE MARSHMALLOW CHALLENGE

This team-building exercise was originally invented by Peter Skillman and popularized by Tom Wujec: https://marshmallowchallenge.com.

Materials: marshmallows, uncooked spaghetti, masking tape, string, large envelopes, measuring tape

Goal: Build the tallest structure from the materials provided.

1. Assemble a kit for each team. Teams of four work well, so plan on one kit for every four people. Place the following materials in large envelopes:
    - twenty sticks of spaghetti
    - one yard of masking tape
    - one yard of string
    - scissors
    - one marshmallow
2. Review the rules:
    - The entire marshmallow must be on the top of the structure; no cutting it up into smaller pieces.
    - Use as much or as little of the kit materials as you'd like.
    - You can break up the spaghetti and cut up the string and tape.
    - The winning team is the one with the tallest freestanding structure, measured from the table to the top of the marshmallow.
3. Set a time limit. Fifteen minutes is a reasonable time frame, but you can adjust it to fit your schedule.
4. Create a fun atmosphere. Play some lively music. ("Ain't No Mountain High Enough" by Marvin Gaye and Tammi Terrell is a good option!)
5. Count down. Provide five- and two-minute warnings.
6. For a fun follow-up to this activity, watch and discuss this video:

    "How Kindergartners Outperform CEOs—Marshmallow Experiment," www.youtube.com/watch?v=7BExiToJFGg

OPTION TWO: PAPER BRIDGES

Materials: For each group, provide the following: thirty sheets of white printer paper, a roll of tape, and a ruler or measuring tape.

Goal: The team that makes the longest bridge in the allotted time is the winner.

1. Divide the group into teams of three or four.
2. Review the rules:
    - Tape can only be used in the structure of the bridge. It cannot be used to attach the bridge to the table.
    - The bridge can have a maximum of two support columns.
3. Set a time limit. Ten minutes works well for this activity.
4. Create a fun atmosphere. Play some music to set the tone. (Two good options are "The Brooklyn Bridge" by Frank Sinatra or "Burning Bridges" by Garth Brooks.)
5. Count down. Provide five- and two-minute warnings.

Debrief

- Group Reflections. For either building option, ask the participants to reflect on how their team worked. Consider asking any or all of these questions:
    - *Describe how people organized themselves. How were roles/jobs delegated?*
    - *How were the available resources used?*
    - *How was the group led? Did a group leader emerge? How?*
    - *How were problems solved?*
    - *Describe the communication between group members.*
    - *What are you wondering about the ways your team worked together?*
- Wrap-up. Discuss with the group key elements of teamwork that were evident during the exercise. Highlight how effective communication and leadership skills played an important role in the building exercise. Encourage participants to share how this exercise relates to teamwork in their programs. Here are some guiding questions:
    - *What surprised you most about this activity?*
    - *What did you learn from this activity?*
    - *What made your teamwork effective?*
    - *How might you apply what you learned to your work with colleagues and children?*

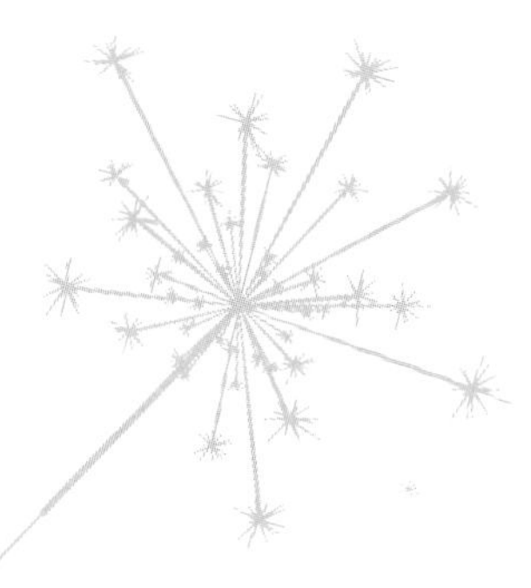

Individualize

- Ask each group to appoint an observer. The observer does not participate in the building but rather uses the reflection questions to guide their thoughts and share feedback with the group when they have finished building.
- To vary the activity, ask teams to use materials from their classrooms (unit blocks work well) or outside (sticks or other natural items) to build a structure.

Investigate

- The following article explores insights from the Marshmallow Challenge:

  "Innovation Leadership Lessons from the Marshmallow Challenge" by Scott D. Anthony
  https://hbr.org/2014/12/innovation-leadership-lessons-from-the-marshmallow-challenge

Illuminate

- Watch a clear overview of the Marshmallow Challenge:

  "Team Building Activity at Work (The Marshmallow Challenge)"
  www.youtube.com/watch?v=7ZMuHZv47bQ

Big Rocks

Things that matter most must never be at the mercy of things that matter least. —Often attributed to Johann Wolfgang von Goethe

Intention

This visual activity helps individuals and teams focus their time and energy on what is most important to them. The big rocks represent the things in life we truly value—core values, goals, and aspirations. The demonstration and reflective questions help participants see why they need to prioritize their big rocks. The origin of the "big rocks" concept is unknown, but it was popularized by Stephen Covey in his book *The Seven Habits of Highly Effective People.*

Implementation

Materials: one quart jar, ten to twelve rocks (golf ball size), a bag of smaller rocks (large pebble size), and a bag of tiny rocks

Step One: Begin by sharing your intent for this activity. Take the glass jar and place it on a table in front of the group and explain that the glass jar will represent all aspects of your professional life.

Step Two: Ask participants what core values shape their work. Prompt them with follow-up questions: What brings you the greatest joy? Why do you work in the early childhood field? What gets you out of bed and into work every day? The answers to these questions will generate the "big rocks." For each response, put a big rock in the jar and use flip chart paper to record the "big rocks" of the program.

Step Three: Next ask the group what day-to-day tasks fill up the jar of their professional lives. The group will have many responses (paperwork, planning, meetings, and so on). For each response, throw in a small handful of the medium-size rocks.

Step Four: When the jar is almost full, ask the participants to share the small tasks of their professional life that fill up the jar. I often refer to this as the minutiae of our daily work. Participants will have many responses (wiping noses, diapers, cleaning, and so on). For each response, throw in a small handful of the tiny rocks.

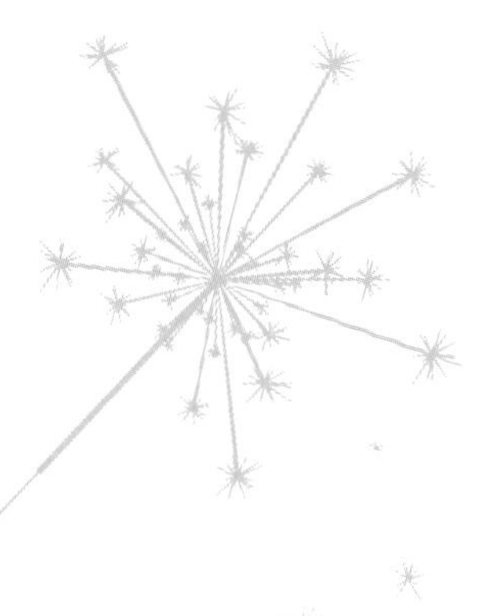

Step Five: When the jar is full to almost overflowing, stop, hold up the jar, remind the group that the jar represents their professional life, and ask the pivotal question: What would happen if the big rocks were not placed in the jar first? The responses tend to focus on the challenges of fitting our big rocks into our busy work lives.

Step Six: Debrief the key message from the exercise: we need to keep the big rocks, the reasons for doing the important work we do with children, families, and one another, at the center of all we do.

You can end the exercise here or complete the following steps to take this exercise to a more vibrant conclusion.

Step Seven: For in-house workshops, conduct team reflections. Divide the participants into groups of four to six people. Ask them to work in their groups to discuss their big rocks as a team, using these questions:

- *What are the big rocks for your team? What do you care most about? What are your top priorities?*
- *Are you willing to commit, right now, to put those big rocks in the glass jar of your life? What steps will you take to be sure the big rocks get in your jar of life first?*

Step Eight: Perform team skits. Ask each team to develop a list of "big rock rules" that will help them to remember to put their big rocks in first. Then ask them to create a short skit (think poem, story, wordplay, or rap) that reflects their big rock rules. Encourage the groups to use any props available. Have a camera on hand to take pictures and videos of these performances!

Step Nine: Debrief the skits with a follow-up discussion. What did we learn about our big rocks? Do we have more big rocks to add to the initial list? What are the most important things we can do to keep the big rocks in the "jar" of our professional life?

Adapted from: MacDonald, Susan. 2016. *Inspiring Early Childhood Leadership: Eight Strategies to Ignite Passion and Transform Program Quality.* Lewisville, NC: Gryphon House, pages 14–16.

SOAR (Strengths, Opportunities, Aspirations, Results) Analysis

Intention

A SOAR analysis helps participants quickly reflect on their current strengths, future aspirations, new opportunities, and results that they would like to achieve. The SOAR framework is a strengths-based approach for generating reflection and dialogues focused on innovation and growth. This activity was adapted from *The Thin Book of SOAR* by Jacqueline M. Stavros and Gina Hinrichs.

Implementation

- Create a SOAR template with questions for each section. This sample was developed for a workshop on creating innovative professional development projects:

Strengths	**Opportunities**
What do you excel at? What makes you unique? What are you proudest of? What are your greatest accomplishments?	What could you create to support the early childhood field? What changes and trends are occurring that you could help to navigate?
Aspirations	**Results**
What are you passionate about? How can you make a difference? What do you want to achieve in the future?	How do you translate your vision of success into achievable outcomes? What measures will tell you that you are on track to achieve success? How will you know when you have achieved your goals?

- Create a slide with the SOAR template to share with the group or copy the template for each individual. You can use the sample above as is or customize the questions to reflect the focus of your workshop. Provide a second template with only the headings (Strengths, Opportunities, Aspirations, Results) for the participants to fill in their responses.
- Put on some background music and give the participants a set amount of time to work on their templates. Six to ten minutes is a reasonable time frame.
- Break the group into partners and give them five minutes to share the highlights of their SOAR map.
- Debrief the activity with questions that connect to the focus of your presentation.

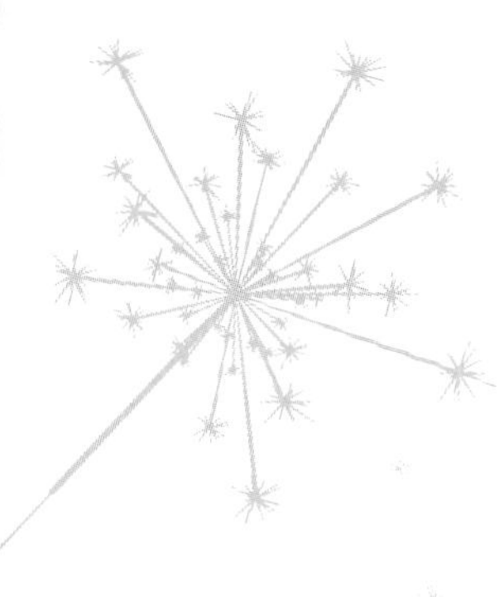

Individualize

- SOAR can also be used at board meetings or parent events as a reflection tool to help develop a strategic plan for the program.

Investigate

- Learn more about SOAR analysis:

  "What is SOAR?" by Jacqueline M. Stavros and Gina Hinrichs www.soar-strategy.com/what-is-soar

  Stavros, Jacqueline M., and Gina Hinrichs. 2009. *The Thin Book of SOAR: Building Strengths-Based Strategies.* Bend, OR: Thin Book Publishing.

Definition of an Early Childhood Educator

Intention

Early childhood educators play a variety of critical roles in providing quality care and education. This activity helps teachers and leaders identify these roles and affirm how each one benefits children, families, colleagues, and their program. It also provides an opportunity to consider how we define our profession and how the language we use influences both the public perception of the important work we do and the policies that regulate our work. This activity can be used in workshops that address a variety of topics to highlight how teachers' roles and responsibilities affect the quality of early childhood education and care.

Implementation

- Have the group brainstorm the roles they play as early childhood educators.
- Show "Definition of an Early Childhood Educator" (on a slide, as individual handouts, or on a poster). You can use this one or customize it to make it relevant and relatable to your group:

  Early Childhood Ed·u·ca·tor (ej•u•kād•r) *n. chef, maintenance worker, hygiene specialist, valet, protector, dishwasher, storyteller, inspector, aerobics instructor, entertainer, record-keeper, self-esteem builder, comforter, traffic controller, inventor, musician, technician, dietitian, plumber, analyst, artist, environmentalist, negotiator, friend . . .*

- Give people a couple of minutes to read it on their own or ask for a volunteer to read it out loud.
- In the large group, or in smaller groups or pairs (depending on group size), invite participants to comment on these roles.
  - Which roles can they relate to?
  - Ask them to give examples of how they play these roles in their daily practice.
- Debrief with the whole group:
  - Discuss how these roles benefit children and families and how they contribute to quality care and education. Imagine how quality would be affected if these roles were not filled.
  - Explore how these roles relate to program values, licensing regulations, and accreditation standards.
  - Consider the importance of language.
    - What words do we use to describe ourselves and our colleagues?

- How do these descriptions influence the perception of early childhood educators and the policies that are enacted?
- How do we feel when we hear other people describing our work (for instance, as babysitting)? Generate a list of strategies that can be used to better educate the public about what our job entails and why it's important to children and families.

Individualize

- Provide a variety of hats and other props and invite participants to choose one and explain what role it represents and how it is played out.
  - For example, traffic controller props might include an orange vest and traffic cones. A prompt might be for someone (or a small group) to role-play a script that depicts a transition (perhaps from circle time to outside play). What would it look like with effective teaching (or traffic control)? What would happen if teachers did not perform that role?
- Group the roles according to program values, licensing, or accreditation standards.
- Encourage participants to create a documentation board illustrating teachers engaged in these roles to make them visible to families and other visitors, or play a slideshow at family and community events.
- Develop advocacy strategies to illuminate the importance of early childhood education and educators.

Investigate

- Discover how language sends a message and influences perceptions:

  Artis, Berna, and Sally D'Italia. 2021. "Consider This: Language Matters—Early Childhood Educators Deserve Respect." *Child Care Exchange.* www.childcareexchange.com/article/consider-this-language-matters-early-childhood-educators-deserve-respect/5026288/.

  Ranck, Edna Runnels. 2020. "Our Proud Heritage. Can We Change Early Care and Education?" *Young Children* 75 (5). www.naeyc.org/resources/pubs/yc/dec2020/change-early-education.

Supporting Children's Play with Intentionality

When he worked, he really worked . . . but when he played, he really PLAYED! —Dr. Seuss

Intention

Research continues to show that the richest learning experiences for children come from their play. Teachers need to support children's play through the intentional use of materials, the environment, and interactions. What better way is there for teachers to learn than through play of their own? In this activity, teachers also explore playful strategies to use in their daily interactions with children. Consider the words of Fred Rogers: "Play is often talked about as if it were a relief from serious learning. But for children, play is serious learning."

Implementation

- Have displays of a variety of play materials set up: for example, recycled items, sensory items, nature items, boxes, blocks, and household items. Make sure they are organized in an inviting, attractive manner. Use materials that reflect the diverse cultures that make up your learning community.
- Invite teachers to individually explore and play with the materials. Provide a list of guided questions. Leave a good amount of time for this—twenty to thirty minutes works well.
    - *What is engaging about the materials?*
    - *What activities could you design with them to support skills and development in all domains?*
    - *What open-ended questions could you ask?*
    - *What vocabulary words could be incorporated?*
    - *What could you add to expand the learning?*
    - *How would you adapt the materials for children with diverse learning styles or individual needs?*
- Next, form small groups and have participants discuss their experience.

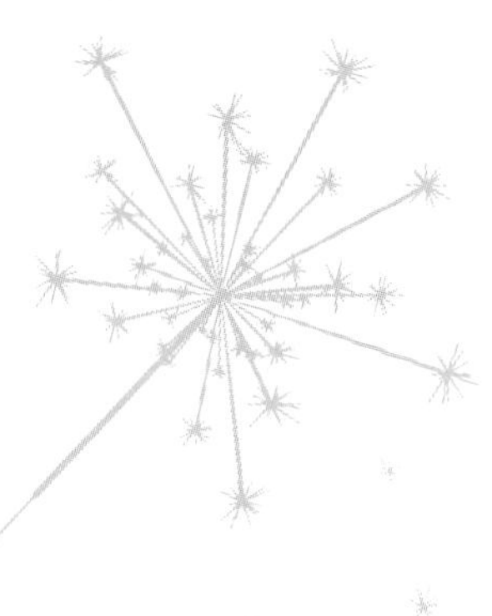

- Bring the whole group together to debrief:
  - Share observations. What did people notice? What were their favorite materials? Why?
  - How does play change when there is more time?
  - What makes a good play material to facilitate learning?
  - What are some ways you incorporate diverse play materials that allow children to see themselves reflected in authentic ways?
  - How does a child's culture and background influence their play?
  - How does play transform interactions, materials, and activities into tools that support children's cognitive, language, physical, and social-emotional development?

Individualize

- If time is constrained, have pairs or small groups do the initial explorations.
- If there is time, invite participants to share any activities they designed with the materials.
- Provide teachers with "play journals" so they can document how they are using play to support children's learning.
- Encourage teachers to create "play boards" to document the amazing things they see children doing through their play. (See Strategy #13—Celebrate! Document and Share Ongoing Stories of Growth and Change.)

Investigate

- Find information and resources about play and advocacy:

  Defending the Early Years
  https://dey.org

Taking Brain and Body Breaks

Short brain breaks help refresh, refocus, and reenergize participants. Consider adding a mixture of energizers and mindfulness exercises to your workshops to boost creativity, enhance learning, and add some fun!

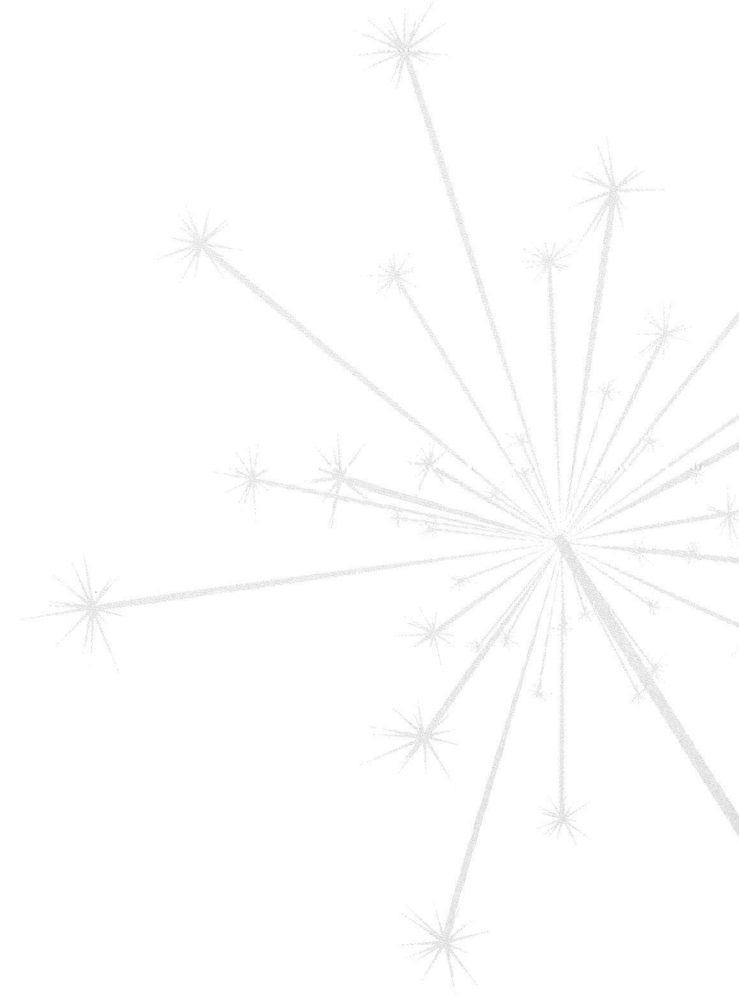

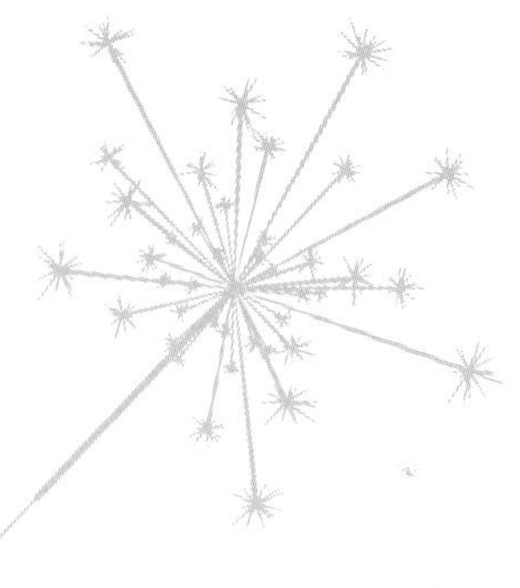

Activity #61

Energizers

Intention

Energizers are short activities that refresh and refocus the group. Keep participants engaged by having a variety of activities ready to go. Having ready a variety of activities that reinvigorate the group and keep participants engaged.

Implementation

- Pause the training and acknowledge what you notice. Try to make this a natural part of the workshop. Simple statements like "It looks like everyone needs an energy break to refocus" or "I can see that it is time to get up and moving" will help transition into the energizer.
- The energizer can be related to the topic of the presentation or simply a break.
- Select and practice energizing activities that you are comfortable with. The group will feed off your spirit and enthusiasm. Be sure to introduce the activity with positive energy and confidence.
- Some quick and lively ideas to try:
    - **Have a short dance party.** Pick a song that will get everyone up and moving. "Happy" by Pharrell Williams or "Conga" by Gloria Estefan are always a hit, or try one of your favorites.
    - **Have a sing-along.** Select a lively adult or children's song. "We Are the Champions" by Queen or "Fight Song" by Rachel Platten are good options to get people singing. You can find many videos of your favorite songs with lyrics on YouTube. It is also fun to ask for a volunteer to lead the group in an upbeat sing-along. You will often find a talented singer in the group.
    - **Play a game.** A few fast-paced rounds of musical chairs; head, shoulders, knees, and toes; or similar games will help get everyone up and moving.
    - **Encourage a good laugh.** Have participants stand up in groups of three and have them play two truths and a lie—sharing two statements that are true and one lie. Provide a focus for the statements—you won't believe this (leadership or teaching challenges they faced), the funniest thing that happened to them at work, why I became a teacher, or add your own ideas. After each person shares, the group has to guess the lie. A quick variation is to play a few rounds of "you never would have guessed." Have everyone stand up and quickly find someone who was not at their table and share one thing that most people would not know about you. Switch partners two or three times.

- **Keep the energy high.** Cheer on the groups, participate in the fun yourself, and keep the activities short.

Individualize

- If you feel comfortable with the group, consider soliciting a volunteer to lead an energizer activity.

INSIGHT FROM THE FIELD

from Luis A. Hernandez

- Include large-group physical activities or individual stretches for virtual formats.
- Energized, well-caffeinated presenters/facilitators help to "wake" folks up either early morning or after lunch.
- Watch YouTube segments of fitness icon Richard Simmons for inspiration!

Watch a video clip of Luis A. Hernandez sharing some of his favorite large-group physical/movement activities (scan QR code or type URL into web browser).

https://vimeo.com/851708915

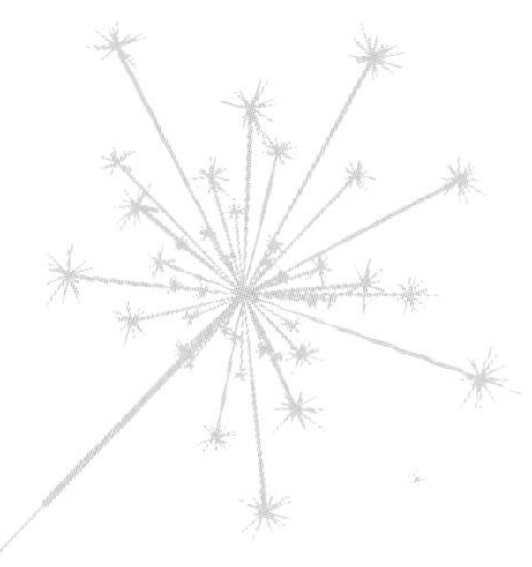

Activity #62

Shake Down, Warm Up!

Intention

When the group's energy is low, this short exercise will quickly reenergize everyone. You can use it at the beginning of a session to jump-start the group or anytime you notice participants looking tired or lacking engagement.

Implementation

- Practice this exercise a couple of times on your own to build your confidence in facilitating this fun, fast-moving exercise.
- Provide an overview:
    - The movement countdown starts at eight and then decreases to one.
    - Start the countdown with eight shakes of the right hand (with hand in the air), then eight shakes of the left hand (with hand in the air). Then eight shakes of the right foot, followed by eight shakes of the left foot.
    - Next, go back to the right hand and do seven shakes, then seven of the left hand, then seven of the right foot, and so on.
    - Continue the countdown until you reach one shake of each.
    - The actions get quicker with this energizer as the numbers decrease, and it really wakes people up.
- Get everyone up and spread out before you begin. It helps to get everyone in a circle, but it is not necessary.
- Stand in front of the group and ask for volunteers to help you lead the activity. It helps build excitement and engagement to have a few people up front.
- Kick off the activity with a high-energy tone and movements. The group will take their cues from you, so show them your passion and excitement for the activity.
- Cool down. Give participants a minute to recover. Ask them how they feel after the activity.
- Resume the training session!

https://vimeo.com/861359312

Illuminate

- Watch a video of Susan and Nancy demonstrating this activity (scan QR code or type URL into web browser)!

Activities #63–66

Be Mindful

Intention

Sometimes you just need to pause and recenter yourself so you can pay attention to learning. As a facilitator, you have the responsibility to recognize the energy of the group and provide opportunities to refocus attention. These short mindfulness exercises revitalize participants when you notice they need a break.

Implementation

Use a mindfulness activity to help participants take a break and return ready to be more present and with sharper focus. You can also incorporate them into your agenda to be implemented at certain key points in the session. Make sure to choose an activity you have practiced and are comfortable with yourself.

Here is a sample of some commonly used mindfulness exercises and practices that you can adapt to your style and audience.

Activity #63: S.T.O.P.

- **S**top. Take a moment to pause your activity and thoughts.
- **T**ake a breath. Focus on your breathing and connect with the moment you are in right now.
- **O**bserve. Notice your internal and external environment and feelings. Where are you? What are you feeling?
- **P**roceed. As you regroup, remind everyone of the importance of taking a break and refocusing. This provides the energy to continue with the agenda or tasks you are engaged with.

Activity #64: Focus on the Space around You

- Invite participants to take a moment to shift their attention to their five senses. Ask them to take two deep breaths (count in for four, out for four) and then observe their environment and notice/describe to themselves:
  - five things you can see
  - four things you can touch/feel
  - three things you can hear
  - two things you can smell
  - one thing you can taste
- Take one deep breath (count in for four, out for seven)

Activity #65: Hear the Bell

- Material: a chime or a bell to create a reverberating tone
- Instruct the participants that you are going to ring the bell (or chime).
- Ask people to raise their hands when they stop hearing the tone.

Activity #66: Square Breathing

- Invite participants to draw a square in the air with their fingers.
    - As they go up one side of the square, breathe in for four counts
    - As they go across the top, hold for four counts
    - As they down the other side, breathe out for four counts
    - As they go across the bottom, hold for four counts

Investigate

- Explore mindfulness activities you can use with participants or share with participants to use with children:

    www.mindfulteachers.org/library

Illuminate

- Watch demonstrations of the 5, 4, 3, 2, 1 exercise:

    "5, 4, 3, 2, 1 Grounding Exercise" by University Health Services
    www.youtube.com/watch?v=Mse-Yg9wyiM

    "5-4-3-2-1 Grounding Method: 5 Senses Grounding to Manage Anxiety" by Lewis Psychology
    www.youtube.com/watch?v=WQg7seUGDUc

- Watch a demonstration of the S.T.O.P. practice:

    "The STOP Practice" by NowEffect
    www.youtube.com/watch?v=EiuTpeu5xQc

Fostering Meaningful Interactions

Creativity seems to emerge from multiple experiences, coupled with a well-supported development of personal resources, including a sense of freedom to venture beyond the known.
—Loris Malaguzzi

Include opportunities for intentional interactions to boost the confidence of participants and help them retain knowledge. Select and adapt activities that will enhance the material you are presenting by encouraging exploration and thought-provoking dialogues.

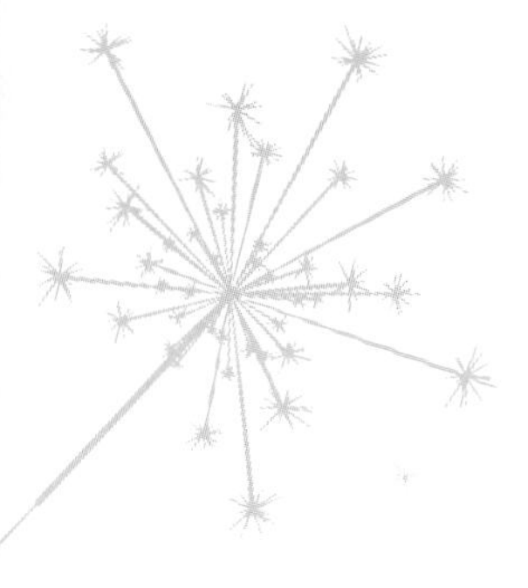

Activity #67

Sharing Our Viewpoints

Intention

Working as a team requires recognizing and aligning our values and viewpoints. This exercise provides a way to begin discussions among educators about their values and views related to their program (or early childhood in general) and their beliefs about program components and philosophy. Considering others' perspectives leads to greater understanding and enhanced communication. This activity can be used in a team-building or communication workshop. It can also be adapted to be used in any other topic-related training by making the statements focused more on the specific topic. (See Activity #71—What's Your Perspective?)

Implementation

- Prepare a list of statements that reflect varied views about early childhood. For example:
    - Children need to get messy in order to learn.
    - Toddlers need to learn how to share.
    - Parents are the experts on their child.
    - It is important for children to connect with nature.
    - Young children need the opportunity to try new things that challenge them and take safe risks.
- Explain that the purpose of this activity is to generate vibrant discussion and dialogue and dig deeper into the nuances around the issues. For instance, someone may agree that children should be allowed to get messy but maybe not all the time. Or an educator may wonder if parents are really the experts on their child, even though the educator has a master's degree in child development.
- Ask participants to consider the degree to which they agree or disagree with each statement.
- Have people stand up and make a continuum line; on one end are people who fully agree with the statement and on the other end are those who fully disagree. People who are somewhere in between can place themselves along the line.
- Break the group into pairs or small groups to discuss the statements, including how they fit in with early childhood philosophy and values and why they agree or disagree with them.
- Bring the group back together to debrief.

- Our own beliefs and values influence how we communicate and interact and lead us to judgments about others' intentions or actions. Recognize that we all approach situations from our own point of view, and that sometimes a teacher's personal values differ from the program philosophy or parents' child-rearing beliefs. It is important for these differences to be acknowledged and for people to be able to have open and honest discussions to resolve differences.
- How do each of the statements affect quality early care and education?

INSIGHT FROM THE FIELD

from Toni Christie

I like to work on shared values as a team. Once we have decided which values we share, they become integral to everything we do as a team and we can create a team contract or agreement that addresses what those values might look like in practice with children, families, and one another. Because it is worked out together, people take ownership and the contract becomes a lived experience.

https://vimeo.com/850976034

Individualize

Instead of participants forming a line, try one of these methods for indicating agreement:

- Have people stand up to the degree that they agree with the statement. People can stay seated or stand up partially or fully.
- Have a line on the floor with everyone standing on one side. People step over or behind the line, depending on the degree to which they agree or disagree with the statement.
- Have statements posted around the room. Participants can rotate around to discuss each statement.

Illuminate

Watch a video of Toni Christie discussing her approach to exploring shared values (scan QR code or type URL into web browser).

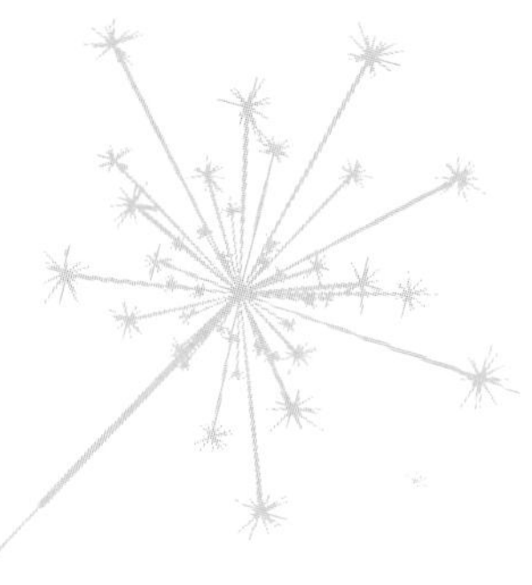

Activity #68

Exploring Culture and Identity

Intention

We all have a culture—our own background, ethnicity, values, beliefs, and traditions that shape our individual identity. Behavior that is different from what we consider "normal" can be confusing or unsettling to us and may make interactions and communication challenging. Recognizing, accepting, respecting, and celebrating our differences creates an environment that helps individuals have the courage to contribute their thoughts and ideas. This exercise helps teachers explore the many aspects of culture and identity and incorporate diversity into their interactions (with children, families, and one another), environment, and activities. Acknowledge to the group that this activity may elicit many feelings and emotions.

Implementation

- Begin with a discussion of how understanding who you are and the factors that influence your identity is crucial to your work with children and families. Consider using a powerful quote to start the dialogue, for example:

  Understanding who you are and how you came to be the person you now are gives you a deeper understanding of how children develop and what factors helped to shape them. This is a lifelong process.—"Examining Teacher Bias," Louise Derman-Sparks and Julie Olsen Edwards, with Catherine M. Goins. 2020. In *Each & Every Child: Teaching Preschool with an Equity Lens*, edited by Susan Friedman and Alissa Mwenelupembe. Washington, DC: NAEYC.

- Brainstorm categories of how we are all unique and different. The responses will likely include things like race, religion, culture, ethnicity, language, gender and sexuality, ability, and taste in music, art, fashion, and food. Fill in other variables to consider. (These may include differences in the concept of time and personal space, hobbies, physical activities, or communication preferences.)
- Encourage participants to reflect on their own personal culture and identity and how those inform their behavior and interactions. What are some of the values and beliefs that guide them? What are some traditions and rituals that are part of their family and community culture? How are their preferences in lifestyle influenced by their culture?

- Identify visible (tangible or surface) versus invisible (learned/experienced or deep) behaviors, values, and activities related to culture. Brainstorm these elements with the group.
- Invite participants to create a visual representation of their personal culture, identity, and current factors that are important in their decision-making. Encourage them to consider both the visible and invisible components, and how strongly those components influence their lives.
    - Have a variety of materials for people to use, including art materials, nature items, loose parts, magazines, and catalogs.
- In pairs or small groups, have people share and discuss how culture influences their behavior and beliefs, giving one example.
- Bring the group back together to debrief.
    - Solicit feedback about the process. Were there any surprises for people? How did it feel to think deeply about their own culture? Describe the experience of sharing with another person.
    - What insights did you gain—either about yourself or about someone else's behavior?
    - How will you use this concept and knowledge in your daily teaching practice? Are there any aspects of your curriculum, environment, materials, or interactions you might adjust?

Individualize

- Provide a reflection sheet to participants before the workshop so they can start thinking about their personal culture before the training.
- Include an iceberg graphic with the other materials for the visual representation activity. Some participants may find that easier to use for their project.
    - "The Iceberg Concept of Culture" graphic (with words) https://mass.pbslearningmedia.org/asset/c12c1a0a-9195-4124-93f4-230f10363a33
    - "The Iceberg Concept of Culture" graphic (without words) https://mass.pbslearningmedia.org/asset/e708741c-9e56-4a87-a047-3ef249dc256e
- Consider using Activity #54—Yarn Web to help explore individual cultures and identities.
- Combine this activity with Activities #43—"Where I'm From" Poem, #67—Sharing Our Viewpoints, or #85—Gallery Walk.

Investigate

- Resources for expanding your knowledge related to culture and identity:

  Revisiting and Updating the Multicultural Principles for Head Start Programs Serving Children Ages Birth to Five
  https://eclkc.ohs.acf.hhs.gov/culture-language/article/multicultural-principles-early-childhood-leaders

  "The Cultural and Linguistic Competence Self-Assessment Checklist for Early Head Start and Head Start Programs"
  www.ecmhc.org/assessment/staff.html

  "Avoiding Cross-Cultural Faux Pas: Understanding the Impact of Cross-Cultural Differences"
  www.mindtools.com/asez5br/avoiding-cross-cultural-faux-pas

  NAEYC Position Statement: Advancing Equity in Early Childhood Education
  www.naeyc.org/resources/position-statements/equity

  "Recommendations for Early Childhood Educators"
  www.naeyc.org/resources/position-statements/equity/recommendations-ECE

  "Recommendations for Everyone"
  www.naeyc.org/resources/position-statements/equity/recommendations-everyone

- For insights about surface and deep culture, see this book, especially chapter 3:

  Sullivan, Debra Ren-Etta. 2022. *Learning to Lead: Effective Leadership Skills for Teachers of Young Children*. 3rd edition. St. Paul, MN: Redleaf Press.

Illuminate

- Lead teachers in a culture activity:
  www.youtube.com/watch?v=9YMglx79I_0
- Watch a video about differences and similarities:
  "Understanding and Accepting Differences" by MyWorkplaceHealth
  www.youtube.com/watch?v=yaNGfWrRHuE
- For a lighthearted look at how children perceive differences:
  Facebook Live from the BBC Family and Education News Network
  www.facebook.com/watch?ref=search&v=1426740300746015&external_log_id=922c13bd-43cb-45c0-b6ad-2db335916380&q=bbc%20family%20and%20education%20news%20kids%20differences

INSIGHT FROM THE FIELD

Supporting Linguistic Diversity

Shared by Karen Nemeth

Professional development providers need to update their recommendations to be sure they are supporting the linguistic diversity of participants and their students. We know that about one-third of young children are dual or multilingual learners, and Head Start, for example, found more than 80 percent of classrooms had at least one DLL/MLL.

Help participants support linguistic diversity by including these, and similar, recommendations in your workshops. The strategies work well for virtual or in-person presentations.

- Instead of saying, "Ask children open-ended questions," you might say, "Learn to ask some open-ended questions in the home languages of the children."
- Instead of saying, "Give children feedback," consider saying, "Provide nonverbal feedback and verbal feedback in English and home languages."
- Instead of saying, "Explain to children . . . ," consider providing options for showing a video or demonstrating for children along with verbal explanations.
- Provide specific guidance on effectively using visuals and props to build meaning and comprehension for young multilingual learners.
- Encourage participants to come up with their own ideas for wording and materials they would use to support learning in children's home languages.
- Additional supports could include enhancing professional development for bilingual assistants, volunteers, or family members so they can provide the same high-quality interactions in the children's home languages that the teacher might do in English.
- See Karen's new book for more ideas:
  Nemeth, Karen. 2022. *Educating Young Children from Diverse Languages and Cultures*. New York: Routledge.
- See Karen's website with lots of blogs for new professional development activities:
  www.languagecastle.com

Karen also suggests the following resources:

- Ready-DLL app for mobile devices, free from Head Start
  https://eclkc.ohs.acf.hhs.gov/culture-language/article/ready-dll-mobile-app
- "The Gift" by Atlanta Speech School
  www.youtube.com/watch?v=WOFMDspl2tA

https://vimeo.com/850972247

- Watch a video of Karen Nemeth sharing her tips for creating opportunities to support linguistic diversity (scan QR code or type URL into web browser).

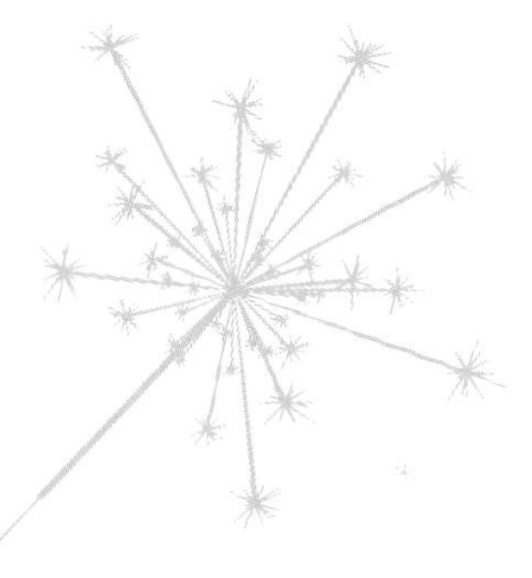

Activity #69

Hopes and Dreams

Fill your heart with your hopes and dreams; dreams that will someday leap and soar into the sky. —Michael Bassey Johnson

Intention

This easy-to-implement activity guides you in facilitating an insightful conversation about each individual's hopes and dreams for their work or the program. You can use this activity to kick off a new school year, as part of a vision workshop, or anytime the group would benefit from reconnecting with their professional aspirations.

Implementation

Materials: index cards, markers, pens

- Establish the focus: Explain to the group that you would like to learn more about their hopes and dreams. This activity can be done for individuals or for the program.
  - For individuals, ask, "What are your hopes and dreams for your work and professional growth?"
  - For the program, ask, "What are your hopes and dreams for the program? What impact do you hope the program will have on children, families, educators, and the community?"
- Distribute index cards. Ask each participant to write their hopes and dreams on index cards, one idea or thought per card.
- Share in groups. Divide the participants into small groups and have them share their hopes and dreams. Ask for a volunteer to list the group's responses, and then share them back to the whole group.
- Share as a large group. Participants are often reluctant to share and read their own cards. Collect the cards, shuffle them up, and ask for volunteers to come up and read or distribute the cards back to the group and take turns reading them.

- Debrief. Ask the group what they noticed about any common themes. Discuss how the hopes and dreams relate to individual professional growth and to the continued growth of the program.
- Develop some next steps:
  - Write up the collection of hopes and dreams into a document to share among participants or post in the program staff room or office.
  - Designate an area where staff can post their hopes and dreams (for themselves or for their program/classroom).
  - Create and print out a word cloud for participants to post in their programs.
  - Create action steps that will move the hopes and dreams into reality.

Individualize

- This activity can be replicated for parent or board meetings.

Adapted from: MacDonald, Susan. 2016. *Inspiring Early Childhood Leadership: Eight Strategies to Ignite Passion and Transform Program Quality*. Lewisville, NC: Gryphon House, pages 16–17.

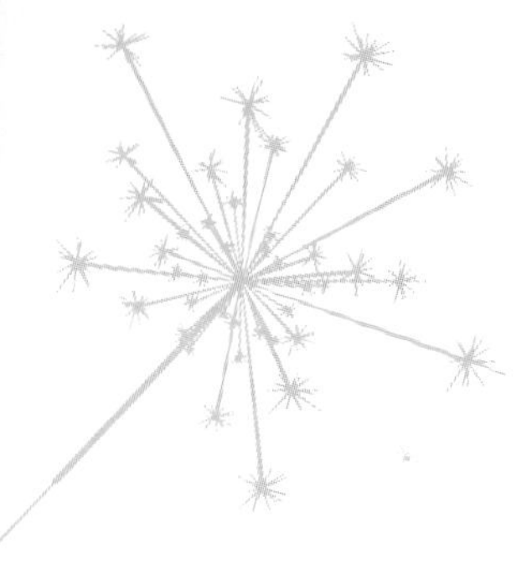

Activity #70

Choose an Item

Intention

This activity gets participants moving around and encourages them to reflect on the training topic or concept, using objects to represent positive aspects of their work. Making these connections helps participants integrate the learning and insights they are discovering into their everyday practice.

Implementation

- Preparation: Collect a variety of objects. Examples include a slinky, a paperclip, a flashlight, a magnifying glass, a prism, nature items (pine cone, shell, feather, and so on)—really anything works! Be creative when considering what objects to use. How could you imagine them relating to your topic?
- Display the items around the room or place a selection on tables.
- Invite the participants to choose an item from those displayed (or something they may have already) that represents or reflects the concept you are discussing. The following are examples:
    - For team building or communication: the strength of a colleague or parent
    - For taking care of yourself: something that brings you joy
    - For curriculum: something that you enjoy doing with young children or a practice of yours that supports children's development
    - For challenging behavior: a strength of a child who exhibits challenging behavior
- Have participants share answers to the following reflection in pairs or small groups: what object did they choose and what does it represent?
- Bring the group back together to debrief and summarize.
    - Note the connection between the objects and what they represent for people. Acknowledge and add in any other connections you might see.
    - How did it feel to have to use an object to represent a concept? (You can compare this to children using representational objects in their play.)
    - Discuss the idea of focusing on the positive and starting from strength. This is another parallel process—we talk about using children's strengths as the foundation on which to build their skills. We need to use the same philosophy when working with adults. How would this affect participants' work environments and their practice?

Individualize

- If you don't have actual objects, you can use pictures of items.
- If all the participants are from the same program, discuss how the items and what they represent connect to the program's vision and goals.

What's Your Perspective?

We don't see things as they are; we see things as we are.
—Frequently attributed to Anais Nin

Intention

Our observations and perceptions are influenced by our values, background, culture, education, and experiences. Even when we all see the same thing, we process it differently. This activity helps teachers understand that people look at things through their own lens and what they bring to any interaction. The key is to recognize the different perspectives and use them to enrich our discussions and problem solving. This activity can be used in any workshop that includes team-building and communication topics, as well as observation or taking care of yourself.

Implementation

- Prepare in advance an array of pictures that depict a variety of people involved in many situations and activities. Be intentional about selecting images that represent individuals of different races/ethnicities, genders, abilities, ages, and so on.
- Group participants in pairs and give each pair one of the pictures.
    - Each person should look at the picture individually and determine their first emotional reaction to the picture.
    - Invite partners to talk with each other about their reaction and why they had that reaction.
    - Partners can discuss what they saw in the picture that elicited the response.
    - Each person should consider what other factors influenced their reaction.
- Bring the group back together. Ask each pair to show their picture and describe their perspectives. Did each person in the pair have the same reaction and response to the picture? What were some of the factors that influenced their perspective? Ask if anyone knows someone who would have a different response to their picture than they had.

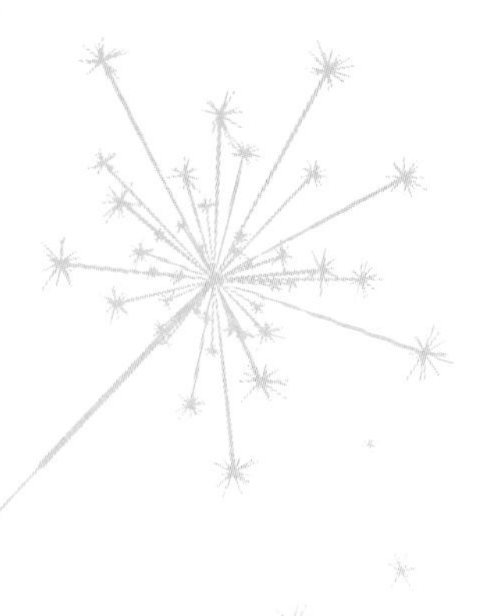

- Wrap up by summarizing the factors that influence people's perspectives, including but not limited to experience, education, personal beliefs, values, background, culture, and knowledge of a situation. Discuss the importance of knowing and understanding people's different perspectives so that we can more effectively interact with one another.

Individualize

- Instead of pictures, use a video for this activity. Have everyone watch the same video; then use the same format to have the discussions.

Investigate

- Explore this website for many pictures that illustrate how people have different perspectives and perceptions:

  Which One Doesn't Belong?
  http://wodb.ca/index.html

Hot Buttons

Intention

We all have our own personalities, communication styles, and temperaments. To work productively as a team and to effectively communicate with others in our organizations (parents, supervisors, and so forth), we need to understand ourselves and one another. This activity helps educators recognize and be aware of their own and others' personalities and communication styles and develop strategies to strengthen teamwork and communication.

Implementation

This activity can follow a discussion or presentation about teamwork or communication that includes information about effective communication techniques.

- Hand out a piece of brightly colored paper (perhaps in the shape of a button) to each person.
- Invite people to write one of their "hot buttons" on it. What is something that gets in the way of constructive communication? (You will likely notice phrases like "interrupting," "not listening," and similar.)
- Participants walk around the room holding up their "hot button." People with similar hot buttons can form small groups to discuss. Or group people in pairs to have them discuss their hot buttons.
    - Encourage participants to share stories of how the hot button has affected their communication with a person who pushes it.
    - How do they react or respond when a hot button is pushed? How does it make them feel about the other person?
- Bring the group back together to debrief.
    - Solicit volunteers to share any insights from their discussions.
    - Did anyone recognize one of someone else's hot buttons in themselves?
    - Summarize key points about how hot buttons impact communication and interactions.
- Follow this exercise with more presentation and discussion around strategies to defuse hot buttons during interactions.

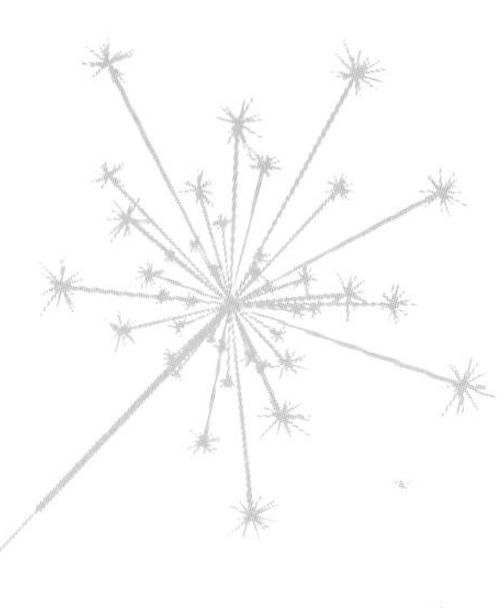

Individualize

- Do a group brainstorm of hot buttons. Write each hot button on a chart paper and post around the room. People can gather by the hot button that resonates with them to discuss and chart the responses.
- Invite participants to create role plays that depict the effects of the hot button.
- Use this activity as a way to discuss hot buttons about other topics (for instance, what is a hot button related to parent interactions or child behavior?).

Investigate

- For a variety of resources (articles and webcasts) on communication and teamwork, see the following website:

  Gallup
  www.gallup.com/Search/Default.aspx?q=communication

- For tips on effective communication, see the following blog posts:

  "Are You Just Talking or Are You Communicating?" by Sandy Abell
  https://insidejobscoach.com/are-you-just-talking-or-are-you-communicating

  "What is Effective Communication?" by Laurie Brown
  https://lauriebrown.com/guides/communication-skills/what-is-effective-communication

Listening Exercise

Intention

Listening is a key component in effective communication. In this exercise, participants practice and reflect on the elements of active listening skills and build their understanding of how strong communication is essential for creating a positive, productive work environment.

Implementation

- Identify a topic to be the focus of the exercise. Examples include the following:
    - *"Describe the best professional development event you have experienced and why."*
    - *"Describe a positive interaction you have had with someone and how it made you feel."*
- Break the group into pairs. Each person will have a chance to be both the speaker and the listener.
- Participants determine who in their pair will be the first speaker.
- Both partners take a minute to reflect on the topic.
- Partner 1 shares their story (two minutes).
- Partner 2 listens to the story without interrupting or asking questions (no talking).
- Partner 2 gives a synopsis of the story back to Partner 1 (one minute).
- Switch roles and repeat the process.
- Bring the group back together to discuss the art and practice of listening.
    - **How did it feel to be listened to?** Responses may include that people felt uncomfortable because they weren't used to a listener not saying anything. Others will say they enjoyed having the undivided attention of the listener.
    - **How did you know you were being listened to?** Responses will likely include eye contact, body language, and similar. Make sure to add appropriate tone of speech, body language (relaxed, fully facing person, arms and legs uncrossed, leaning forward, smiling, nodding, friendly hand gestures), and accurate retelling of the story.
    - **How did it feel to listen without talking?**
- Using the same process (Partner 1 speaks, Partner 2 listens; then switch), tell the same story. This time, the listener can speak, but tries to get more information ***without* asking questions**—so they have to use other strategies.

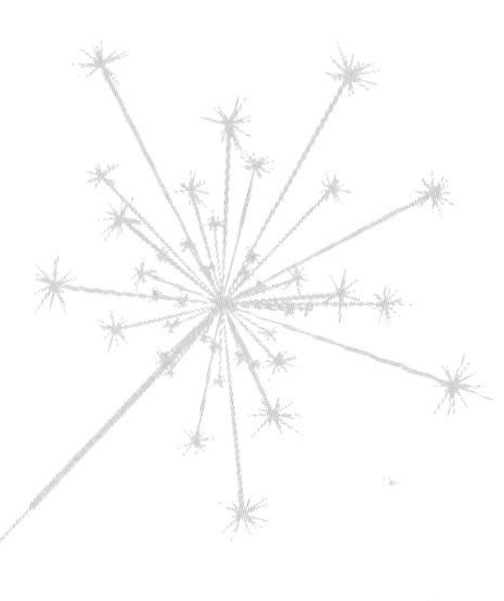

- Bring the group back together to debrief:
  - How was the second part of the exercise different?
  - Why is it important to get more information without asking questions? (Questions can sometimes derail a conversation, making it more about the listener.)
  - How did the listener get more information without questions?
    - Make sure responses include leading or clarifying statements, such as "Tell me more about that" and "What I hear you saying is . . . "
- Summarize the exercise and tie it back to the original concept (for example, elements of effective professional development, elements of positive interactions).

Individualize

- If there is time, you can use a triad for this exercise with the third person being the observer.

Investigate

- For more on active listening, see the following blog post:

  "Working Together: Communicating Effectively" by Marcia Hebert
  www.marciahebert.com/2011/07/working-together-communicating-effectively-2

How Children Learn (the Apple Activity)

We learn by example and by direct experience because there are real limits to the adequacy of verbal instruction. —Malcolm Gladwell

Intention

The value of play as a vehicle for learning has been well documented. This activity provides a concrete illustration of how children learn through exploration. Teachers will have a better understanding of the learning process as interactive and experiential, and of the importance of play. This activity can be used in any workshop that addresses development or curriculum.

Implementation

Materials: real apples (one per participant), fake apples, paper plates, napkins, plastic knives, paper or index cards, a picture of an apple, a large card with the word *apple* written on it

- Use this activity as a lead-in or follow-up to a presentation or discussion of how children learn.
- Brainstorm how an infant learns about something new (in this case, an apple). Responses will likely include touching it, smelling it, seeing what they can do with it, tasting it, and so on.
- Pass out the following items to each participant: paper plate, plastic knife, napkin, piece of writing paper or index card, and a real apple.
- Review the instructions. The first step is an individual activity:
    - Pretend that you do not know what an apple is.
    - Explore your apple in any way you choose.
    - Based *only* on your own exploration, write down words that describe your apple.
    - When you have finished, count how many words you have and write down the total.
- Ask participants to share how many words they have and note the range of numbers (for instance, 4–12) on a chart under a heading titled "Individual." Next, form pairs.

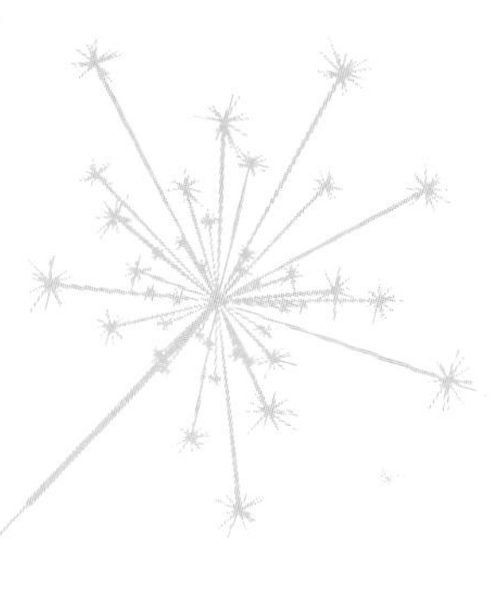

Each partner shares their words, adding words that they don't have to their own list. The end result is that both partners will have the same list of words. Ask what the new number of words is and note the range on the chart under a heading for "Pairs."

- Go around the room and have each person share one word from their list (they should share a word that hasn't been listed yet). As each person shares a word with the group, write every distinct word on a chart, even ones that are similar. Continue this process until all words have been shared.
- Tally the complete list of words charted. Note the total number of words on the chart under the heading "Group."
- Now pass out fake (plastic, plush, and so on) apples to participants, with instructions for participants to individually explore them in any way they choose. (Depending on the number of participants, they may have to share these.)
- Based on these explorations, go through the list of words on the chart and have the group determine which ones no longer apply. Cross off those words with a marker.
- Now show the group a picture of an apple. Based on this, the group will again determine words left on the chart that no longer apply. Cross those off the list.
- Finally, show the group the word *apple*. The remaining words will be assessed for relevance (and likely all will be crossed off).
- Debrief by asking for participants' reactions and realizations. Summarize and add any of your own observations that were not brought up. Note the relationship to children's learning and developmentally appropriate practice.
    - People explored their apples in a variety of ways. (Children have individual learning styles.)
    - Many words mean similar things. (We need to include a rich vocabulary in our conversations with children.) There was an increase in the number of words going from individual to partner to group. (Children need opportunities to learn in a variety of settings.)
    - Learning takes place within a context—activities should be intentional and support children learning about their world through real-life experience whenever possible.
    - Learning is deepened when children have time to explore and real items to manipulate.

Individualize

- This is a great activity to do with parents to help them understand the value of play.
- Use some of the words that come up in a mind-mapping activity. (See Activity #36—Mind Mapping.)
- Create a word chart or word wall to increase vocabulary.

Investigate

- Read more about how to encourage open-ended play and exploration:

  Duncan, Sandra. 2022. "The Honeycomb Hypothesis: A Fresh Perspective on the Color Orange for Infants, Toddlers, and Twos." *Exchange Magazine*. January/February 2022. www.childcareexchange.com/article/the-honeycomb-hypothesis-a-fresh-perspective-on-the-color-orange-for-infants-toddlers-and-twos/5026360.

  Fox, Heather, and Susie Wirth. 2015. "The Learning in Loose Parts." Community Playthings. June 2, 2015. www.communityplaythings.com/resources/articles/2015/Loose-Parts.

  Daly, Lisa, and Miriam Beloglovsky. 2015. *Loose Parts: Inspiring Play in Young Children*. St. Paul, MN: Redleaf Press.

  Daly, Lisa, and Miriam Beloglovsky. 2017. "Loose Parts 2: Inspiring Play with Infants and Toddlers." Community Playthings. October 31, 2017. www.communityplaythings.com/resources/articles/2017/Loose-Parts-play-for-Infants-and-Toddlers.

For virtual presentations, ask participants to imagine or visualize their apple exploration. Use a whiteboard feature to list the words during the round-robin.

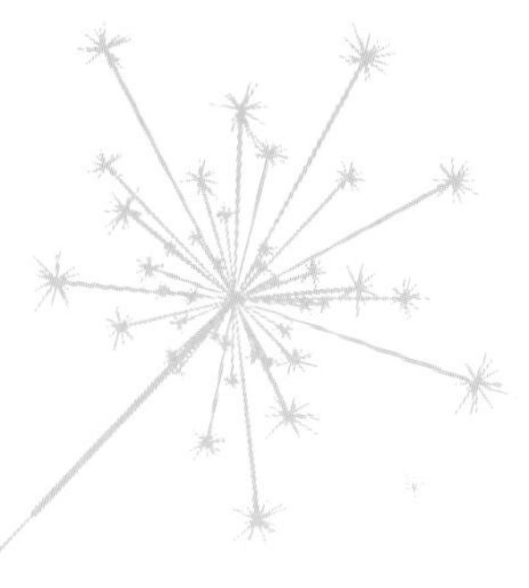

Activity #75

Reflecting on Gratitude

Intention

This activity creates opportunities for individuals to reflect on what they are grateful for and to express gratitude to one another. Focusing on what we are grateful for improves relationships, builds engagement, and creates a more positive work environment.

Implementation

Materials: Provide a variety of paper, markers, and sticky notes. If you have the space, you can place sheets of large flip chart paper on the wall for each person.

Step One: Individual gratitude lists

- Put on some background music (consider "Thank You for Being a Friend" by Andrew Gold or "What a Wonderful World" by Louis Armstrong) and ask participants to create a list of everything they are grateful for in their professional lives.
- Encourage them to include every single thing they can think of, regardless of how big or small.

Step Two: Group discussion

This can be done in a large group or small groups of four or five people followed by a large-group debrief.

- *What are you most grateful for?* Encourage participants to share two to three highlights from their lists.
- *What surprised you as you were creating your list?*
- *How does it feel to see everything you are grateful for on one list?*

Step Three: Building practices of gratitude

- Wrap up this activity by having the group brainstorm responses to this question:
  - *What can you do in your school community to build gratitude practices into your daily work?*
- Capture the responses from the participants.

  (Here are some ideas to get them started or to add to the list: have a basket of thank-you cards and stamps available to send to staff, parents, and community members; create a gratitude bulletin board for staff and families to post notes; post gratitude quotes in the staff room; begin staff meetings by sharing one thing you are grateful for.)
- Commit to trying two ideas in the next month.
- Establish check-ins to see how the gratitude ideas are being put into practice and what new ideas you can try for the next month.

Individualize

- For in-house groups that are familiar with one another, you can wrap up by creating opportunities to express gratitude. Use Activity #78—Mix and Mingle, considering the following prompts or your own:
    - *I am grateful for what you did . . .*
    - *I am grateful for how you . . .*
    - *I am grateful for your positive energy around . . .*
    - *I am grateful for your commitment and dedication to . . .*
- This activity can be adapted and used for parent or board meetings.
- Encourage teachers to create a similar activity with children.

Investigate

- Discover different ways for expressing gratitude and showing appreciation:

  Chapman, Gary, and Paul White. 2012. *The Five Languages of Appreciation in the Workplace: Empowering Organizations by Encouraging People.* Chicago, IL: Northfield Publishing.

For virtual meetings, use the following adaptations:

- Ask participants to have paper and markers available.
- Use breakout rooms for small-group discussions.
- For brainstorming, encourage participation through the chat box or use a whiteboard feature.

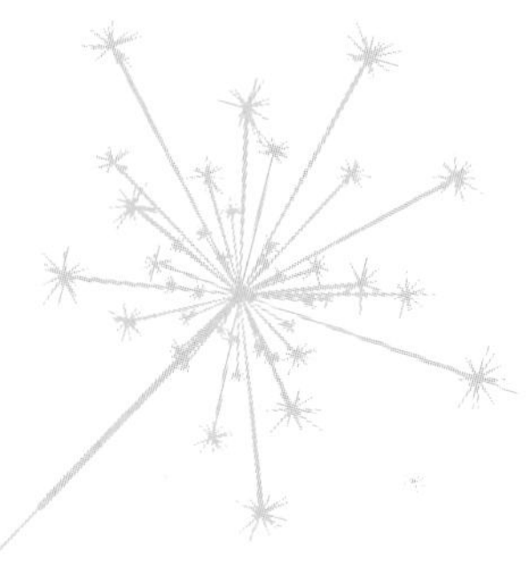

Activity #76

Chapters of Our Professional Lives

Intention

This activity provides a fun and creative way for individuals to think about how they would like to move beyond the status quo of their day-to-day work and gain clarity about what goals they would like to accomplish.

Implementation

- Provide an overview of the activity. It helps to make these prompts visible on a slide or flip chart:

  Think of your professional life as a book.

  - *What would the title be?*
  - *What is the name of the chapter you are in right now?*
  - *What do you want the next chapter to be called?*
  - *What excites you about the next chapter?*
- Ask participants to silently reflect on each prompt. Remind them that they do not need to stress over the perfect answer; often what pops into their minds first will provide key insights. It also helps to let participants know it is okay to have creative answers.
- Divide participants into groups of three to four to share their responses. Ask that one person record the key themes that come up in the group. Give the groups a minimum of ten minutes for their discussions.
- Engage in a vibrant debrief by having participants share responses to the questions. To highlight the desire for professional growth, it helps to focus the most time on the names of the next chapter and what excites participants about moving into that chapter of their professional life.

Individualize

- If working with an in-house group, record the names of the next chapters and post them somewhere visible to the staff. Use the titles as ideas for future professional development.
- This activity can be used to focus a professional development conversation with individual staff. It generates new ideas and meaningful goal setting and helps staff feel that you are interested in their thoughts and ideas related to their growth.
- These questions are also helpful in the interview process to get a sense of an individual's desire to grow and develop.

Carousel

Intention

Get people moving! This activity generates ideas in a collaborative activity that helps people share in a nonthreatening format. Everyone has an opportunity to express a perspective.

Implementation

- Prepare charts with headings that relate to the topic and information you aim to gather. The number of charts will depend on how many participants there are. For example:
  - To generate ideas for how to include literacy in your curriculum, the information you will want to gather is "activities and materials that support literacy." Have charts labeled with activity areas and routines found in an early childhood program (art, blocks, outdoors, arrival/departure, snack, and so on).
  - To generate ideas about effective communication, charts can be labeled with headings such as "Tips for active listening," "Barriers to constructive communication," or "Strategies to elicit more information."
- Post the charts around the room, leaving enough room in between for movement.
- Divide into small groups (three to five people each). Give each group a different-colored marker.
- Assign each group to one of the charts to start. Participants brainstorm ideas and answers.
  - One person acts as the recorder and adds the ideas to the chart, making sure to leave room for other groups to add their ideas.
  - Allow three to four minutes per chart.
- After three to four minutes, groups rotate to the next chart.
- At each chart, participants can add ideas and star those they agree with that are already there.
- Groups rotate until each group has had a turn at each chart.
- Groups end by going back to their original chart to see if they want to add anything else and considering any themes in the responses. Ask them to choose their top three ideas.
- Debrief:
  - Each group reports their top three ideas on their original chart.
  - Invite others to add anything that hasn't been mentioned.
  - Discuss any points that are raised or incorporate them into the rest of the session.

Individualize

- After the training, you can create a document from all the charts to send as a follow-up.

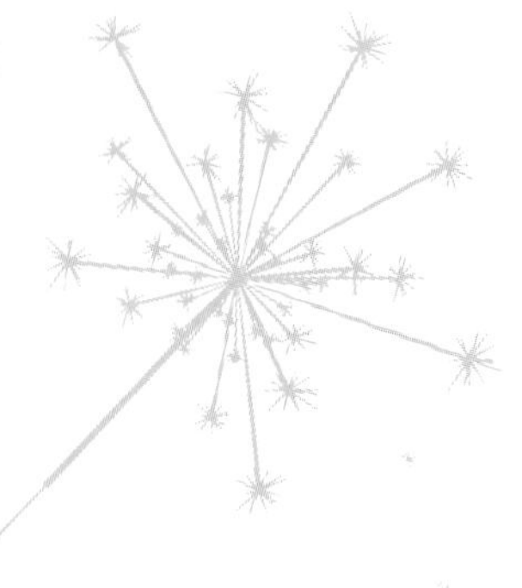

Activity #78

Mix and Mingle

Intention

This energizing, fast-paced activity gets participants up, moving, and engaging with one another. It provides short time frames for participants to share a key idea or concept with multiple partners.

Implementation

- Provide a clear prompt. You can put the prompt on a slide or flip chart for reference (if available). Here is an example:
    - *Introduce yourself and share a high point of your professional experience from the past six months (a project you completed, a breakthrough you experienced, a positive mentoring moment, and so on).*
- Play upbeat music.
- Ask everyone to get up from their seats and move around the room until the music stops.
- When the music stops, have them speak to one or two of their near neighbors.
- Give participants five minutes to share with partners, and then ask them to switch partners and share again. Keep the energy fun and upbeat!
- Debrief: Ask participants to share what it felt like to share their thoughts with others. Share what you observed about the interactions. Record a list of words to describe the energy in the room!

For virtual groups, place partners in breakout rooms for five minutes and then change the partners and place them in a different breakout room.

Individualize

- Create prompts for discussions that link to the specific topic you are discussing and give participants a chance to share their knowledge and ideas. Examples:
    - For a workshop on challenging behaviors:
        - *Share your most helpful strategy for calming a child who is upset or stressed.*
    - For a workshop on positive change:
        - *What brings you joy and a sense of satisfaction in your daily work?*
        - *What is one story from your classroom that captures what you are proudest of as an early childhood educator?*
        - *What motivates you to do your very best?*

Your Professional Year in Review

Intention

To end the school year in an intentional way, engage educators in a rich dialogue about the past year's highlights and challenges. The questions provided allow each individual to pause and reflect on their work and will fuel meaningful group dialogues.

Implementation

- Welcome: State in your own words how important it is to end the school year by reflecting on what went well, the challenges teachers faced, and their goals for the coming year.
- Individual reflection: Share these questions and ask participants to take ten to fifteen minutes to reflect on the questions and write down their thoughts:
    - *What were the moments that made you inspired, energized, and deeply connected to your work in the early childhood field?*
    - *What strengths and skills did you use this year to achieve all that you did (courage, determination, kindness, patience, and so on)?*
    - *What was the best thing you did for yourself?*
    - *What was the best thing you did for someone else?*
    - *The one thing you would like to redo in a better way is . . .*
    - *Who were the people that made this year a better year for you? How did (or will) you thank them?*
    - *What is your number one professional goal for the next school year? Why is this goal important to you?*
- Set the tone: Play soft music and provide a variety of pens and paper.
- Short debrief: Gather everyone back together and ask for some feedback on the exercise. Use general questions about the experience:
    - *How did it feel to reflect on the past year?*
    - *What was an aha moment for you?*
- Group discussion: If your group is larger than eight, break it down into small groups of four to five people to discuss their responses to the questions. Have a note keeper capture the answers. Remind everyone that they are invited to share their responses, but they can pass on any questions they are uncomfortable sharing with the group. Allow a minimum of twenty minutes for groups to discuss.

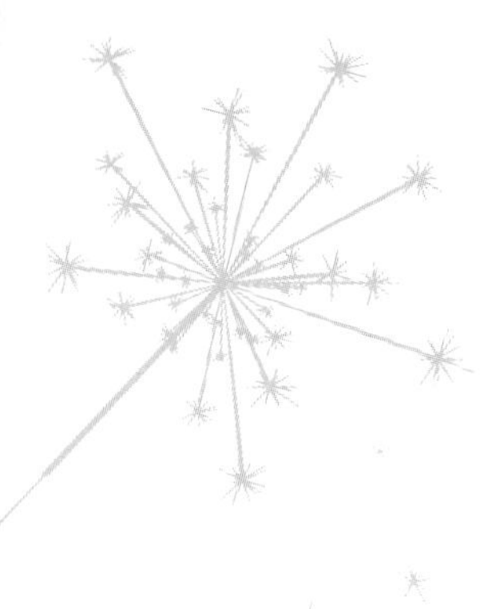

- Group sharing: Have a spokesperson for the group share the highlights of their discussion with the larger group. The following are some prompt questions:
  - *What was a common theme in your group?*
  - *What was most energizing?*
  - *What are some areas in which you would like to do better next year?*
- Wrap-up: Have the groups share the goals that were discussed in their group. Offer your reflections on what was shared and your excitement about supporting everyone in the coming year. End the discussion in a way that focuses on positive growth and hope for the future.

Individualize

- This activity can be adapted for a midyear review.

Envisioning Future Success

Whatever we believe about ourselves and our ability comes true for us. —Susan L. Taylor

Intention

This engaging and celebratory exercise provides participants the opportunity to imagine their goals and dreams coming to life at a set time in the future as they envision their accomplishments becoming a reality. This activity works well with any training centered on creating and achieving goals.

Implementation

- Set the tone. Create a joyous atmosphere! Consider adding some celebratory items to the space. Signs with the date in the future, balloons, champagne-type glasses to toast everyone's success (no alcohol needed; sparkling cider or seltzer is fine), party hats, or a special food can help to get everyone in a festive mood.
- Create the focus. A clear frame-up for the activity keeps everyone engaged. Here is a sample for a vision and goals workshop:
    - *Imagine it's twelve months from now, and you have stayed focused on achieving your goals. Think about how it feels to see your intentional work successfully bringing your vision to life!*
    - *Join your group as if it is ______ (date). Introduce yourself to your group by sharing the high points of your ______ (dreams, goals, vision) as if they have come to life! (The course you completed, the new classroom techniques you are utilizing, the time management strategies you have implemented, and so on.)*
    - *Encourage everyone to embrace the futuristic spirit of this activity and to portray themselves as if it were the future date established for this activity. Remind everyone to stay in the present tense!*
- Establish groups. Groups of four work well for this activity. Allow plenty of time for each person to share, a minimum of five minutes per person. Have the groups create a highlight list of all that they have accomplished.

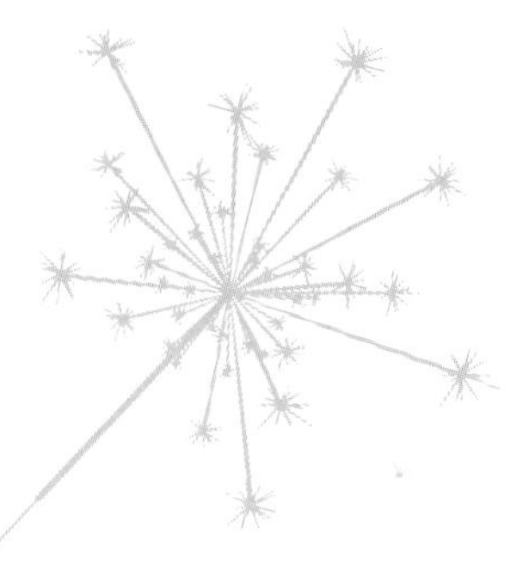

- Encourage group sharing. Play some upbeat music to kick off the group sharing. ("Ain't No Stoppin' Us Now" by McFadden and Whitehead works well.) You could also ask each group to find a theme song that relates to the group's accomplishments and have them play a clip from the song before sharing their lists.
- Wrap up. Congratulate everyone on all they have accomplished! Ask everyone what it felt like to achieve their goals. Record a list of words to describe the energy and emotion in the room. Encourage everyone to share one thing that will help them stay on track to achieve their goals.

Individualize

- This activity can be adapted for a variety of workshops by creating a relevant focus statement.

INSIGHT FROM THE FIELD

The Power of Kind and Unkind Words

Shared by Leland O. Clarke

This activity could be used in a workshop on team building, communication, or empathy. Help participants reflect on and recognize the power of words. Using bubbles creates an interactive and concrete way to introduce the concepts of cooperation, kindness, and empathy.

- Have a conversation about kind and unkind words and how they make you feel.
- Invite participants to imagine the bubbles as unkind words.
- Blow bubbles and have participants try to put the bubble back into the bottle. They will find this nearly impossible to do.
- Explain how difficult it is to take back hurtful words once you say them. Be careful how you use words.
- Watch a video of Leland O. Clarke sharing communication activities (scan QR code or type URL into web browser).

https://vimeo.com/861370102

Cultivating a Collaborative Learning Environment

Individually, we are one drop. But together, we are an ocean.
—Widely attributed to Ryunosuke Satoro, Japanese poet

We all know the saying "Two heads are better than one." Adult learning is enhanced when people work with others on applicable learning tasks, much like social psychologist Lev Vygotsky theorized that interaction and communication are critical to children's learning. Interacting with colleagues with a variety of diverse backgrounds, perspectives, and skills deepens teachers' individual comprehension. Collaborative learning activities engage participants in gaining new information through dialogue and sharing ideas and knowledge. They come away with a richer understanding of the topic and concept that is being discussed.

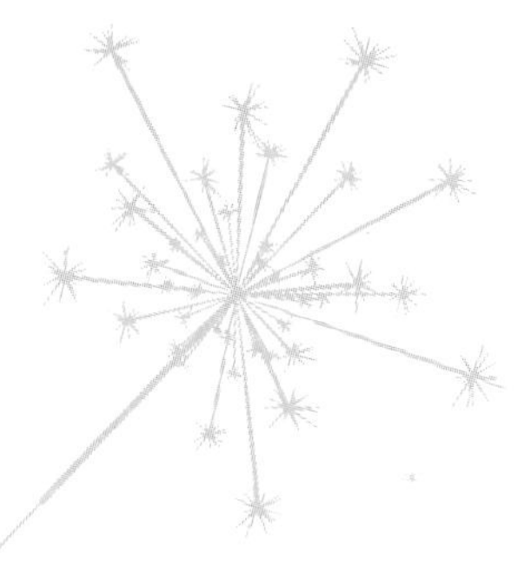

Activity #81

Create a Vision Statement

Intention

This interactive activity provides an opportunity for staff to contribute to a shared vision for the program. First, each person creates a vision board that illustrates the program at its very best. Then participants engage in concrete and inspirational dialogues about the program's future by sharing their vision boards. A program director or outside facilitator can lead this activity.

Implementation

Materials: heavy card stock, markers, stickers, magazines to cut up, images or photographs

- Create vision boards. You can create the vision boards during the meeting or provide the materials ahead of time and have participants come to the meeting with a vision board. Invite participants to imagine it is one year in the future and to depict their vision of what makes your program vibrant, energized, and an amazing place for children and educators to live and learn together.
- Facilitate a vision-focused discussion. Share some thoughts on the importance of having a shared vision. Use any of these or add your own ideas:
  - Provides clarity on where the program is headed
  - Fuels the energy needed to move away from the way we have always done it to what we desire to happen
  - Paints a clear picture of our program operating at its highest level of success
  - Highlights the professional aspirations of everyone in the program
  - Increases the passion, intentionality, and engagement of everyone in the program
  - Builds collaboration that is essential to program-wide transformation
- Divide the staff into groups of four to five people and have them do the following:
  - Share their vision boards.
  - Summarize the key points of the participants' visions on a flip chart.
  - Share their key points with the larger group.
- Form a vision committee. Ask for a couple of volunteers to join you in crafting a draft vision statement. The committee can begin by creating a summary of the key points from all the groups and then work on a draft vision statement that is clear, compelling, empowering, and motivational. Share the draft(s) with the staff and ask for feedback before finalizing it.

- Live your vision! Create visually appealing posters with the vision statement and post them with photos that capture the vision coming to life throughout the program. Use the vision as the foundation for creating relevant professional development goals and learning experiences. Successfully weaving the vision into the daily life of the program will build a renewed sense of purpose and increase engagement.

Individualize

- Replicate this activity to inspire insightful reflections and dialogue for parent events, board meetings, or classroom teams.

Investigate

- Learn more about creating empowering vision statements:

  MacDonald, Susan. 2016. *Inspiring Early Childhood Leadership: Eight Strategies to Ignite Passion and Transform Program Quality*. Lewisville, NC: Gryphon House.

  Seale, Alan. 2003. *Soul Mission, Life Vision: Recognize Your True Gifts and Make Your Mark in the World.* San Francisco, CA: Red Wheel.

Illuminate

- Watch this video for an overview of creating a vision board:

  "How to Create a Vision Board" by Jack Canfield
  www.youtube.com/watch?v=iamZEWox3dM

- Watch a video of Susan MacDonald sharing ideas for vision board workshops (scan QR code or type URL into web browser).

https://vimeo.com/893354140

Activity #82

Scenarios/Case Studies

Intention

Providing a specific scenario with some guided questions allows participants to apply knowledge and new ideas to practice. In small groups, they consider the scenario and bring their collective wisdom and perspectives to help resolve an issue or broaden their understanding.

Implementation

- Create scenarios or case studies that depict examples of specific situations, individuals, or a set of circumstances that reflect diverse cultural perspectives.
- Provide a handout with the scenario and guided questions pertinent to the content being discussed.
- Case studies and scenarios can be based on your own experiences or examples from colleagues, or created from a variety of sources to illustrate a point.
- Participants can be asked to volunteer a scenario or case study to be addressed by the group.
- Below are a couple of examples for different topics.

DEVELOPMENT/CURRICULUM

It is a warm, breezy day. Two-and-a-half-year-old Jessie is sitting outside on the grass, sometimes pulling the grass and sometimes moving his hand across the top of it. He stops suddenly when a butterfly goes by and watches it for a moment. He looks down at the grass again, sees some ants, and laughs aloud. When you approach him, he points at the ants and says, "Look! Ants marching!"

- *What is Jessie doing? What can you surmise about his development (cognitive, social-emotional, physical, language)?*
- *What is Jessie trying to understand? Practice?*
- *What is Jessie interested in?*
- *How would you respond to Jessie?*
- *What activities/materials would you plan to extend Jessie's interest and learning?*

SEPARATION

Mrs. Lee seems to have a harder time than her child with separation anxiety. When she brings three-year-old Sam to the program, Sam gives his mom a hug and gets involved right away with an activity. Mrs. Lee, however, continues to hang around, and at times hovers until Sam becomes anxious himself. The teacher tries to usher Mrs. Lee out the door, with reassurances that she can call anytime during the day to check in. When Mrs. Lee finally leaves, it takes Sam a few minutes to become reengaged in the program.

- *What is your first reaction?*
- *What factors may be contributing to Mrs. Lee's behavior?*
- *What message does Mrs. Lee's behavior convey?*
    - *To the staff:*
    - *To Sam:*
- *In what way is this creating a problem for the following people:*
    - *Sam:*
    - *Mrs. Lee:*
    - *The staff:*
- *How could Mrs. Lee better prepare herself and Sam for this transition?*
- *What strategies can the staff use to help Mrs. Lee feel more comfortable and create a more positive separation routine?*
- *Once strategies have been developed, who needs to know about them?*

- Divide the large group into smaller groups of four to five people.
- Provide instructions and a time frame for the activity and assign a group leader who will manage time and record the responses.
- Participants discuss the scenario and guided questions.
- Bring the full group back together. Groups share their scenarios and solutions. If each group has the same scenario, have each share one thing in a round-robin until all responses have been recorded.
- Summarize and point out any themes. Relate the discussion back to the work that was done before the case study exercise and refer back to the exercise as appropriate for the remainder of the session.

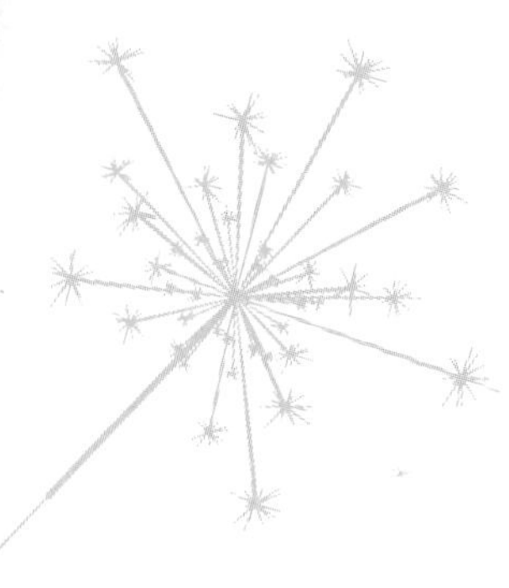

Individualize

- Create a case study or scenario for each age group, based around the same topic.
- For multi-session topics, ask participants to prepare a scenario or case study in advance of the next session. Provide a framework for participants to share their scenarios in small groups.

Investigate

- Find sample case studies here:

  "Case Studies and Scenarios" by the College of Early Childhood Educators
  www.college-ece.ca/members/case-studies-and-scenarios

Getting to Know Families

Families are of primary importance in children's development. Because the family and the early childhood practitioner have a common interest in the child's well-being, we acknowledge a primary responsibility to bring about communication, cooperation, and collaboration between the home and early childhood program in ways that enhance the child's development.

—NAEYC Code of Ethical Conduct

Intention

Family engagement begins with knowing the families. We need to recognize and value the diversity of the families we serve and consider a variety of strategies to get to know them beyond outward appearances.

Implementation

- This activity might follow a discussion or presentation about families, including the definition of *family*.
- Have pictures of diverse families posted around the room or pass some out to small groups. Make sure to include pictures of all kinds of families doing a variety of activities in many settings.
- Note the importance of communicating and collaborating with families based on the NAEYC Code of Ethical Conduct.
- Brainstorm all the ways that families (in general) might be diverse.
  - Try using an alphabet chart for this (see Activity #19—Alphabet Chart).
- Invite participants to look at the pictures. If the pictures are posted around the room, people can do a walkabout individually. If the pictures are distributed to small groups at tables, participants can look at and reflect on them individually first. Provide some guided questions to consider as they look at the pictures.

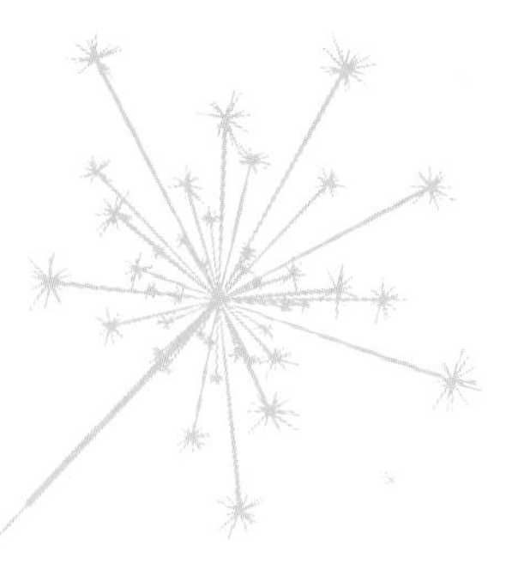

- *What can you infer about this family and their values?*
- *What clues lead you to these conclusions?*
- *What other factors contribute to your conclusions?*

- In pairs or small groups of three to four, have participants discuss the following questions:
  - *Did everyone in the group have the same idea about the families?*
  - *What kinds of things did you see in the pictures that influenced your perception of the family?*
  - *How does your own background and experience influence your first perceptions and reactions to a family?*
  - *What are some other things you would need to consider before having a more accurate understanding of the family?*
  - *What are some ways you can get more information?*
  - *How does your image of the family impact your relationships and interactions with them?*
- Bring the whole group back together to share ideas and summarize. Discuss how you can use the diversity of families to benefit and strengthen programs.
- Make an action plan for getting to know families better.

Individualize

- Develop a questionnaire to gather information about families.
- Encourage teachers to engage families in their programs in a variety of ways.
  - Invite families to share their heritage, rituals, and culture through stories, songs, food, and so on. Sharing could be in person or through video or written materials.
  - Ask families to share important words in their home language(s).
  - Arrange activities to bring families together, such as a potluck, music event, family play event, or art show.
- Suggest that teachers create a family wall or bulletin board highlighting family relationships.

Investigate

- Resources from NAEYC on working with families:

  Steen, Bweikia Foster. 2022. "Five Rs for Promoting Positive Family Engagement." *Teaching Young Children* 15 (2). www.naeyc.org/resources/pubs/tyc/winter2022/fiver-rs-family.

Friedman, Susan, and Alissa Mwenelupembe, eds. 2020. *Each & Every Child: Teaching Preschool with an Equity Lens.* Washington, DC: NAEYC. See especially Part 5: Engaging Diverse Families.

NAEYC Code of Ethical Conduct and Statement of Commitment. See Section II: Ethical Responsibilities to Families.
www.naeyc.org/sites/default/files/globally-shared/downloads/PDFs/resources/position-statements/Ethics%20Position%20Statement2011_09202013update.pdf

Illuminate

- Scenarios and reflective questions to use for staff development on engaging families of dual- and multi-language learners:

  "Cultural Perspectives in Caregiving: Applying Relationship-Based Practices"
  https://eclkc.ohs.acf.hhs.gov/culture-language/article/cultural-perspectives-caregiving-applying-relationship-based-practices

- Webinar:

  "Webinar: Facilitated Leadership and Family Engagement—Learning with and from Families" by Debbie LeeKeenan and Iris Chin Ponte in collaboration with NAEYC
  www.youtube.com/watch?v=xCNLykelNNQ&t

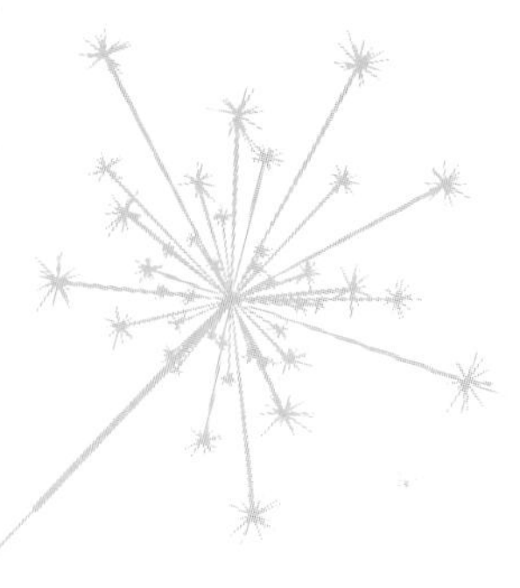

Activity #84

Scavenger Hunt

Intention

A critical element of teamwork is strengthening connections—with one another and with the program. A scavenger hunt can help people learn about one another and discover more about their program and environment. It is also a great way to engage teachers, infuse fun, and get people moving!

Implementation

- Create scavenger hunt forms or cards according to the topic of your training. For instance:
    - To help people learn about one another's strengths, talents, and skills, include items such as "good at technology," "involved in the arts," "background in special education," and "nature buff." This helps build an internal resource base so teachers know who they can turn to for assistance or ideas.
    - To encourage teachers to really look at their classrooms or total program environment, ask them to find items such as something that reflects the program values, diversity, literacy support, or other positive qualities.
- Explain the instructions, according to your purpose, including the time frame.
    - People can work individually or in pairs/small groups/teams.
    - Make sure people know how to document that they found the item or person. They could take a picture or a selfie with what they found, describe it, or bring it back with them.
- Bring the group back together to debrief.
    - Invite people to share what they found and how it demonstrates the stated purpose of the hunt.
    - Discuss how to modify or expand the item, or add more items, to further support the purpose.

Individualize

- Have teachers make up their own scavenger hunts for their classrooms. They could also make one for the children.
- Suggest follow-up tasks and encourage participants to make an action plan to address what they have discovered (for instance, how to add more diverse books and materials to their environment or how to incorporate educators' strengths and talents into the program planning).

Sample Templates:

Note: You will want to customize the list of items based on what you know about the participants and what is relevant to them and their programs. The goal is for teachers to be able to discover more about one another and their programs and to connect what they are learning to their practice.

HUMAN SKILLS AND EXPERIENCES SCAVENGER HUNT

Find Someone Who . . .	Name:
Speaks more than one language	
Is knowledgeable about nutrition	
Is a nature buff	
Is a passionate sports fan	
Knows a lot about STEM	
Has great computer skills	
Is familiar with community resources	
Has worked with children with special needs	
Is a visual artist or musician	

LITERACY SCAVENGER HUNT

Find something in each area that supports language and literacy:

AREA	ITEM	HOW TO USE
Greeting		
Blocks and Building		
Art		
Snack/Lunch		
Sensory		
Science/Nature		
Outside		
Manipulatives		
Bathroom		

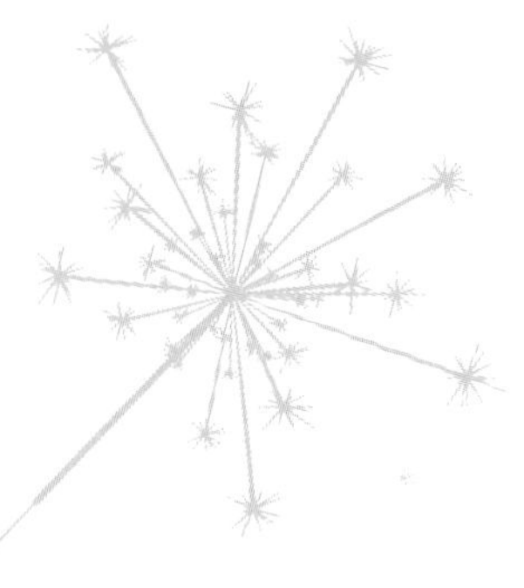

Activity #85

Gallery Walk

Intention

A gallery walk gets participants actively involved with content and with one another. Use this as a culminating activity after participants have worked on a project. Much like a museum exhibit, participants have the opportunity to view, reflect on, give feedback about, and go deeper into the materials and projects that are shared. Plus, it gets participants up and moving! Teachers who are reluctant to speak in a group are apt to feel more comfortable contributing their ideas in this manner.

Implementation

- Use a gallery walk to showcase any project that your participants have engaged in, whether individually or in a small group. Examples include Activities #43—"Where I'm From" Poem, #44—Create a Professional Shield, #51—Drawing, #55—Create a Success Board, and #56—Collaborative Building Tasks.
- Explain the process of the gallery walk at the beginning of a collaborative or individual project. Let participants know they will be exhibiting their work and they will have the opportunity to view and comment on others' work.
- After completing the project, invite teachers or groups to post their projects or materials around the room (or display them on their tables).
- All participants walk around the room to view the displays. They can do this individually and discuss with others as they move through the exhibit.
    - Provide sticky notes to participants or have a blank chart next to each project so people can post comments or clarifying questions. Responses can also be made to previous comments or questions.
- Bring the group back together to debrief.
    - Ask each individual or group representative to answer any clarifying questions about their display.
    - Engage in a discussion about any conclusions or recommendations related to the project.
    - Make sure to express appreciation for everyone's engagement and participation.

Individualize

- Provide a reflection sheet for participants to record their responses or questions. These can be used for follow-up activities or discussion.
- Use this activity to engage families. Have a family night where teachers display their classroom's or group's work. Families do a gallery walk and have an opportunity to talk with the teachers about their work.
- This would also be a great way to exhibit a long-term professional development project. The process and final outcome could be exhibited for the whole staff and other interested stakeholders (board, funders, and so on).

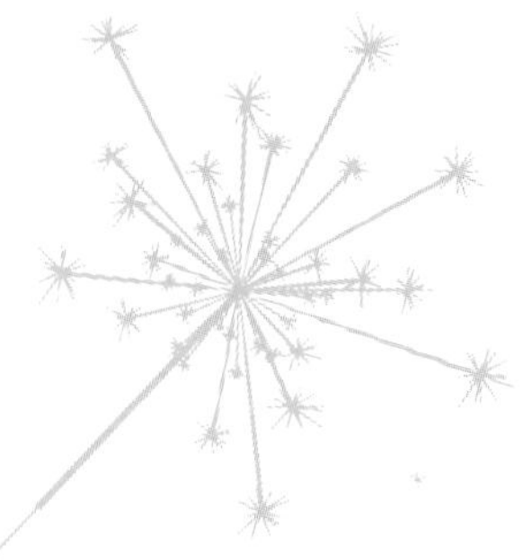

Activity #86

Developmentally Appropriate Practice (DAP) for Adults

Intention

Creating a trusting, respectful, creative, equitable program environment for adults can be thought of as a parallel process to what we do for children. Reinterpreting DAP through an adult-focused lens provides concrete examples that help guide how we interact with and provide support for our colleagues and can help teachers to come together as a team to develop a work environment in which everyone can thrive.

Implementation

- Begin with a discussion of developmentally appropriate practice for children.
  - What is it? Brainstorm with the group and add information as needed.
  - Review the foundational standards and values/beliefs that DAP is built on.
  - Share examples of how DAP is implemented. Solicit ideas from the participants about how it is demonstrated in their own practice and program.
- Explain that the group will now consider how to apply those same standards to our work with adults by substituting the word *educator* or *leader* (or other appropriate word) for *child*.
- Break the large group into smaller working groups (three to four people). Make sure each group has a recorder and reporter.
- Distribute a DAP handout (see sample below) with instructions for the group to consider each standard in relation to adults instead of children, and discuss the following:
  - *What would it look like if the standard was fully met?*
  - *Give examples of how it is currently being met in your program.*
  - *Think about steps you could take to reach full success.*
- Determine the best first step toward full success and create an action plan to make it happen.
- Bring the group back together to debrief:
  - Invite each group to share highlights of their discussion and their first next step.
  - Summarize by noting the importance of each standard and how each one impacts the early childhood work environment.

Individualize

- If time is constrained, assign each group one standard to focus on.
- Instead of a handout, you could use this as a carousel activity. Write each standard on a separate chart paper. Have small groups rotate around the charts to add ideas. (See Activity #77—Carousel.)
- If all the participants are from the same program, invite them to document how they are implementing DAP for adults (particularly the first step in their action plan) and share at a staff meeting.

Investigate

- Find helpful insights and clear language related to developmentally appropriate practice:

  NAEYC Position Statements

  www.naeyc.org/sites/default/files/globally-shared/downloads/PDFs/resources/position-statements/dap-statement_0.pdf

  www.naeyc.org/resources/position-statements/dap/principles

  www.naeyc.org/sites/default/files/globally-shared/downloads/PDFs/resources/position-statements/Ethics%20Position%20Statement2011_09202013update.pdf (See Section III: Ethical Responsibilities to Colleagues)

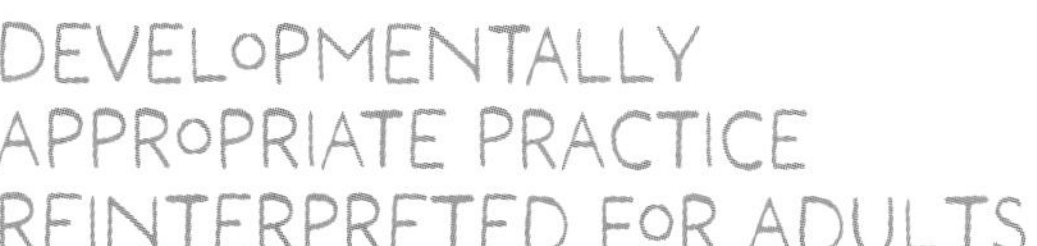

DEVELOPMENTALLY APPROPRIATE PRACTICE REINTERPRETED FOR ADULTS

This activity is based on the NAEYC Position Statement on Developmentally Appropriate Practice, adopted April 2020. (www.naeyc.org/resources/position-statements/dap/guidelines)

1. CREATING A CARING, EQUITABLE COMMUNITY OF LEARNERS

- Each member of the community is valued by the others and is recognized for the strengths they bring.
- Relationships are nurtured with each child (educator), and educators (leaders) facilitate the development of positive relationships among children (educators).
- Each member of the community respects and is accountable to the others to behave in a way that is conducive to the learning and well-being of all.
- The physical environment protects the health and safety of the learning community members, and it specifically supports young children's (educators') physiological needs for play, activity, sensory stimulation, fresh air, rest, and nourishment.
- Every effort is made to help each and every member of the community feel psychologically safe and able to focus on being and learning. The overall social and emotional climate is welcoming and positive.

2. TEACHING TO ENHANCE EACH CHILD'S DEVELOPMENT AND LEARNING

- Educators (leaders) demonstrate and model their commitment to a caring learning community through their actions, attitudes, and curiosity.
- Educators (leaders) use their knowledge of each child and family (educator) to make learning experiences meaningful, accessible, and responsive to each and every child (educator).
- Educators (leaders) effectively implement a comprehensive curriculum (professional development event or system) so that each child (educator) attains individualized goals.
- Educators (leaders) plan the environment, schedule, and daily activities to promote each child's (educator's) development and learning.
- Educators (leaders) possess and build on an extensive repertoire of skills and teaching strategies.
- Educators (leaders) know how and when to scaffold children's (educators') learning.
- Educators (leaders) know how and when to strategically use the various learning formats and contexts.
- Educators (leaders) differentiate instructional approaches to match each child's (educator's) interests, knowledge, and skills.

What does full success look like?

What do you do currently?

What are your next steps to achieve full success?

What? So What? Now What?

Intention

Use this exercise to reflect on a situation or event. Participants work in teams to bring diverse perspectives and understanding to the event and consider how to move forward. This can be used to analyze a real-life situation (for staff from the same program) or to debrief a role play or scenario. This activity is adapted from research in *Critical Reflection for Nursing and the Helping Professions: A User's Guide* by Gary Rolfe, Dawn Freshwater, and Melanie Jasper (2001).

Implementation

- Form small groups of three to four people. Each group can work on the same situation or use different ones customized for each group.
- At each stage, allow two minutes for individual reflection and five minutes for each group to collect their ideas and share across groups.

WHAT?

- Present the event or situation and ask guiding questions to get the details of what happened: for instance, a conflict with a parent. This phase is all about the facts, not interpretations. Sample questions:
    - *What did you notice or observe?*
    - *What stood out to you?*
    - *What surprised you?*
    - *What was your role?*
    - *What was your reaction?*
- Invite participants to first reflect individually on the situation. They can write their thoughts on sticky notes to post on a chart or appoint a notetaker to capture them during sharing.
- Participants share their thoughts with their small group.
- Each group shares their thoughts with the whole group.

SO WHAT?

- Small groups engage in an analysis of the event. Begin with individual reflections; then in small groups, develop some interpretations and consider the implications for practice.

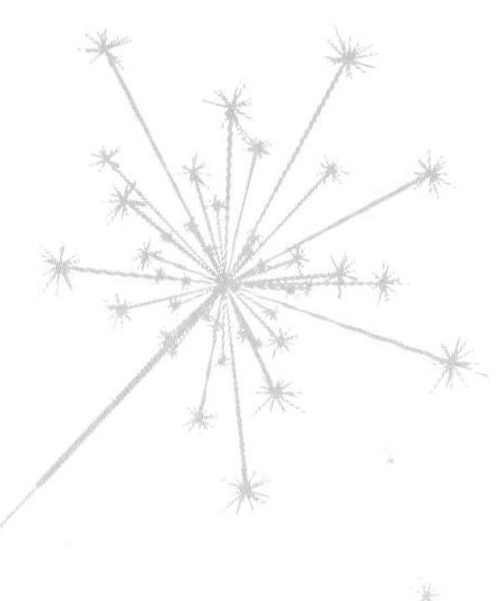

  - *How did it affect you?*
  - *How did you feel?*
  - *What did you learn?*
  - *What questions did this bring up?*
  - *What conclusions can you draw?*
  - *What patterns emerged?*
- Consider the importance of this experience—to the group, the program, and the community.
- Share with the whole group. Note themes and common perspectives.

NOW WHAT?

In their small groups, participants consider the following questions: *What would you do differently next time? How will what you learned influence your practice?*

Each small group shares with the whole group.

WRAP-UP

Debrief with the whole group. Note the parallel process to observing children—addressing the facts first and then analyzing to discover patterns and make interpretations. How did this process help you understand the situation? It doesn't always matter if an issue is resolved; sometimes it is helpful to shift your mindset and learn from experience.

If this is an in-house workshop to consider a specific issue, develop an action plan: *What action will you take next? What resources will you need?*

Individualize

- See Activity #42—Questions and Reflections for Energized Interactions for ideas.

Investigate

- Learn more about the What? So What? Now What? protocol:

  "What? So What? Now What?" by Gustavo Razzetti at the Fearless Culture blog
  www.fearlessculture.design/blog-posts/what-so-what-now-what
- See a sample template from Miro:

  https://miro.com/templates/what-so-what-now-what/
- Explore a further explanation of the protocol:

  "Explanation of Rolfe et al.'s (2001) Reflective Model" by the University of Cumbria Academic Services and Retention Team
  https://my.cumbria.ac.uk/media/MyCumbria/Documents/ReflectiveModelRolfe.pdf

The Importance of Routines and Rituals

Rituals are a powerful way of using gestures, actions and our behavior to bring positive energy and intention into our daily rhythms. In early childhood settings, a focus on rituals will set the tone for peace, love, pace, care, and beauty.

—Toni Christie and Memory Lyon

Intention

This activity helps teachers realize the learning potential in our daily routines and rituals so they can plan to embed intentional experiences. Children are always learning no matter what they are engaged in!

Implementation

- Brainstorm with the group a list of routines and rituals that occur during their day.
  - This will likely include arrival, handwashing, toileting/diapering, snack/lunch, nap, and departure.
  - Add any you have thought of that participants do not come up with on their own.
  - Note that planned activity times (art, free play, circle time, outdoor play, and so on) do not count as a routine or ritual.
- Break participants up into small groups (three to five people).
- Assign one to three routines or rituals to each group (depending on time). Provide these guided questions for teachers to consider:
  - *What are children doing during that time? (Be specific: What actions and interactions are children engaged in?) What is the role of the adult? (How is the adult creating moments of connection and joy? How is the adult interacting with children?)*
  - *What are children learning and feeling during that time? For instance: learning concepts, fine- and gross-motor skills, or language; feeling secure, loved, cared for, and valued.*

    - *What are some actions you could take to enhance these routines and rituals?*
- Bring the group back together to debrief.
    - Share highlights from each group's chart.
    - Share one action to enhance the routine or ritual.

Individualize

- Do this as a carousel activity. Post large pieces of paper around the room with one routine or ritual on each. Small groups can rotate through the charts to add their ideas. (See Activity #77—Carousel.)
- Add a column that directly relates to the workshop topic. For instance:
    - For a workshop on literacy, add "What new language and vocabulary can be used?"
    - For a workshop on STEM, add "What materials would enhance learning about STEM concepts?"
    - For developing social-emotional skills, add "How can you support these skills?"
- Encourage teachers to reflect at the end of the day (or week) to consider how they have incorporated intentional learning experiences into their routines and rituals. These can be shared in staff meetings or one-on-one supervision meetings.
- Recommend that teachers create a list of learning experiences for each of the routines and rituals to help them be intentional in their interactions with children during those times.

Investigate

- Learn more about the importance of rituals and routines:

    Burman, Lisa. 2023. *A Culture of Agency: Fostering Engagement, Empowerment, Identity, and Belonging in the Early Years.* St. Paul, MN: Redleaf Press. See especially chapter 3: "Rituals of Belonging and Identity."

    "Making Everyday ECE Routines into Extraordinary Rituals" by the Educa blog www.geteduca.com/blog/making-everyday-rituals-extraordinary

    "Routines: Extraordinary Learning in Everyday Opportunities." Tip Sheet # 9. *The Education State.* www.education.vic.gov.au/Documents/childhood/providers/edcare/Three-Year-Old-Kindergarten-Teaching-Toolkit/Tip-Sheet-9-Routines-V4.pdf.

Illuminate

- Watch this webinar to learn more about the importance of rituals:

    "Toni Christie on Rituals: Making the Everyday Extraordinary in ECE" https://app.livestorm.co/educa/making-rituals-extraordinary-christie

Wrapping Up Workshops with Intention

You started your workshop strong, and a powerful ending is just as important! Use these activities to help participants recall how the content of the session resonated with them and consider how they will integrate their new knowledge and ideas into their work. Encourage teachers to share their insights with their colleagues and to delight in how their practice will be strengthened. Your closing should ignite participants to take action!

Evaluations and feedback are critical for you to determine the effectiveness of your training. Even the simplest forms of evaluation provide information about participants' reactions to the training content and the presentation itself. Use a combination of rating scales and open-ended questions. You can create a general evaluation form to be used for any session and customize it with some additional questions for collecting specific information about a particular topic or training event.

Additional feedback may be obtained after the workshop through follow-up activities. How will you connect with participants next week or next month? What methods will inspire participants to put their new ideas into practice and continue their learning journey? How can you assess the impact your workshop had on the participants, and through them on the children and families they serve? Consider how you can help participants sustain the energy from the workshop.

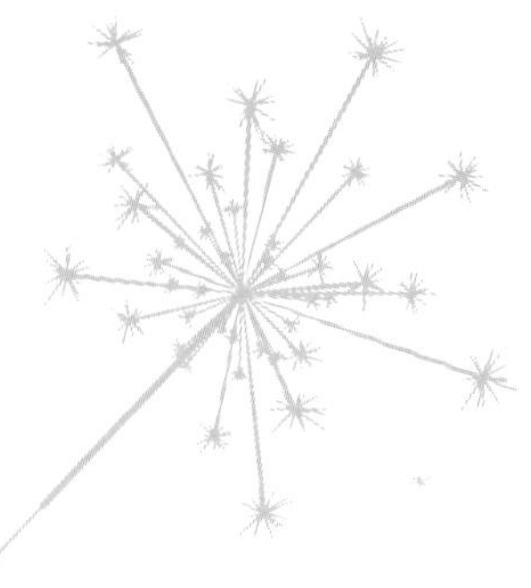

Activities #89–97

Wrap-Up Activities

Intention

Wrap-up activities synthesize the workshop content, connect teachers with the new knowledge, and help participants articulate how they will incorporate the new information and ideas into their daily practice and promote professional accountability. Close with a positive message about how the changes participants make will benefit the children and families in their program, as well as enhance their own joy and passion for their work. Make sure to leave enough time for these activities!

Implementation

Activity #89: Round-Robin

Go around the room and have everyone share one idea for bringing what they learned into practice.

Activity #90: The Top Ten

Making a top-ten list is a fun way to frame a closing brainstorming session. Depending on the group size, you can do this as a whole group or break larger groups down into smaller groups. Ask the participants to come up with ten ways to __________ (something directly related to your topic). If this activity is done in groups, have the groups share their top two ideas with everyone.

Activity #91: Create a Six-Word Story

Ask participants to reflect on and write down their key takeaways from the session. Then invite them to write a short, inspirational story using six words from their reflection. Encourage participants to share their six-word stories as a powerful closing activity.

Activity #92: Infographic or Headline

Have participants create a visual representation or headline highlighting something that stood out for them from the content.

Activity #93: FTE (First Time Ever)

Invite participants to share a "first time ever" moment—the first time they heard one of the ideas presented, or they realized something about the topic, or they considered something from a different perspective.

Activity #94: Commitment Statement

Provide a commitment statement form for participants to record one action they are committed to undertake that uses what they learned.

Activity #95: Elevator Pitch

Ask each participant to create and share a thirty-second elevator pitch based on what they learned. This could also be done in pairs.

Activity #96: What, Why, How?

Ask participants to complete a form that gives them the opportunity to identify what they learned, why it is important, and how they will apply it in their practice.

Activity #97: One to Four

Create four columns on a chart or whiteboard. Ask each participant to share:

- One thing they now know that they didn't know before
- One thing they would like to know more about
- One new insight (aha moment)
- One action they will take to apply their new discoveries to their practice

Individualize

- Invite participants to express what they learned and are taking away through their own creative expression (dance, rap, song, art).

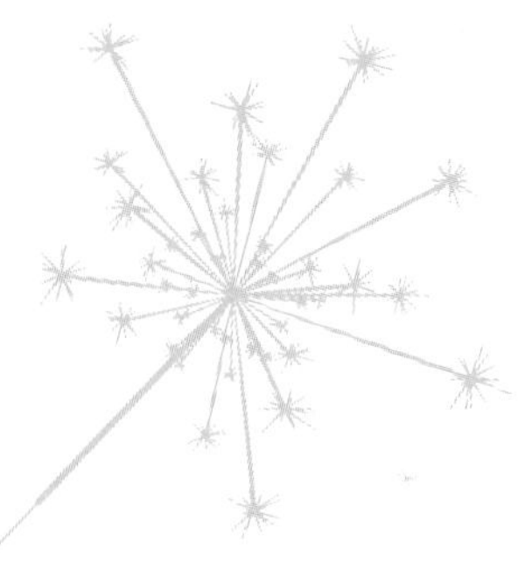

INSIGHT FROM THE FIELD

One-Word Wrap-Up

Shared by Joelfré L. Grant and Debra Sosin

The following wrap-up or closure activity can be used for a onetime professional development (PD) event or for a multiday event or series. The activity serves both as an assessment for the facilitator and a unifying reflection for the participants.

- At the end of the session, the facilitator asks the participants to reflect on the PD event, thinking about one thing they are feeling or considering about the information, and then come up with one word that reflects where they are in the process of learning or shows their perspective about the event.
- The facilitator invites participants to share whatever word is on their mind and asks them to begin sharing, popcorn style.
- After each participant shares, the facilitator repeats the word and writes down the word as it is spoken (ideally on large flip chart paper in front of the group).
- The facilitator adds their own word at the end, then reads the entire list.
- For a virtual training, this can be done in the chat box. The facilitator can type the words into the chat box as they are spoken.
- When reading the words at the end, share them as a poem. State something like "This is such a dynamic list. We have created a poem today."
- Watch a video of Joelfré L. Grant explaining this wrap-up activity (scan QR code or type URL into web browser).

https://vimeo.com/851756940

Get Feedback

Intention

How do you know if the professional development you provided was effective and achieved your intended outcomes?

Designing evaluation forms and methods that provide meaningful feedback for you is critical for your own growth as a facilitator and leader. It is important to get feedback about the workshop content as well as the presentation methods and activities. What worked? What can you modify or improve for the next time?

Implementation

- At the end of the session, thank the participants for their attention and explain how the evaluation will be done. Let the participants know how important their feedback is to help you assess the training and modify it as needed. Stress that we are all life-long learners and this assessment is part of your learning process.
- Offer participants an evaluation form. See the appendix for sample evaluation forms you can customize.
    - Make sure to leave enough time at the end of the session for participants to thoughtfully complete the form.
    - Include the basic information (title of the event, date and time, facilitator name) on the form.
    - Design evaluation forms to obtain the specific feedback you want to receive.
    - Use statements that can be rated on a continuum (agree–disagree, or poor–excellent) that elicit information that will help you assess both the content and the mechanics of the training, such as participant engagement and involvement, your presentation skills, training activities, time management, the space, and whether the training objectives were defined and met. For example:
        - *The facilitator was well prepared and knowledgeable in the content.*
        - *The activities were relevant to the content of the workshop.*
        - *The workshop reflected diversity, equity, and inclusiveness.*
        - *I learned something that I can apply to my work.*
        - *The facilitator was responsive to participants' questions, ideas, and needs.*
        - *There was ample time for discussion.*
        - *The facilitator had a positive attitude.*
        - *There was enough time to adequately cover the content.*

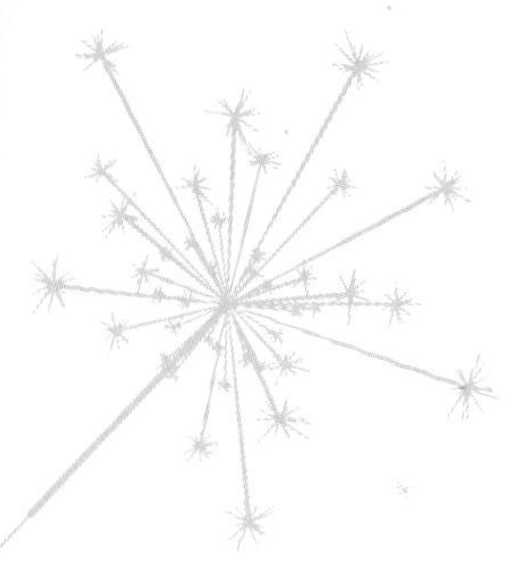

    - *The content was current and relevant.*
    - *The facilitator used a variety of strategies to engage participants.*
    - *The workshop flowed in a logical way.*
  - Use open-ended questions to understand what was most useful or interesting about the content, what could be improved, and what ideas participants will apply to their practice. You can also find out what questions the participant still has and what they would like to explore further. These responses can help you develop future sessions on the topic or develop new topics, particularly if you are working with teachers who are from the same program. For example:
    - *What did you come here wanting to learn?*
    - *What was most/least useful information for you?*
    - *What is one thing specifically you will use in your daily practice?*
    - *Was there something you particularly connected to?*
    - *Did anything surprise you?*
    - *What is one thing that would improve this workshop?*
    - *What do you still have questions or would like additional information about?*
    - Include space for participants to add their thoughts and comments that are not directly related to the questions you asked. *Is there anything additional you would like to add?*
- Use a variety of methods to get evaluation responses. Paper surveys can be completed and collected at the end of your session. Online surveys can be set up to allow responses within a specific time period (not to exceed a week).
- For larger groups, it can be helpful to offer a drawing or incentive for everyone who completes the evaluation.
- For a quick evaluation, you can have chart paper posted and invite participants to use sticky notes to express something they learned or connected to.

Individualize

- Have an attractive notebook available for participants to write any additional personal notes to you.
- Do a round-robin response to a statement such as “The thing I most appreciated about this workshop was . . .”

Activities 99–101

Follow-Up

Professional accountability is a good thing. Without it, excellence is merely a pipe dream and even average performance isn't a realistic expectation. —Leon Ellis

Intention

Research tells us that professional development has the most impact when participants have a chance to put the new information and ideas directly into their practice with follow-up and support. Providing some follow-up tasks and reflective activities will help participants use what they take away from the training in their work. Try one of these activities to maximize the effectiveness of your workshop.

Implementation

Activity #99: Postcards

Give each participant a stamped postcard with two prompts on it (if all are staff from the same program, they don't have to be stamped—just provide a place for them to be collected). Ask that participants complete the prompts and return the postcards to you in a specified time frame (not longer than one month). Use prompts that relate to the topic of the training to get an idea of how teachers are transferring their new knowledge and ideas into their practice. For example, for a workshop on language and literacy, you could include prompts such as these:

- *I added these books to our library:*
- *I used these open-ended inquiry questions with the children:*
- *Here is a conversation I had with a child:*
- *I connected words with an action or experience by . . .*

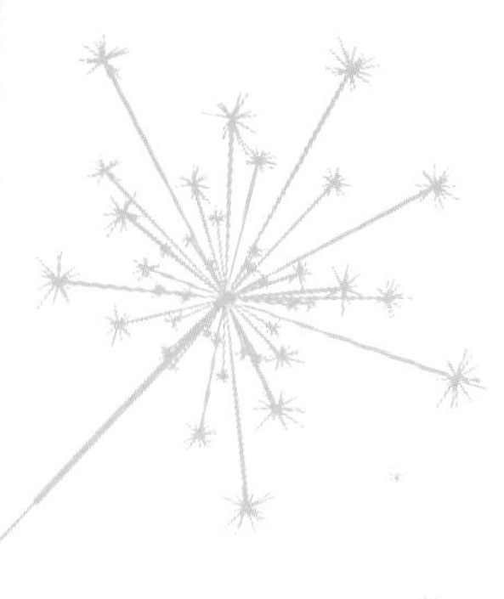

Activity #100: Commitment Statement

- Ask participants to review the commitment statement they completed as part of your session wrap-up, and to email you with a story of how they kept their commitment (and include pictures if appropriate).
- Have each participant write their commitment and address on a postcard, and collect the postcards at the end of your session. Mail the postcards back to participants after one month to remind them of their commitment. (Or scan the postcards and email them to the participants.)

Activity #101: Post-Workshop Activities

- Coaching: Offer to hold a thirty- to sixty-minute coaching call with each participant within a specified time frame (up to four months) to clarify any information or provide guidance on how to implement any of the ideas from the training.
- Virtual follow-up meeting: Include a one-hour virtual meeting as part of the training. Use this meeting for participants to provide feedback about how the ideas are working in their program and share success stories or get guidance about any challenges.
- Social media: Create a dedicated social media group for participants to continue to share ideas and successes.

Individualize

- If you are presenting this as a program leader to staff from the same program, follow up with some focused observations or set up a buddy system for staff to work together to implement and reflect on new ideas.

Section Three

Appendices

Workshop Preparation Checklist

Workshop Planning Template

Sample Workshop Schedules

Sample Workshop Evaluation Forms

Professional Development Reflection Sheet

Tips for Facilitators

Resources for Videos

Supercharge Video Clips

Resources for Professional Learning—Courses, Workshops, Conferences

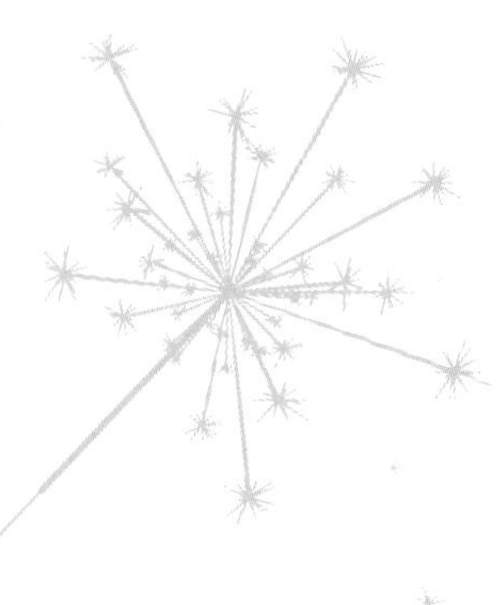

Workshop Preparation Checklist

Event: ______________________ Date of Event: ______________

Presentation Title: ______________________________

Audience: ______________________ Number of Participants: ________

Host Organization: ______________________________

Contact Person: ______________________________

Email: ______________________________

Office Phone: ______________________ Cell Phone: ______________

Location: ______________________________

Presentation Preparation:

- ❑ Slide decks
- ❑ Evaluations
- ❑ Contact sheets
- ❑ Presentation backed up to the cloud
- ❑ Materials to be printed sent to host by: ____________
- ❑ Handouts
- ❑ Certificates
- ❑ Presentation on backup flash drive
- ❑ Presentation on travel computer
- ❑ Binder with all materials and travel documents set up

Travel:

- ❑ Detailed directions (if driving)
- ❑ Hotel booked
- ❑ Flight booked
- ❑ Airport transfer arranged
- ❑ Passport/REAL ID/necessary ID and travel documents

Packing:

- ❑ Binder with all materials
- ❑ Index cards
- ❑ Cell phone and backup chargers
- ❑ Small speaker
- ❑ Flip chart pad (local)
- ❑ Power strip and cord (local)
- ❑ Snacks or meal (if necessary)
- ❑ Wireless presentation clicker and backup batteries
- ❑ Computer, adapters and power cords
- ❑ Large Sharpie markers
- ❑ Sticky notes
- ❑ Gift for host and card
- ❑ Business cards
- ❑ Projector (local)
- ❑ Water bottle
- ❑ Specific materials for activities: ____________

Workshop Planning Template

Workshop Title: ______________________________

Key Goal(s): ______________________________

Date: ______________ Time: ______________

Organization: ______________________________

Time:	**Focus:** Presentation, Activity, Video Clip, Discussion	Slide	Materials Needed or Handout Referenced

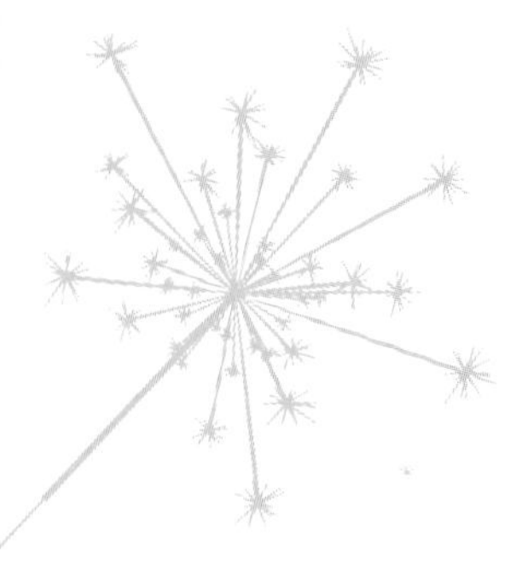

Sample Workshop Schedules

Designing engaging and inspiring workshops requires that you are intentional about planning the workshop for the time available. Regardless of the amount of time, you want to follow a consistent format that includes the following:

- Welcome and overview
- Reflection / centering activity
- Presentation and/or discussion of key issues
- Opportunity to practice applying ideas
- Closing reflection

This format can be expanded for longer presentations. We have provided a sample workshop that utilizes the activities for a ninety-minute and two-hour workshop session.

Illuminating the Magic and Wonder in Each Child

SCHEDULE FOR A 90-MINUTE PRESENTATION

00 Welcome:

Two-minute overview of the intent of the workshop

Two-minute introduction of the presenter and their passion for the workshop topic

05 Video Reflection: Ask everyone to take a few deep breaths and watch a video clip of Red Grammer singing "See Me Beautiful" (https://www.youtube.com/watch?v=03F-qZChiA0). Review Activity #37—Video Clip Reflections.

When the song ends, ask everyone to think of one person in their life who saw their unique beauty and strengths. Then ask them to introduce themselves to a partner and share how that person influenced their life. Allow each person two minutes to share.

15 Presentation: Prepare slides with information highlighting the importance of seeing the strengths in each child. Review Strategy #6—Design Compelling Presentations.

25 Interactive Activity: Guide participants through the Your Image of the Child activity (Activity #46).

60 Presentation: Share concrete strategies for illuminating the magic and wonder in each child. Review Strategy #6—Design Compelling Presentations.

70 Group Brainstorm: Encourage participants to brainstorm additional ways to bring out the best in each child. Utilize Brainstorming Techniques (Activity #31). Have each group share two of their ideas with the larger group.

85 Wrap-Up: Affirmation Statements (See Activity #47.)

Ask participants to write an affirmation statement that clearly reflects how they will illuminate the best in each child. Ask for volunteers to read their affirmation statements to the group.

90 End

To extend this workshop to a two-hour workshop (120 minutes), you can:

- Select an Introduction (Activities #23–26) and allow ten minutes for participants to introduce themselves.
- Add ten minutes to the "See Me Beautiful" reflection. Have the participants share their thoughts in small groups of four and allow time for the groups to share the key themes of their discussion with the larger group.
- Ask each person to create an Affirmation Statement (Activity #47) related to how they will illuminate the magic and wonder of each child. Ask participants to share their affirmation statement with the large group.

You can easily adapt your workshops to fit any schedule by carefully selecting activities that enhance the topic, keep participants engaged, and help you achieve the desired outcomes for the workshop. Be creative as you design your workshops, try new ideas, and expand your repertoire of activities that you enjoy facilitating!

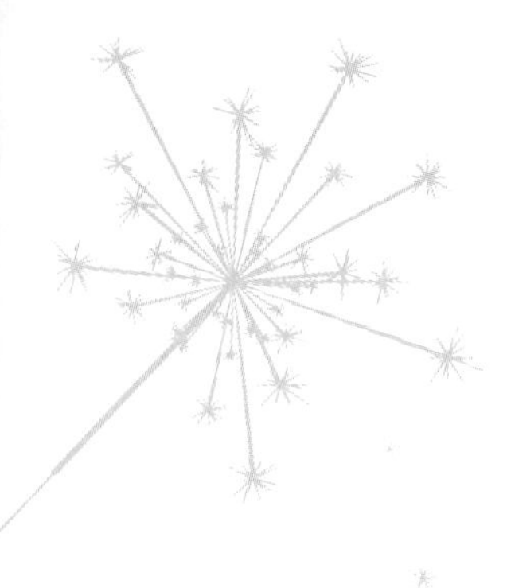

Sample Workshop Evaluation Forms

Workshop evaluations can be designed to provide feedback on the workshop content, the materials, and the presenter. Facilitators can customize the questions and format for gathering feedback. Detailed information on creating workshop evaluations is available in Activity #98—Get Feedback. These samples provide options to get you started.

Sample One: General Evaluation

What were the highlights of this workshop for you?

What new skills or strategies will you incorporate into your work?

What suggestions do you have for improving this workshop?

Overall, how would you rate the content and delivery of this workshop:

5	4	3	2	1
Excellent	Very Good	Good	Fair	Poor

Additional Comments:

Sample Two: Workshop-Specific Evaluation

Illuminating the Magic and Wonder in Each Child

1. What were the highlights of this workshop for you?

2. Outcomes:

Below are the stated outcomes for this course. Please assess, based on your own learning, whether the outcomes (what you have learned or will have changed as a result of your experience) have been achieved.

4. Achieved More than Expected—you have learned more than you expected, the instructor and content were excellent.

3. Achieved—you feel you can successfully complete the activities described in the outcome statements.

2. Partially Achieved—you are able to successfully complete some of the activities described in the outcome statements.

1. Not Achieved—the outcomes are not attainable based on what you learned.

Outcome: At the completion of this course, participants will have . . .	**Rating**
Strengthened their knowledge of the importance of building positive relationships with children	
Identified new strategies for building positive relationships with children	
Enhanced their understanding of the principles of Appreciative Inquiry as a tool for illuminating children's strengths	
Engaged in a variety of reflective learning experiences	
Created an Illuminating the Magic and Wonder in Each Child Action Plan to guide their daily work	

3. Describe the new skills or strategies that will have the greatest impact on your daily work:

4. List two new resources you discovered through this workshop that will enhance and support your work:

5. What suggestions do you have for improving this workshop?

Additional comments:

Workshop Evaluation Resources

- You can view a variety of workshop evaluation templates on the Jotform website: www.jotform.com/form-templates/search/workshop%20evaluation%20forms

Professional Development Reflection Sheet

Professional Development Event:

Facilitator:

Sponsoring Agency:

Date:

OR
Research/Reading Topic:

Title/Description:

1. What was most useful/interesting?

2. What specifically did you learn that you will apply to your practice?

3. What questions do you still have? What would you like to explore further?

4. How did this affect or shift your perspective?

Tips for Facilitators

Whether you are new to facilitating training or have many years of experience, you want to be intentional about designing and delivering a powerful workshop every time! You can use this checklist (and customize it to include any other personal items) both before and after the session, to make sure you are following a model that maximizes effectiveness and participant engagement.

- ❑ Prepare and practice—Do your research, develop the outline and objectives, and practice for timing and tone.
- ❑ Ensure the workshop and all activities are aligned with the workshop's purpose.
- ❑ Contact the site/host to discuss logistics, directions, technology, and other needs.
- ❑ Know your audience—Connect with them beforehand to find out about their backgrounds, experiences, and learning styles so you can create activities that will resonate with them.
- ❑ Be authentic—Use your strengths to relate to participants in a genuine way.
- ❑ Be present and passionate—Know your *why* and relay that to participants to create a learning community.
- ❑ Deliver a strong opening—Hook people right from the start to get them invested.
- ❑ Include variety—Provide a balance of activities, vary the pacing and movement, and include brain and body breaks.
- ❑ Avoid jargon and lingo—Be clear with your language and be careful of acronyms.
- ❑ Use examples, visuals, and resources that reflect diversity, equity, and inclusion goals.
- ❑ Tap into the wisdom of the group—Be a partner in learning.
- ❑ Be flexible—Have contingency plans for unexpected situations.
- ❑ Be aware of your own and your participants' facial expressions, body language, and tone of voice.
- ❑ Choose your words carefully.
- ❑ Honor silence—Adults, like children, may need time to process information and formulate questions or responses.
- ❑ Engage in wrap-up and evaluation—Leave enough time for thoughtful reflection and response.
- ❑ Follow up—Provide any follow-up communication with participants.
- ❑ Perform a self-evaluation and review your outline to make any modifications based on your experience and participants' feedback.

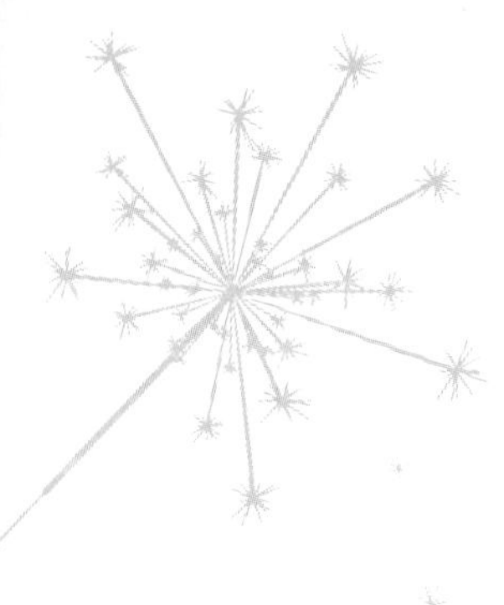

INSIGHTS FROM OUR CONTRIBUTORS:

- From Holly Elissa Bruno: Remember, your mistakes, failures, and embarrassing moments will help you grow.
- From Linda Schumacher: When you ask a question of a small or large group, count to ten before speaking again. It will seem like forever, but you will get more responses by allowing this processing time.
- From Joelfré L. Grant: Trust the group and trust the group process, because they hold the ideas and answers, and you hold the space for their ideas and answers to emerge.
- From Luis A. Hernandez: Don't let them see you sweat. When presenting virtually, smile and look into the camera.
- From Debra Sosin: You don't need to have all the answers. Use the knowledge of the participants to enhance the information you share.
- From Debbie LeeKeenan: Be sure everyone can take something away to use tomorrow. Have multiple entry points in your sessions.
- From Toni Christie: Keep current in practice so you understand the reality that participants are living in.

Resources for Videos

Video clips add new insights and energy to workshops. It is essential to prescreen videos to be sure that they are current, are related to your topic, and represent diverse perspectives. Show only the portions of the video that will highlight the message you want to share. You can find relevant videos online. Check whether any permissions from copyright holders are necessary given your situation and usage. Here are some useful sources:

- Author Videos: Many authors create videos highlighting their book's key points. You can find them by searching for their book online, viewing their websites, or searching video repositories such as YouTube. These are two examples of author videos:
  - "Barbara Fredrickson: Positive Emotions Transform Us" by Greater Good Science Center
    www.youtube.com/watch?v=hKggZhYwoys
  - "Carol Dweck: The Power of Believing that You Can Improve" by TED Talk
    www.youtube.com/watch?v=_XomgOOSpLU&t=15s
- Research Videos: Including current and relatable research can enhance your presentation. These sites are good sources for early childhood research videos:
  - Center on the Developing Child at Harvard University
    These videos focus on the science behind early childhood development, brain research, and toxic stress.
    https://developingchild.harvard.edu/resourcecategory/videos
  - Project Zero at Harvard University
    These videos relate to learning, creativity, and curriculum.
    https://pz.harvard.edu/pop-teacher-education-resources/video-library
  - The Colorado Department of Education's Results Matter Video Library Catalog includes a comprehensive listing of 177 video clips focusing on assessment, observations, using technology, and supporting kids just being kids.
    www.cde.state.co.us/resultsmatter/rmvideolibrarycatalog
- TED (Technology, Education, and Design) Talks. You can search for a topic related to your presentation on the TED talk site. www.ted.com
- YouTube. Allows you to search for videos by specific topic. You can also set up a YouTube library to organize your videos by topic. www.youtube.com
- Additional sources for videos include:
  - SoulPancake
    https://participant.com/soulpancake
  - Playing For Change
    www.playingforchange.com

Supercharge Video Clips

This book includes QR codes to connect readers to short video clips of the following training activities and interviews with thought leaders:

- Creating a Sense of Welcome—Beth Fredericks (page 48)
- Facilitating Vision Board Workshops—Susan MacDonald (page 165)
- Sharing "Where I'm From" Poems—Susan MacDonald (page 91)
- Supporting Linguistic Diversity—Karen Nemeth (page 141)
- Who Saw Your Uniqueness?—Holly Elissa Bruno (page 110)
- Shake Down, Warm Up! Demonstration—Susan MacDonald and Nancy Toso (page 132)
- Supporting Diverse Learners—Linda Schumacher (page 14)
- Wrap-Up Activity—Joelfré L. Grant (page 186)
- Large-Group Physical/Movement Activities—Luis A. Hernandez (page 131)
- Exploring Shared Values—Toni Christie (page 137)
- Communication Activities—Leland O. Clarke (page 162)

Resources for Professional Learning—Courses, Workshops, Conferences

Committing to your ongoing professional growth requires expanding your knowledge of the myriad opportunities available. We have included this listing of resources to help you begin to explore the many options available. View this list as a starting point and add resources in your community, state, or particular interest area.

Online Webinars and Courses

The CAYL Institute: CAYL Catalyst Webinar Series
www.cayl.org/webinars

Early Childhood Investigations Webinars
www.earlychildhoodwebinars.com

Educa Webinars
www.geteduca.com/webinars

edX: Free Online Courses from the World's Best Universities
www.edx.org/course?course=all

- Our favorite course: The Science of Happiness from the University of California, Berkeley
  www.edx.org/course/the-science-of-happiness-0

Harvard Graduate School of Education: Certificate in Early Education Leadership (CEEL)
www.gse.harvard.edu/ppe/program/certificate-early-education-leadership-ceel

Inspiring New Perspectives: Online Courses and Workshops
https://earlychildhoodprofessionaldevelopment.com

Kaplan Early Learning Online Courses
www.kaplanco.com/ProfessionalDevelopment

NAEYC Webinars
www.naeyc.org/events/trainings-webinars/recorded-webinars

Penn State Extension: Better Kid Care On Demand Courses
https://extension.psu.edu/programs/betterkidcare/on-demand

Redleaf Press Webinars
www.redleafpress.org/Webinars.aspx

Think Small Institute
www.thinksmall.org/institute

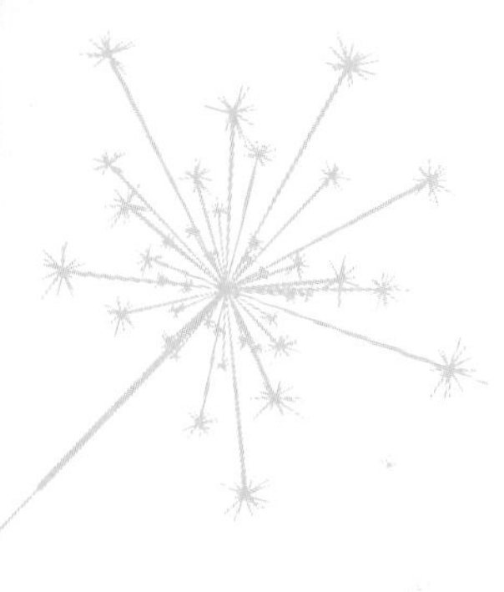

Early Childhood Conferences

Child Care Aware: Symposium and Leadership Institute
www.childcareaware.org/events

Council for Professional Recognition: Early Educators Leadership Conference
www.cdacouncil.org/en/annual-conference

Early Learning Leaders Annual Conference
www.earlylearningleaders.org

McCormick Center for Early Childhood Leadership: Leadership Connections Conference
https://mccormickcenter.nl.edu/leadership-connections-national-conference-2024

NAEYC (National Association for the Education of Young Children): Annual Conference and Professional Learning Institute
www.naeyc.org/events

- This calendar lists conferences run by NAEYC affiliates: https://app.smartsheet.com/b/publish?EQBCT=ec55eecdcb904f5d954133c9812a2c2e

NAFCC (National Association for Family Child Care): Annual Conference
https://nafcc.org/news-events

NAREA (North American Reggio Emilia Alliance) Conferences
www.reggioalliance.org/conferences

The World Forum Foundation Events
https://worldforumfoundation.org/all-events

Wunderled: Free to Play Summit (virtual)
https://wunderled.com

Zero to Three Conferences
https://go.zerotothree.org/signature

References and Resources

Adams, Robert L. 2017. "15 Time Management Tips for Achieving Your Goals." *Entrepreneur*, September 22, 2017. www.entrepreneur.com/article/299336.

Aguilar, Elena, and Lori Cohen. 2022. *The PD Book: 7 Habits That Transform Professional Development*. Hoboken, NJ: Jossey-Bass.

Bergen, Sharon. 2009. *Best Practices for Training Early Childhood Professionals*. St. Paul, MN: Redleaf Press.

Brown, Peter C., Henry L. Roediger III, and Mark A. McDaniel. 2018. *Make It Stick: The Science of Successful Learning*. Cambridge, MA: Belknap Press.

Burman, Lisa. 2023. *A Culture of Agency: Fostering Engagement, Empowerment, Identity, and Belonging in the Early Years*. St. Paul, MN: Redleaf Press.

Burnett, Bill, and Dave Evans. 2016. *Designing Your Life: How to Build a Well-Lived, Joyful Life*. New York: Knopf.

Byington, Teresa A. 2019. *Lose the Lecture: Engaging Approaches to Early Childhood Professional Learning*. Lewisville, NC: Gryphon House.

Canfield, Jack, Brandon Hall, and Janet Switzer. 2020. *The Success Principles Workbook: An Action Plan for Getting from Where You Are to Where You Want to Be*. New York: William Morrow.

Carter, Margie, Deb Curtis, and Elizabeth Jones. 2002. *Training Teachers: A Harvest of Theory and Practice*. St. Paul, MN: Redleaf Press.

Chapman, Gary D., and Paul E. White. 2012. *The 5 Languages of Appreciation in the Workplace: Empowering Organizations by Encouraging People*. Chicago: Northfield Publishing.

Coughlin, Anne Marie, and Lorrie Baird. 2022. *Creating a Culture of Reflective Practice: The Role of Pedagogical Leadership in Early Childhood Programs*. St. Paul, MN: Redleaf Press.

Coyle, Daniel. 2022. *Culture Playbook: 60 Highly Effective Actions to Help Your Group Succeed*. New York: Random House Business.

Dirksen, Julie. 2016. *Design for How People Learn*. Indianapolis: New Riders.

Drago-Severson, Eleanor. 2009. *Leading Adult Learning: Supporting Adult Development in Our Schools*. Thousand Oaks, CA: Corwin Press.

Drago-Severson, Eleanor, and Jessica Blum-DeStefano. 2017. *Tell Me So I Can Hear You: A Developmental Approach to Feedback for Educators*. Cambridge, MA: Harvard Education Press.

Dweck, Carol S. 2006. *Mindset: The New Psychology of Success*. New York: Random House.

———. 2015. "Carol Dweck Revisits the 'Growth Mindset.'" *Education Week*, September 22. www.edweek.org/leadership/opinion-carol-dweck-revisits-the-growth-mindset/2015/09.

Gordon, Jon. 2007. *The Energy Bus: 10 Rules to Fuel Your Life, Work, and Team with Positive Energy*. Hoboken, NJ: Wiley. http://theenergybus.com.

Heath, Chip, and Dan Heath. 2017. *The Power of Moments: Why Certain Experiences Have Extraordinary Impact*. New York: Simon & Schuster.

Hirschy, Sharon Thompson. 2016. "Creating a Personalized Learning Network for Professional Development and Growth." *Exchange*, May/June: 73–76.

Kegan, Robert, Lisa Laskow Lahey, Matthew L. Miller, Andy Fleming, and Deborah Helsing. 2016. *An Everyone Culture: Becoming a Deliberately Developmental Organization*. Cambridge, MA: Harvard Business School.

Liedtka, Jeanne, and Tim Ogilvie. 2011. *Designing for Growth: A Design Thinking Tool Kit for Managers*. New York: Columbia University Press.

MacDonald, Susan. 2016. *Inspiring Early Childhood Leadership: Eight Strategies to Ignite Passion and Transform Program Quality*. Lewisville, NC: Gryphon House.

———. 2019. *Inspiring Professional Growth: Empowering Strategies to Lead, Motivate, and Engage Early Childhood Teachers*. Lewisville, NC: Gryphon House.

Malaguzzi, Loris. 1993. "For an Education Based on Relationships." Translated by Lella Gandini. *Young Children*, November: 9–12. https://reggioalliance.org/downloads/malaguzziyoungchildren.pdf.

———. 1994. "Your Image of the Child: Where Teaching Begins." *Child Care Information Exchange*, 96. http://reggioalliance.org/downloads/malaguzzi:ccie:1994.pdf.

Maurer, Robert. 2015. *One Small Step Can Change Your Life: The Kaizen Way*. New York: Workman Publishing.

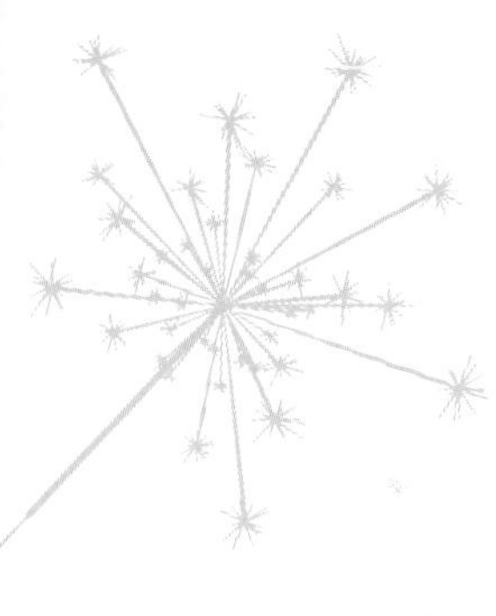

McArthur-Blair, Joan, and Jeanie Cockell. 2018. *Building Resilience with Appreciative Inquiry: A Leadership Journey through Hope, Despair, and Forgiveness*. Oakland, CA: Berrett-Koehler.

McKeown, Greg. 2014. *Essentialism: The Disciplined Pursuit of Less*. New York: Crown Business.

Meyers, Eva Jo. 2019. *Raise the Room: A Practical Guide to Participant-Centered Facilitation*. El Cerrito, CA: Spark Decks.

NAEYC (National Association for the Education of Young Children) and NACCRRA (National Association of Child Care Resource and Referral Agencies). 2011. "Early Childhood Education Professional Development: Training and Technical Assistance Glossary." Washington, DC: NAEYC. www.naeyc.org/sites/default/files /globally-shared/downloads/PDFs/our-work/public-policy-advocacy/glossarytraining_ta.pdf.

The National Institute for Early Education Research. *Preschool Matters* (blog). http://nieer.org/publications/blog.

Nelson, Ken, David Ronka, Lesli Lang, Liz Korabek-Emerson, and Jim White. 2020. *Designing & Leading Life-Changing Workshops: Creating the Conditions for Transformation in Your Groups, Trainings, and Retreats*. Kittery Point, ME: Cliffhouse Press.

Ozenc, Kursat, and Glenn Fajardo. 2020. *Rituals for Virtual Meetings: Creative Ways to Bring Connection, Meaning, and Joy to Online Work, Teams, and Relationships*. Hoboken, NJ: Wiley.

Palmer, Parker J., and Megan Scribner. 2017. *The Courage to Teach Guide for Reflection and Renewal*. Hoboken, NJ: Wiley.

Parker, Priya. 2018. *The Art of Gathering: How We Meet and Why It Matters*. New York: Riverhead Books.

Rolfe, Gary, Dawn Freshwater, and Melanie Jasper. 2001. *Critical Reflection for Nursing and the Helping Professions: A User's Guide*. New York: Palgrave.

Rothstein, Dan, and Luz Santana. 2014. *Make Just One Change: Teach Students to Ask Their Own Questions*. Cambridge, MA: Harvard Education Press.

Seale, Alan. 2003. *Soul Mission, Life Vision: Recognize Your True Gifts and Make Your Mark in the World.* San Francisco, CA: Red Wheel.

———. 2018. *Transformational Presence: The Tools, Skills, and Frameworks.* Newburyport, MA: Center for Transformational Presence.

Sinek, Simon. 2011. *Start with Why: How Great Leaders Inspire Everyone to Take Action*. New York: Portfolio Penguin.

Stavros, Jackie, and Cheri Torres. 2018. *Conversations Worth Having: Using Appreciative Inquiry to Fuel Productive and Meaningful Engagement*. Oakland, CA: Berrett-Koehler.

Stavros, Jacqueline M., and Gina Hinrichs, 2009. *The Thin Book of SOAR: Building Strengths-Based Strategies.* Bend, OR: Thin Book Publishing.

Vanderkam, Laura. 2011. *168 Hours: You Have More Time Than You Think*. New York: Penguin.

Washington, Valora, Brenda Gadson, and Kathryn L. Amel. 2017. *The New Early Childhood Professional: A Step-by-Step Guide to Overcoming Goliath*. New York and Washington, DC: Teachers College Press and NAEYC.

Whitney, Diana, Amanda Trosten-Bloom, and Kae Rader. 2010. *Appreciative Leadership: Focus on What Works to Drive Winning Performance and Build a Thriving Organization.* New York: McGraw-Hill.

Podcasts

A Bit of Optimism hosted by Simon Sinek. https://simonsinek.com/podcast

Disrupt Yourself Podcast hosted by Whitney Johnson. https://thedisruptionadvisors.com/podcast

Happier with Gretchen Rubin hosted by Gretchen Rubin. https://gretchenrubin.com/podcasts

Positivity Strategist hosted by Robyn Stratton-Berkessel. https://positivitystrategist.org/podcast

The Preschool Podcast hosted by Jo Sinanan and Maddie Hutchison, presented by HiMama. www.himama.com/blog/category/podcast

"Q&A with Chip Heath: The Power of Moments" on the *Craig Groeschel Leadership Podcast*. www.youtube.com/watch?v=q65DjuUTDIo

Ten Percent Happier hosted by Dan Harris. www.tenpercent.com/podcast

That Early Childhood Nerd hosted by Heather Bernt-Santy. www.thatearlychildhoodnerd.com

Unlocking Us hosted by Brené Brown. https://brenebrown.com/unlockingus

Websites

AI Commons: https://appreciativeinquiry.champlain.edu
Resources (articles, videos, books, and workshop materials) focused on Appreciative Inquiry and Positive Change.

Authentic Happiness: https://authentichappiness.org
Learn about positive psychology through readings, videos, research, surveys, opportunities, and more.

CDC: www.cdc.gov/ncbddd/actearly/
"Learn the Signs. Act Early"—children's milestones.

Center for Leadership and Educational Equity (CLEE [School Reform Initiative]): https://www.schoolreforminitiative.org/protocols
Protocols and processes to support communication and collective understanding

Center on the Developing Child at Harvard: http://developingchild.harvard.edu
Podcast and resources.

Child Care Exchange: www.childcareexchange.com
Articles, videos, professional development about early childhood and leadership topics; other resources available with membership.

Dale Carnegie: www.dalecarnegie.com
Webinars, videos, articles on leadership and communication.

Endurance Learning: https://trainlikeachampion.blog
Concrete tips and strategies for training activities.

Greater Good Magazine: https://greatergood.berkeley.edu
Science-Based Insights for a Meaningful Life. Includes articles, quizzes, videos, and a podcast.

Inside Jobs Coaching: http://insidejobscoach.com/resources
Free downloadable worksheets and resources related to business and management planning, communication, and personal well-being.

McCormick Center for Early Childhood Leadership: https://mccormickcenter.nl.edu
Articles, videos, blogs, and other resources focused on leadership.

National Association for the Education of Young Children: www.naeyc.org
Articles, videos, and blogs on all topics related to early childhood topics and advocacy.

National Center for Pyramid Model Innovations: https://challengingbehavior.org
Resources, training guides, and videos around social-emotional development and behavior.

Positive Psychology: https://positivepsychology.com
Resources, including tools, techniques, courses, and tips, to help you bring positive psychology into your daily practices.

Teachers Resisting Unhealthy Children's Entertainment (T.R.U.C.E.): www.truceteachers.org
Blog posts and play/materials guides.

Acknowledgments

Our professional journeys have been fueled and shaped by individuals who have dedicated their lives to empowering and inspiring early childhood educators to bring their best to children, families, and colleagues. This book would not be complete without expressing our appreciation for the many people who guided and supported our desire to find impactful ways to design and facilitate professional development experiences for the early childhood field.

This book has been made richer by the professional insights and strategies from the dedicated professionals who generously shared their expertise and wisdom. We appreciate their contributions to this book and all that they have done to support the early childhood field.

We deeply appreciate Holly Elissa Bruno for being a source of ongoing inspiration. We are delighted and honored to have her write the foreword. Holly Elissa's willingness to help us and many others find ways to bring their strengths to the early childhood field is a true gift.

We are thankful to have Melissa York as our editor at Redleaf Press. She was a constant source of wisdom and insights as we strategized our plans for this book. We are grateful for her belief in this book, amazing editing skills, and ongoing availability.

We want to acknowledge that this book would not have been possible without the positive influence of the thought leaders and mentors who guided us.

Susan is forever grateful for having Mary Mindess as one of her first professors at Lesley University. Mary's wisdom, kindness, and heartfelt conversations shaped Susan's work for over forty years. Susan's passion for professional development was sparked by the possibilities that Karen Shaeffer, a longtime colleague, provided her in the initial phases of designing a training system for the Commonwealth of Massachusetts. She cherishes the opportunities she had to interact with and learn from Paula Jorde Bloom, Holly Elissa Bruno, Lella Gandini, Lillian Katz, Ellen Hall, Alan Seale, Bob and Megan Tschannen-Moran, and so many other gracious individuals who provided encouragement and support.

Nancy is so appreciative of Susan MacDonald, a longtime mentor and friend, for igniting the idea for this book and including her in its creation. Susan has been supportive and motivating throughout the process and has inspired Nancy to find new ways to share her experiences.

Nancy's interest in the early childhood field was kindled by many rich and thought-provoking conversations with Meg Barden Cline, her adviser and one of her first professors at the University of Massachusetts Amherst. She helped Nancy develop a deep understanding and appreciation of the importance of the early years, as well as the value of advocating for the field. Nancy was privileged to work with Marlies Zammuto for many years; her energy, positivity, and spirit continue to be a driving force in Nancy's work. She treasures the interactions she has had with a wide range of facilitators and speakers who have shared their ideas and encouraged her, especially Joanna Doyle, Suzanne Wildman, Andrea Urbano, Josephine Holmboe, and colleagues in the Massachusetts Association for the Education of Young Children.

We are thankful for our family and friends who made up our support networks. Their belief in us gave us the courage to create this book. Without their behind-the-scenes support, interest, and flexibility, this book would not have been possible.

Last and most important, we express our deep gratitude for the educators who showed up and participated in our trainings over the past thirty years. Their engagement and feedback helped us develop and continually enhance the professional development strategies and activities that infuse our practice and that we have shared in this book.

Contributors

We are grateful to this amazing group of thought leaders, authors, highly regarded speakers, and researchers who enhanced this book with their inspirational tips and strategies.

HOLLY ELISSA BRUNO

Holly Elissa Bruno, MA, JD, served as Maine's assistant attorney general and University of Maine at Augusta's academic dean and associate professor before becoming a best-selling, award-winning author on emotionally intelligent leadership, managing legal risks, and translating trauma's harsh legacy into healing. She is an in-demand international keynoter.

www.hollyelissabruno.com

TONI CHRISTIE

Toni Christie is the director of the Childspace Early Childhood Institute in Wellington, New Zealand. She is passionate about early childhood education, leadership, environments, infants, teamwork, communication, and advocacy for children, families, and early childhood educators. Toni holds a master of education with merit from Victoria University in Wellington.

https://childspace.nz/

LELAND O. CLARKE

Promoted to full professor of education and music at Wheelock College, Leland O. Clarke taught and created many education and music courses over an eighteen-year period. He is presently Professor of the Practice in the School of Music in the College of Fine Arts at Boston University.

BETH FREDERICKS

Beth Fredericks is a lifelong early childhood activist who sparks inspiration wherever she goes. Beth is a master trainer for Mind in the Making, which shares the science of learning, and she works with the Singapore Zoo to bring this neuroscience to visitors from all over the world.

JOELFRÉ L. GRANT

Joelfré L. Grant, a descendant of the Confederated Salish and Kootenai Tribes, has dedicated his career to the care and education of young children. Teaching and training in Head Start, in campus child care programs, and as a facilitator for the National Center for Parent, Family, and Community Engagement, he has focused on relationships with families, providers, and community partners. Joelfré believes in lifelong learning and is particularly interested in cultural humility and social justice in learning and development.

LUIS A. HERNANDEZ

Luis A. Hernandez's professional development work focuses on a wide range of early childhood education and management topics. His expertise includes early literacy, dual-language learning, adult learning practices, family engagement, and leadership topics. As a regular presenter and keynote speaker at national, state, and local conferences, Luis is highly regarded for his motivational and energizing presentations.

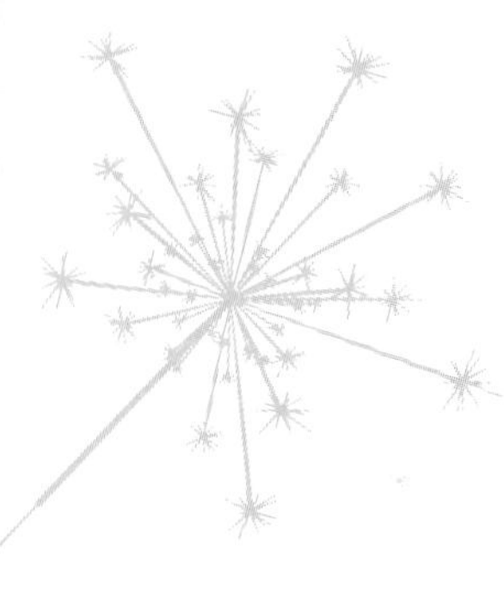

DEBBIE LEEKEENAN

Debbie LeeKeenan is a lecturer, consultant, and author. She has been in the field of early education for over fifty years, including as the director of Eliot-Pearson Children's School at Tufts University from 1996 to 2013. In addition, she has been a faculty member at Lesley University and the University of Massachusetts Amherst. Debbie is the producer of the film *Reflecting on Anti-bias Education in Action: The Early Years* (2021).

KAREN NEMETH

Karen Nemeth is an author and professional development presenter focusing on early education for multilingual learners. She hosts the Language Castle resource website and has held national association leadership roles in NAEYC (National Association for the Education of Young Children), TESOL (Teaching English to Speakers of Other Languages), and NABE (National Association for Bilingual Education). She has presented more than a thousand hours of professional development for schools, conferences, universities, and webinar audiences, always working on ways to elevate professional learning experiences.

https://languagecastle.com

LINDA SCHUMACHER

Linda Schumacher has been in the early childhood field for over forty years and has been a trainer for the past sixteen years. She offers both in-person and virtual professional development to centers, to family child care agencies, and at state and national conferences. In addition to her own trainings, Linda has facilitated training on Environmental Rating Scales, Ages and Stages Questionnaires (ASQ and ASQ-SE), National Association for Family Child Care (NAFCC) Accreditation, and the Pyramid Model.

www.lindaschumacheronline.com

JAYNE SINGER

Dr. Jayne Singer is a clinical psychologist with more than forty years of experience in hospital, school, and community-based settings, with families and children with a wide variety of medical, developmental, emotional, behavioral, and familial challenges, including trauma. She is a past president of the Massachusetts Association for Infant Mental Health. She is engaged in continuous national and international teaching and intensive mentoring as an International Trainer of the Brazelton Touchpoints Approach and the Newborn Behavioral Observations system as relationship-based care techniques in service of child development and parent-provider partnerships.

DEBRA SOSIN

Debra Sosin, a clinical social worker, Infant and Early Childhood Mental Health Consultant (IECMHC), and special educator, has worked with children, families, and providers in a wide range of settings for over forty years. She brings a deep commitment to a relational approach to all of her work. She is currently affiliated with the Brazelton Touchpoints Center at Boston Children's Hospital.

About the Authors

Susan MacDonald is the founder of Inspiring New Perspectives, a consulting group focused on empowering school leaders and educators to create learning environments that deeply respect and nurture the possibilities that lie within each teacher, child, and parent. Susan's passion and expertise for creating positive change are reflected in her professional speaking and coaching and in her books, *Inspiring Early Childhood Leadership: Eight Strategies to Ignite Passion and Transform Program Quality* and *Inspiring Professional Growth: Empowering Strategies to Lead, Motivate, and Engage Early Childhood Teachers.*

Susan is a lifelong learner, continually adding to her own knowledge through the exploration of new research and literature, allowing her to provide educators and leaders with the tools to effect positive change in their own organizations. Susan holds a master's degree in instructional design and multiple professional coaching certifications. Susan has been developing and delivering inspirational courses, keynotes, and workshops for over twenty-five years throughout the United States, Canada, Italy, Jamaica, Wales, and Ireland.

Susan's background encompasses a wide range of experiences, including director of a Reggio-inspired preschool program; adjunct faculty at Lesley University, Wheelock College, and Southern New Hampshire University; and Commonwealth of Massachusetts licensing supervisor. She is the past president of the Boston Area Reggio Inspired Network and past vice president of the Massachusetts Association for the Education of Young Children.

Away from work, Susan can be found reading, cooking, traveling, or simply enjoying life's rich everyday moments with her husband, Patrick, and their four children.

SPEAKING

Susan has developed a wide variety of workshops and keynote presentations designed to inspire educational professionals to weave new approaches, ideas, and strategies into their daily work. Susan creates engaging and inspiring professional development experiences for individuals, small groups, and large audiences.

COACHING

As a professionally certified coach, Susan works with educational leaders to create opportunities for them to develop and execute a vision that aligns with their core beliefs. Susan's individual coaching services are designed to cultivate the skills and dispositions that leaders need to improve program quality, increase positive energy, enhance professional working relationships, and create inspirational learning environments for children, educators, and families. Her deep knowledge of early childhood quality standards combined with her unique professional background give her an unrivaled ability to successfully guide leaders through the coaching process for bringing their goals to life in concrete ways.

AUTHOR

Susan's goal as an author is to write books that encourage leaders to explore new possibilities and provide them with tools to create high-quality learning environments fueled by positive, engaging energy. Her books, *Inspiring Early Childhood Leadership*—winner of the AAP REVERE Awards (Classroom: Professional Resources—School Climate)—and *Inspiring Professional Growth* are focused on empowering early childhood leaders to embrace new strategies for leading with passion, intention, and purpose.

To learn more about Susan's work, you can visit her website: www.inspiringnewperspectives.com.

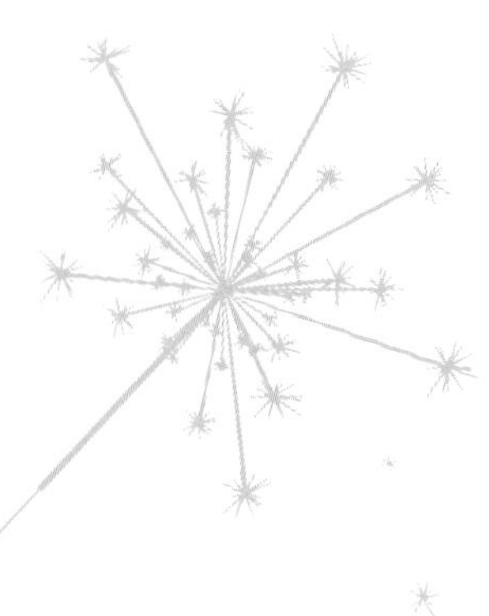

Nancy Toso is the founder and director of the Nancy L. Toso Consulting Group, committed to providing relevant and meaningful professional development to early childhood educators and leaders. Nancy's work involves conceptualizing, developing, and implementing customized professional development and coaching that meets the needs of educators and programs at all levels in the field of early care and education.

Nancy became passionate about early childhood as a college student and intern at the Massachusetts Office for Children. Nancy holds a master's degree in early childhood and continued her learning through postgraduate courses and her year as a Community Advocates for Young Learners (CAYL) Fellow, allowing her to stay current with research and trends in the field. She has been deeply involved with NAEYC, from her graduate school project of establishing the Western Massachusetts affiliate to her role as governing board member of MAAEYC. Her activities in the organization have included developing and writing distance learning courses, establishing guidelines and reviewing applications for CEU courses, planning and implementing conferences, and collaborating with other statewide organizations to advocate for quality early learning opportunities for children and to provide quality professional development opportunities for early childhood educators. Nancy has spent the last thirty-five years developing and presenting timely and dynamic professional development in a variety of settings locally, statewide, and nationally.

Nancy's career has included a wide range of experiences, including teaching infants, toddlers, and preschoolers, directing and owning early learning centers, starting a resource and referral agency, providing consultations to groups starting child care programs, and serving as adjunct faculty at Wheelock College and the Northeast Montessori Institute and as a professional coach for early childhood teachers and leaders.

Nancy's nonwork interests include reading, walking along the beach, hiking, cooking, volunteering for community human services organizations, and enjoying time with family and friends.

SPEAKING

Nancy has spent the last thirty-five years developing professional learning experiences for early childhood educators that are designed to share the most current knowledge and best practices and empower educators to put new ideas and perspectives into their own practice. Nancy's training experiences are highly interactive, encouraging participants to be fully engaged in their learning and to learn from one another. Her training is customized to accommodate groups and learners from all facets of the field and at all levels of experience.

AUTHOR

Nancy's goal as an author is to share the knowledge and skills she has attained through her journey and give leaders the confidence to explore new ideas to energize their presentations and engage audiences. She is excited to provide concrete strategies and techniques for designing and delivering impactful professional development that will empower leaders to inspire and motivate educators and support their growth.